SO-AKA-212

TIES THAT BIND:
PARTIES AND VOTERS IN CANADA

TIES THAT BIND:
PARTIES AND VOTERS IN CANADA

James Bickerton, Alain-G. Gagnon, and Patrick J. Smith

OXFORD
UNIVERSITY PRESS

OXFORD

UNIVERSITY PRESS

70 Wynford Drive, Don Mills, Ontario M3C 1J9
www.oupcan.com

Oxford New York
Athens Auckland Bangkok Bogotá Buenos Aires Calcutta
Cape Town Chennai Dar es Salaam Delhi Florence Hong Kong
Istanbul Karachi Kuala Lumpur Madrid Melbourne Mexico City
Mumbai Nairobi Paris São Paulo Singapore Taipei Tokyo
Toronto Warsaw

and associated companies in
Berlin Ibadan

Oxford is a trade mark of Oxford University Press

Canadian Cataloguing in Publication Data

Bickerton, James
  Ties that bind : parties and voters in Canada

Includes bibliographical references and index.
ISBN 0–19–541276–1

1. Electioneering – Canada.   2. Political parties – Canada.
3. Elections – Canada.   I. Gagnon, Alain-G. (Alain-Gustave), 1954–   .
II. Smith, Patrick J.   III. Title.

JL193.B52 1999   324.971   C99–931338–X

Designer: Tearney McMurtry
Composition: IBEX Graphic Communications Inc.

Copyright © Oxford University Press Canada 1999

1 2 3 4 – 02 01 00 99

This book is printed on permanent (acid-free) paper ∞.

Printed in Canada

Contents

Acknowledgements

The authors would like to gratefully acknowledge support and assistance from various sources in the preparation of this book. First of all, we are very grateful to the Social Science and Humanities Research Council of Canada whose grant (SSHRCC #410-94-1617) made this work possible. In addition, we are grateful to the anonymous reviewers of the manuscript for their helpful comments and suggestions. Our colleague and friend, Munroe Eagles, deserves special mention for his unwavering support and many insights at various stages of the project. Other colleagues who deserve mention for their much-appreciated suggestions include Alan Whitehorn, David Laycock, and Ed Broadbent. Kennedy Stewart, from the London School of Economics, provided the charts included in chapters 1, 4, and 5, and provided helpful comments on aspects of the book as well. Appendices A, B, and C were compiled by Tony Coulson. At Oxford University Press Canada, the supportive attitude and hard work on this project of Euan White, Ric Kitowski, Laura Macleod, and Valerie Ahwee are also gratefully acknowledged.

Each of us would like to express appreciation for assistance and support we have received. James Bickerton would like to thank St Francis Xavier University for research support in the form of sabbatical leave and research grant, and the Department of Political Science at Simon Fraser University for hosting him during the final stage of manuscript preparation. Alain Gagnon would like to express his appreciation for the support provided by McGill University through the Quebec Studies Programme. Patrick J. Smith would like to thank Simon Fraser University and the Institute of Governance Studies for research assistance.

Notes on the Authors

James Bickerton is Professor of Political Science at St Francis Xavier University. His publications include *Nova Scotia, Ottawa and the Politics of Regional Development* (1990), The *Almanac of Canadian Politics* (1991, 1995, with Munroe Eagles, Alain Gagnon, and Patrick Smith), and *Canadian Politics* (1990, 1994, 1999, with Alain Gagnon).

Alain-G. Gagnon is Professor of Political Science at McGill University, Director of the Quebec Studies Programme, and Editor of *Politique et société*. His recent publications include *Quebec y el federalismo canadiense* (1998), *Quebec* (1998), and *Canadian Parties in Transition* (1996, with Brian Tanguay).

Patrick J. Smith is Professor of Political Science and Director of the Institute of Governance Studies at Simon Fraser University. His publications include *The Vision and the Game: Making the Canadian Constitution* (1987, with L. Cohen and P. Warwick), *Continuities and Discontinuities: The Political Economy of Social Welfare and Labour Market Policy in Canada* (1994, with Andrew Johnson and Stephen McBride), and *Urban Solutions to Global Problems* (1996, with Peter Oberlander and Tom Hutton).

CHAPTER 1

PARTIES AND VOTERS IN CANADA

Viewed from afar, electoral politics in Canada must appear a strange amalgam of predictability and surprise, stability and volatility. At the close of the twentieth century, the party in power is the same one that governed at the beginning of the century, and for an inordinate amount of the time in between. Yet the contemporary party system seems to bear little relationship to that which characterized either turn-of-the-century or mid-century Canadian politics. In fact, several dramatic upheavals have taken place in the relationship between parties and voters, constituting a restless and potentially dangerous undertow that has threatened the relatively placid surface of one dominant party (the Liberals) temporarily spelled in power by their main opponents, the Progressive Conservatives. Elections clarify for parties and voters alike the current character of their relations, registering both continuities and changes. Partially obscured, vaguely calibrated, or hidden perils in the voter-party relationship will often rise to the surface during election periods, and the ties that bind diverse communities of voters to particular parties are tested. To use Jeffrey Simpson's colourful analogy, 'Politics is like an endless river winding its way through the nation's psychological terrain. Elections are the white-water passages, where political life froths and boils, hurtling the participants at accelerating speeds through a chute of perils towards calm waters at the end'.[1]

Clearly, the relationship between Canadian voters and their political parties has seldom been an easy one, especially at election time. By the same token, to describe it in general terms as unstable or volatile would be misleading. There have always been strong currents of continuity and stability in voter-party relations in Canada. Such continuity is deeply rooted in distinct regional political cultures and party histories, in enduring ties that have developed between ethnocultural or linguistic groupings and particular parties (or parties of a certain type), and in the ever-present economic and class cleavages within Canadian society that underlay and give shape to left-right ideological divisions around which the parties must manoeuvre, both for reasons that are long term and strategic, as well as for short-term tactical advantages.

Competing Models of Party and Voter Behaviour

One reading of the history of the pre-1993 relationship between political parties and Canadian voters is that it was essentially one long tradition of alternately electing one of two national parties, both of which competed for the same policy space and the same electorate. The victor in any particular election was the party that was most successful at brokering voter support in three or four primary dimensions: the class-economic (which roughly translates into a left-right ideological spectrum), the ethnocultural (which encompasses religion, ethnicity, and language), the urban-rural dimension, and the regional dimension. This view of Canadian electoral politics is congruent with the general argument that parties in search of electoral success will converge on the preferences of the median voter, regardless of their ostensible ideology or the particular configuration of their political base. As a consequence, elections become little more than marketing campaigns for the parties as they each seek to outdo each other in making their leaders and policies attractive to the median voter. If they prove not to be, then they will be changed to make them more suitable for the purpose of maximizing votes. The voters are motivated by pure rational self-interest: they will choose the party that promises to maximize their own utilities.[2]

This model, a variant of 'rational choice' theory, assumes that there are no long-term divisions or cleavages within the electorate that can shape the values, beliefs, and political orientations of voters in fundamentally different ways, and therefore interfere with the rational, short-term calculations that voters are expected to make regarding which party best serves their immediate interests. At the very least, the model suggests that such cleavages are eroding or disappearing from society, or have simply ceased to be relevant to political choice. This reflects the modernist ideal of inevitable 'progress' towards a society of homogeneous, middle-class consumers. Parties from this perspective are viewed as little more than election machines, attuned to the straightforward objective of maximizing their share of the popular vote in this increasingly undifferentiated electorate. Policies, issues, personalities, and strategies are all employed towards this end.

This view of voter and party behaviour offers some powerful insights into party and voter rationality that are applicable to all developed, democratic societies. With regard to Canada, a modified version of this model emerged as the most widely accepted view of Canadian electoral politics. Researchers on voting behaviour have asserted that Canadian voters are notably less stable in their partisanship than is the case for comparable jurisdictions. It is also claimed that variables such as class, region, and religion are only weakly related to how people vote and to the party with which they identify.[3] This 'volatility' in the behaviour of individual voters has usually been explained by referring to voter characteristics, or to the character of Canadian parties, or to both.[4] In this way researchers have painted a picture of the Canadian electorate as 'flexible and non-ideological' in its partisanship; in complementary fashion, Canadian political parties—at least the two traditional national parties—are seen as centrist, non-ideological election machines. Usually referred to as *brokerage parties*, their behaviour is dictated by the need to build and rebuild winning electoral coalitions. To do this they must be prepared to poach each other's voters, and to be free of ideological constraints so that they may appeal to the non-aligned or weakly committed voter. In J.A. Corry's formulation, 'they [the parties] are brokers of ideas. They are middlemen who select from all the ideas pressing for recognition as public policy those they think can be shaped to have the widest appeal'.[5] The result is two national parties that are barely distinguishable in terms of their policies, support bases, or electoral strategies. As a result, elections are fought over short-term issues, scandals, and the personal attributes of leaders. On the basis of these superficial and changeable criteria, Canadian voters cast their ballots.

Both the assumptions underlying this model of voter and party behaviour, as well as the model's empirical findings with regard to Canadian parties and voters, are open to criticism. To begin, the modernist ideal of an increasingly undifferentiated, middle-class society has not come to pass. Voters continue to differ from one another in terms of their class background and often identify themselves and their concerns in other than simple consumerist terms. These other identities tend to be much less flexible than that of 'consumer', and therefore can become the basis for relatively stable voter identification with particular political parties. The model can also be criticized for ignoring the weight of party histories that tie parties to particular symbols, ideologies, and policy orientations. These party features are rooted in social, ethnocultural, and geographic bases of party support that endure over decades. As noted by Axworthy and Goldfarb, 'Political parties are not the playthings of leaders. They have collective identities, a core clientele and, above all, institutional memory.'[6] If political leaders must appeal to the non-aligned, weakly committed, and new voters to win elections (and they do), they must do so without alienating their core supporters or risk destroying 'the inheritance passed down from previous generations of partisans. Maintaining the base is a precondition for political success.'[7]

With regard to the empirical description of the Canadian electorate, different positions have been taken on both the question of voter volatility and on the social/ideological contours (or lack thereof) of partisanship. Richard Johnston et al. disagree with the purported size of Canada's cohort of 'flexible partisans', arguing that the instability of voter partisanship has been overstated due to an artificial inflation of the numbers of 'party identifiers' created by faulty measurement techniques.[8] Johnston further argues that Canadian voters are, in fact, 'rooted in tribal loyalties' and that Canadian parties have clear social bases in the Canadian population. In particular, religion has been an important factor in party support that is a cultural phenomenon linked to social forces outside the strict confines of family socialization.[9] Other scholars have used historical, survey, and electoral data to argue that Canadian voters are not as non-ideological as is sometimes suggested, and that both activists and voters support their parties on the basis of certain ideological associations or agendas.[10]

Brodie and Jenson also disagree with the dominant brokerage view of Canadian political parties. They argue that the mainstream brokerage parties did not simply offer voters what they thought they wanted, but actively moulded voter perceptions of politics. The Liberals and Conservatives developed and perpetuated the most salient cleavage within the Canadian electorate: the ethnocultural divide. They did this by providing voters with a definition of politics that defined Canadian politics in cultural terms. This was more congruent with their organizational interests as *bourgeois* parties supportive of the capitalist system than a definition of politics based on class. Every time issues based on class differences threatened to erupt onto the political agenda, the established support bases of these parties were threatened, leading 'the bourgeois parties to divert ... the challenge by reformulating new conflicts in the old familiar discourse of bicultural conflict or regional differences'.[11] The left-wing CCF, followed by the NDP, were only partially successful in introducing class differences as an alternative basis for electoral competition, and increasingly came to accept the prevailing 'definition of politics' and to compete with the bourgeois parties on their own terms.

This conceptualization of parties as shapers of the political discourse and active creators of voter preferences makes an important contribution to our understanding of Canadian parties and the party system. Throughout the history of Confederation, the old-line, bourgeois parties did benefit from the prevailing cultural definition of politics in Canada, while socialist and social democratic alternatives suffered as a result. Certainly parties of the latter ilk failed to fully exploit historic opportunities to substitute a class-based political discourse for the dominant form of cultural politics. As a result, except during certain 'exceptional' periods, elections and voter loyalties at the national level continued to revolve almost exclusively around questions of language, religion, region, and the need for parties to act as brokers across these divisions in order to ensure national unity. However, as Brian Tanguay argues, Brodie and Jenson's central contention that it was the bourgeois parties' constant (and conscious) manipulation of the political discourses of religion, regionalism, and biculturalism that foiled the left by preventing the emergence of a class-based definition of politics 'seems both to carry the Machiavellianism of the established parties to excessive lengths and to overestimate their ability to determine the content of the political agenda unilaterally. It also downplays the independent importance of religious, regional, linguistic and cultural differences among Canadians.'[12]

Nor were the socialist parties of the twentieth century the first to have their electoral aspirations founder on the rocks of ethnocultural and regional divisions in Canada. Robert Laxer has traced the roots of Canada's weak sense of economic nationalism to the nineteenth-century political weakness of its agrarian class, which, contrary to agrarian movements in other countries at a similar stage in their economic development, failed to capture or exercise significant political influence at the national level. Laxer attributes this anomaly (which had a direct, if complex, effect on the Canadian state's formative economic and industrial policies) to agrarian movements' inability to unite farmers across the country's linguistic, religious, and regional divides.[13] The organizing difficulties of Canadian labour parties were compounded by this earlier failure of agrarian movements to establish and institutionalize a strong sense of Canadian nationalism. Agrarian success undoubtedly would have created a more favourable political and ideological climate for the early Canadian labour movement (which eschewed independent development and direct political involvement in favour of the apolitical American model and often under direct American control); in turn, this would have improved the prospects of a socialist political movement seeking to organize itself in alliance with the labour movement.

Clearly, ideology, culture, class, and party politics have coexisted in a complex, reciprocal relationship that retreats far back into Canadian history. Tracing a direct line from class interest to political party to political discourse to electoral outcomes is fraught with difficulties. It may also suffer from rather dubious assumptions, especially if a political discourse based on class is accorded importance in electoral politics (and to electoral outcomes) only when it receives unequivocal party political expression, as with the early CCF. But no party can afford to be the unequivocal instrument of just one class, and 'the struggle between parties is not a tournament with as many parties as there are classes'.[14] As Bourque noted, every party seeks to contain within it and to reflect the whole spectrum of social relations in a society. Even if a party may seek to create the political and ideological conditions most favourable to the economic and class interests it defends, 'the program of a party, much less the policy of a government, cannot be unequivocally identified with the specific interests of its hegemonic class'.[15] Class has been a persistent and salient cleavage in Canadian electoral politics, and it has usually been the mainstream brokerage parties that have been most successful at incorporating class politics into their competitive struggle with one another. Though such incorporation is always symbolic in discursive terms, it clearly has not been only or exclusively this. As Leo Panitch observed:

> When John A. Macdonald's Conservative Party constructed a 'Tory-Producer' alliance around the tariff and mildly progressive industrial relations legislation, it did so not by ignoring class (although certainly by decrying class conflict) but by incorporating working class demands, interests and leaders in their

project. . . . When the Mackenzie King Liberals constructed their industrial rela-
tions and welfare state program in 1944–45, they did much the same thing. . . .
And Pierre Trudeau, seeking to end his dependence on the New Democratic
Party (NDP) in a minority government, and faced with the opportunity of the
Stanfield Conservatives' calling for an incomes and prices freeze, went to
Sudbury during the 1974 election campaign and shouted, 'So what's he going
to freeze? Your wages! He's going to freeze your wages!'[16] Here again was the
incorporation of class, the expression and mediation of working-class interests
within the framework of the Liberal Party.[17]

Understanding Canadian Party and Electoral Politics

In sum, the prevailing models of party and voter behaviour in Canada
provide some valuable insights into the political behaviour of both the
electorate and political parties. However, they do have some deficiencies
and drawbacks. At the very least, it may be said that the volatility aspect in
Canadian voting behaviour often has been overplayed, and that the parties
are generally more constrained by their ties to a core electorate and more
ideological in their electoral appeals than is often recognized. Certainly,
the enduring aspects of the party system and voter behaviour—the underlying continuities of each—have received too little acknowledgement or
attention.

A useful corrective in this regard is the argument made by Donald Blake,
among others, that Canadian electoral history has been marked by a number of 'critical' or 'realigning' elections that have ushered in large-scale
alterations in party loyalties that persist for a number of succeeding elections. Far from being either a constant of Canadian party politics or entirely
absent, volatility has been sharply higher during certain subperiods of
Canadian electoral history. Blake argues that changes in the character and
shape of the Canadian party system can be understood using the concept
of *electoral eras*: 'sets of elections within which party support distributions
are interrelated among themselves, but are unrelated to support distributions outside that era'.[18] A second argument emphasizes the regional
dimension of Canadian electoral parties. Provinces and regions have not
experienced episodes of partisan realignment similarly. In addition to tem-
poral variation in partisan stability patterns, there is also a considerable
degree of spatial variation, with some provinces/regions remaining unaffected by the significant shifts in voter support that mark a critical election, while experiencing their own dramatic shifts at other times when the
overall result otherwise suggests a degree of stability in the pattern of party
support. In sum, as Blake noted, 'wholesale change is rarer than we have
been led to believe by the "textbook theory" and less uncommon than the
theory's critics have suggested'.[19]

A satisfying account of the voter-party relationship in Canada, then, should recognize the tension between the need for parties to retain the support of *a stable and distinctive social and geographic base of supporters in the electorate* while reaching out to the non-aligned or weakly committed median voter. The key to successful brokerage is to attract the support of the latter while maintaining the former.[20] *Brokerage politics* should properly be thought of as a complex, multidimensional process that is fraught with difficulties. First and foremost, the parties must maintain their base of core supporters, who tend to be predisposed (as the result of past electoral campaigns and their own interests and identities) to certain appeals of an ideological or symbolic nature. The parties must also attempt to broker the country's French-English, regional, and class divides, lest their stable voter bases become too narrow to carry them to power and to sustain them there. Finally, they must expand their voter base during election periods by devising ways to reach out to non-aligned or uncommitted voters (sometimes referred to as the 'floating vote'). However, if the parties fail to maintain a core support base from which to broker for this additional support, they risk not merely defeat but electoral disaster.

The explanation for the fate of Canada's oldest national party, the Progressive Conservatives, goes to the core of Canadian political parties' historic practice of brokerage politics. When these parties diverge too much from the basic values and preferences of their core supporters in order to tailor their appeal to attract new constituencies and/or the median voter, they risk exceeding the limits of partisan tolerance. Even when the short-term result is long-awaited electoral success, the bloated party that results may be crippled by the exigencies that accompany the integration of new supporters, activists, and legislators that do not fit comfortably within the party's established social, regional, and ideological parameters. Though often characterized as an important, even heroic function performed in the interests of nation building, brokerage politics taken to such lengths erodes formerly stable lines of partisan division. In 1993 it nearly destroyed one of Canada's great national parties; it may yet prevent the Tories from ever again winning a national majority or mandate to govern.

That such a severe punishment for the Tories can be deemed a possibility rests not only on the party's poor performance in two successive elections but also on the strong evidence of a long-term realignment of party loyalties in 1993, especially in Quebec and the West. As Blake noted, such periodic realignments in the partisanship patterns of provincial or regional electorates typically persist for decades. Such electoral eras are marked by relative stability in the vote shares and geographic support bases that underpin party competition, in effect establishing a new party system. The Progressive Conservatives' place in this new party system (as one of several minor or regional parties) does not bode well for any proximate return to major party status.

All this suggests three things about parties, voters, and the practice of brokerage politics in Canada. *First*, putting aside the question of individual voter volatility, within the Canadian electorate there have been relatively stable 'communities of voters' at the constituency, provincial, and even regional level. Over the years, a significant portion of these constituency electorates have been tolerant of a fair degree of inconsistency on the part of their parties of choice; at the same time, the parties have generally recognized the need to reignite and reaffirm their traditional ties to these particular core support bases, especially during elections. This has been an important determinant of party behaviour. *Second*, parties from time to time have alienated these core support bases by exceeding the normal limits of partisan tolerance, usually in an attempt to transcend the normal boundaries of this traditional electorate. *Third*, established patterns of voter support for parties at the constituency, provincial, or regional level that exhibit stability over long periods of time may become subject to significant and lasting change ushered in by a critical election or over a series of elections. This occurs when the strong ties that bind particular electorates to particular parties are broken through political insensitivity or lack of responsiveness to the core electorate's values and concerns. This break may occur over a relatively brief period of time (as with the Conservatives and western voters between 1988 and 1993) or over an extended period of time (as with the Conservatives and Quebec voters between 1885 and 1896 or the realignment of western voters between 1921 and 1935). The completeness and duration of this break in partisan ties depends on the extent to which a formerly disfavoured party can be transformed into a more attractive alternative, and/or by the emergence of a new party or parties whose express intent is to appeal to the alienated (and therefore available) electorate.

Continuity and Change in Party Support: Three Party Systems

In Canada, where deep ethnocultural and regional cleavages have overlaid and sometimes smothered the usual class and urban-rural divisions of industrial societies, the brokerage party goal of constructing truly national electoral coalitions has been increasingly elusive. The initial two-party system that existed prior to 1921 proved inadequate in representing the country's growing diversity of interests and identities. Thereafter, the demise of national two-party competition and the onset and persistence of discrete regional arenas of party competition suggests that understanding the crisscrossing patterns of partisanship and party competition in Canadian politics can be done only by breaking down the national electorate and party system into a number of discrete parts. At the very least, *Quebec* must be considered as a separate electorate; in addition, the further division of English-speaking

Canada along *regional* or *east-west* lines may be necessary in order to fully comprehend voter behaviour and the dynamics of party competition. Finally, voters at the *subregional* or *constituency* level often constitute distinctive 'communities of voters' that are fairly consistent and predictable in their voting behaviour over long periods of time in terms of their allegiance to one party that holds (or that repeatedly presents itself to them as holding) a particular cultural, ideological, or policy orientation.

At a minimum, then, ethnocultural, class-economic, urban-rural, and regional factors have provided the context for voter-party interaction in Canada. The parties have responded to this context in terms of their organization, finances, leadership, strategies, ideologies, and policies. These are the sinews of 'the ties that bind' particular communities of voters to particular parties. But it is also true that change in these factors force parties to continuously adapt, nurture, and reaffirm their ties to particular electorates. Periodically, the ties have been severed and new voter-party connections established.

Recognizing that voter-party ties within the national party system have taken on different characteristics during different historical epochs, researchers at the University of British Columbia have found it useful to divide the Canadian party system into three historically distinct systems in order to better understand major changes in the pattern of party competition in Canada. The first party system dated from Confederation to the 'conscription election' of 1917; the second party system stretched from 1921 (although it only truly 'settled' into its new alignment in 1935) to the Diefenbaker victories of 1957–8; the third party system ran from 1962 to 1984.[21] Each party system has been different from the previous one in terms of the social and regional bases of party support. The major divisions between parties within each era of party competition have been along four primary dimensions: ethnocultural, socio-economic, urban-rural, and regional. Support for the Liberal Party throughout all three party systems was rooted in the country's Catholic population, especially in Quebec and the Maritimes. Ontario, Manitoba, and British Columbia were the heartlands of Anglo-Protestantism. These religious differences translated into differences over 'the moral and symbolic claims of the British connection', with the Tories supported by Anglo-Protestants championing imperialism and the British connection, and the Liberals supported by Catholics and ethnic minorities resisting the pull of Empire.[22]

The Liberal Party built its political hegemony upon this 'Catholic core' in the twentieth century, including its most recent period of extended rule, from 1963 to 1984 (the third party system). During this period the Liberals also made a centre-left urban appeal and crafted a national unity/national identity strategy based on the policies of bilingualism and multiculturalism, which reinforced the party's traditional support base among French Canadians and ethnic minorities. Diefenbaker's populist appeal enabled the

Figure 1.1 Percentage of Popular Vote by Party

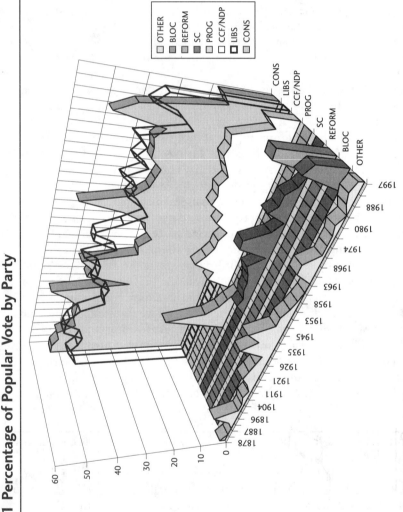

Source: Adapted from Elections Canada results.

Figure 1.2 Governing Parties, 1878–1997, by Popular Vote

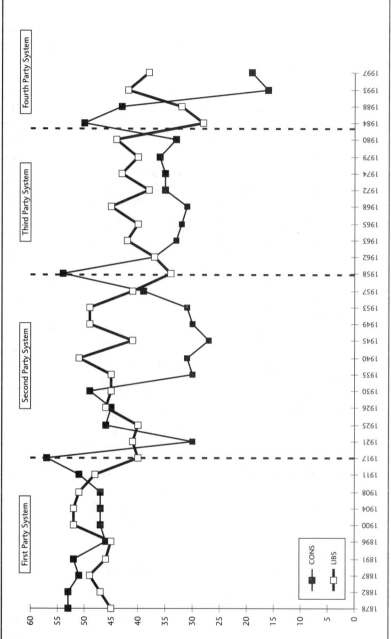

Source: Adapted from Elections Canada results.

Conservatives to break out of the narrow Ontario base to which they had been relegated after 1935 and to displace third parties in the West, as well as the Liberals, who had benefited from four-party competition in that region during the second party system (1921–57). By coalescing the right, Diefenbaker made the Conservatives the dominant party in western Canada.

Diefenbaker's personal charisma and populist rhetoric were not solely responsible for this feat. His accomplishment is attributable in large part to the decline in salience of Canada's British Empire connections and therefore the need or rationale for a protectionist commercial policy. This freed the Conservatives from a policy position that had been unpopular with electorates in the Prairie and Maritime regions, allowing Diefenbaker to appeal to a broader constituency in English-speaking Canada than had theretofore been available to the Conservative Party. The Diefenbaker legacy, however, left the Tories with a voter base that was still 'ethnically and religiously narrow'. The party's appeal remained greatest among the country's English-speaking Protestant population, in particular drawing agrarian and anti-establishment sentiment from this group.[23] The Liberals, with a secure Quebec–Atlantic base but now virtually shut out of western Canada, had to pursue majorities in urban Ontario. The overall result was the absence of a truly national party between 1962 and 1984 and the ever-present possibility of minority governments.

The presumption in this historical periodization of party systems in Canada, as in most systems analyses, is that the component parts of the system are the primary determinants of the attributes and functioning of the parts. In other words, the parts (parties in this case) are distinguishable primarily in relationship to other parts (other parties) and to the whole system and its environment (the voters). It suggests that prior to 1984 there were at least three major orientations of the entire party system during which the character of each party and its support was distinctive. The relationship of primary interest here is that which exists between the parties in competition with one another and their strategic positioning *vis-à-vis* the electorate in this context. It further suggests that while ties have been created between parties and voters within historically demarcated party systems, from time to time they may be done, undone, and redone as the parties strategically jockey with one another.

All this may in fact be the case, but the emphasis on the changes that occur from system to system should not be allowed to obscure the continuities that accompany the changes. Moreover, while ties to particular electorates may be undone, parties that choose to do so (or simply fail to anticipate and act to prevent such an occurrence) are likely to find it exceedingly difficult to later renew these same ties.[24] What is important here will be the character of the ties that have bound electorate and party, the circumstances (when, how, why) of their undoing, and the consequences for the parties in question and the party system as a whole. Finally, what strategic options are parties left with when their ties with a core electorate are severed? How and to what extent can these broken ties be repaired? What other electorates, if any, are available to which parties may seek to bind? Is their competitive status enhanced or eroded as a result?

The Mulroney Interlude and a Fourth Party System

The 1984 election result represented a dramatic change from the previous century in that the Liberal Party's strongholds in the Catholic areas of eastern Canada collapsed. Particularly devastating for the Liberals was their performance in Quebec, where the party lost fifty-six seats and half of its vote share. The Conservatives, on the other hand, gained fifty-seven seats and nearly quadrupled their vote. This dramatic reversal can be attributed to a couple of key factors: the Conservatives' choice of a Quebec leader and the party's less centrist and interventionist orientation compared to that of the Liberals. This laid the basis for a Conservative alliance with Quebec on economic and constitutional issues. As in 1957–8, Liberal policies and governing style had created an electoral opening for the right type of Conservative leader, who cemented his advantage through a shift in ideological positioning so as to better appeal to an electorate alienated from the governing party. This set the stage for the recreation of the original nineteenth-century Macdonald coalition of francophones and francophobes, with the same incoherence and instability that would have to be overcome.[25] It did not take long after 1984 for this to become evident.

It should be noted that while both the Conservatives and the NDP expanded their reach during the third party system compared with the previous period of party competition, the former had no significant presence in Quebec and the latter had none east of the Ottawa River. The Liberals, on the other hand, for much of this period, governed on a narrowed geographic base that had shrunk to eastern Canada and had a virtual monopoly in Quebec. No truly national parties existed, if the criteria for such a designation are having adequate representation from and enough viable political organization in all regions of the country to provide the party with an ongoing presentation of the demands, concerns, and opinions from all parts of the country and to allow the party to be competitive in periodic national elections.

On the surface, the 1984 to 1993 period marked a return from regional to national party politics. The anomalous election of 1984 was followed by the 1988 results when a Free Trade Agreement with the United States polarized the national electorate around a single, predominant issue. But even under those propitious circumstances for generating a truly national debate and common national choice for Canadians, anti-free trade voters in the West strategically chose the strongest Opposition Party in the region (the NDP), while in the East they did the same and moved to the Liberals, denying both parties the claim to speak with a strong national voice; the Conservatives, of course, clearly benefited from not having to split the free trade vote with another party. Even so, they won a majority of seats in only two provinces (Quebec and Alberta), which was an unusually tepid mandate for the national electorate to confer on a majority government.

The 1993 election shattered even this dubious return to a single national arena of party competition. Though the Liberals won seats in every province in 1993, they suffered from a very weak presence in Alberta, BC, and francophone Quebec; more tellingly, the only other party that has ever been able to assert a realistic claim to national party status throughout our history as a country was totally decimated and replaced by two regional parties—the Bloc Québécois and the Reform Party—that represented diametrically opposite points of view on most public policy questions. The New Democrats, who briefly threatened in 1988 to displace the Liberals as the alternative to the Tories and thereby complete the prophecy that Canada would track European history and move towards a nationwide, left-right polarization of its party politics, were similarly devastated by the 1993 results: their seemingly resilient and slowly growing group of social democratic voters—a growing annoyance and obstacle to both Liberals and Tories—was reduced to a pathetic rump that discouraged even the most diehard believers in the inevitability of their party's goal of attaining truly national party status and contesting for power. The election result suggested that a minimum of three arenas of party competition continued to exist in Canada, with English-speaking Canada divided along an east-west gradient between a Liberal-Conservative East and a Liberal-Reform West, while Quebec again stood apart, divided into two one-party dominant systems (the Liberals and the Bloc Québécois) according to language and ethnicity.

The 1997 federal election result suggests a further fragmentation of the Canadian electorate along regional, ethnocultural, and ideological lines. The Liberal support base was narrowed by significant losses in Atlantic Canada and the West, leaving the party to continue governing from an overwhelming and monolithic Ontario base. The Reform Party consolidated and strengthened its position as the dominant party in western Canada, while losing its only seat east of the Manitoba–Ontario border; the Bloc Québécois remained the party of choice of French-speaking Quebecers. The Conservatives and New Democrats were revived and returned to official party status in Parliament on the strength of their support from an Atlantic Canadian electorate angry with Liberal government policies that hurt the region; as well, the NDP saw the return of some traditional seats in the Midwest (Manitoba and Saskatchewan), while Conservative leader Jean Charest's personal popularity in Quebec attracted enough of the 'soft nationalist' vote to give his party at least a foothold in that province. In sum, this national patchwork of party support has created the most regionalized party system and Parliament in Canadian history, with Atlantic Canada, Quebec, Ontario, and the West each constituting discrete arenas of party competition, with different combinations of parties competitive in each region.

One conclusion that can be drawn from this historical overview is that for the past thirty-five years, national party competition in Canada has been sporadic at best, with no indication that the future will be any different. After 1997, no party can lay claim to a national base of support. The two-party vote share of the traditional national parties—the Liberals and the Conservatives—has declined steadily through each period of party competition, reaching a low point of approximately 60 per cent of the vote in 1993 and 1997. The Westminster system of one-party government inherited by Canada was designed for a two-party system—or at least the ruling party and an official Opposition Party that had a reasonable prospect of replacing the government. This is no longer the case in Canada. Even if the Liberals immediately benefit from this by being the only party in a position to govern, a possibly significant long-term result is increasing voter dissatisfaction with a political system that fails to offer them a real alternative.

It may be, then, that more electoral volatility and political insecurity for all political parties are in store. That is certainly one popular reading of 1993 and 1997: that a cranky electorate now has no allegiances to party. However, the evidence is not conclusive; a good case can be made that the situation in which Canadian parties find themselves is more a product of poorly designed political institutions than the result of an increasingly unruly electorate. It can be argued that Canada now exhibits many of the characteristics of a European-style, multiparty system, with parties grouped into ideological families that draw sustenance from relatively stable electorates that are predisposed to either right- or left-wing appeals, with electoral change occurring within these families rather than across family boundaries. However, it does differ in one key facet: Canada has not developed political institutions for accommodating a degree of cooperation and power sharing between parties in the same ideological family; our electoral system and parliamentary practices work against rather than facilitate this, deliberately suppressing and frustrating a fundamental underlying dynamic in the country's electoral politics. Yet any future stability for national parties in Canada, or more appropriately the national party system, requires institutions that will support more interparty cooperation. This is especially the case now because of the almost complete regionalization of Canada's electorate and party system.[26]

Canada: A Regionalized Polity

During the first half-century of Confederation, regionalism in Canada was contained within a national two-party system.[27] Basic political compromises and trade-offs were struck to achieve this: the Maritimes were provided with a regionally controlled railway that structured its freight rates to allow regional manufacturers to compete in central Canadian and western markets; guarantees were given to Quebec to safeguard its language and religious and legal institutions, while English-speaking prime ministers' appointment of a 'Quebec Lieutenant' ensured French Canadians at the minimum a form of deputy prime ministership; western settlers were provided with free land and a railway to connect them with each other and with international markets.

With time these initial compromises and concessions were overturned or negated by the adoption of new policies, which proved contrary to the interests of particular regions. This allowed the party in opposition to corral regional support by taking up the offended region's cause. Thus, Liberals took up the western farmers' call for lower tariffs and tapped the outrage of French Canadians about the hanging of Louis Riel and the wartime imposition of conscription. This gave the Liberals regional voting blocs that would keep them in power for decades. In the 1920s the Conservatives, thrown into opposition as the result of shifting regional and ethnic loyalties, led the Maritime Rights Movement and nurtured local and regional electorates throughout Canada that wanted to retain Canada's affiliation with all things British. These ties between parties and voters were long term and durable, determining the basic architecture of the Canadian party system over many decades. During more recent times, the Tories railed against Liberal agricultural and energy policies that were unpopular in the West and a Liberal constitutional settlement that excluded the government of Quebec. Championing these regional causes created new ties between the Conservatives and regional electorates that had previously been alienated from the Tories, allowing the party to replicate (for a time) the Quebec–West support base that had once served the Liberals so well.

Yet despite such regionalist appeals and seeming political sensitivity to regional concerns (or perhaps because of them, as Porter[28] or Brodie and Jenson[29] argued) on the part of the traditional parties, regionalism in Canada could not be contained (as it had been prior to the First World War) within a national two-party system. Third parties with regional bases of support have been a continuous feature of Canadian politics since the federal election of 1921, making life difficult for political scientists trying to classify the country's hybrid party system,[30] and confounding expectations regarding an eventual return to a more 'normal' state of affairs (the Anglo-American two-party model).

One set of factors reinforcing this tendency to regionalism in Canadian electoral and party politics is the design and operation of Canadian political institutions: federalism, Westminster-style one-party government, the simple plurality electoral system, and the unreformed Senate. It has been argued repeatedly that the design of key national political institutions is central to parties' capacity and willingness to effectively represent regions. For these

critics, Canada's national political institutions too often appear to exac-
erbate regionalism and stoke the fires of regional discontent rather than
facilitate the systematic integration of regional interests and concerns into
the process of governance.[31] In particular, the electoral system and the
Senate have come in for criticism: the electoral system because of its tendency to penalize national parties with widespread but rather thin support
while rewarding regional parties that spatially concentrate their votes; the
Senate because of its inability to perform the role usually designated to
upper houses in the national legislatures of federal states—that of regional
representation. Such distortions and inadequacies have placed an excessive
political burden on the federal cabinet as virtually the only political mechanism for effectively representing regional interests within national political
institutions.

Federalism, combined with Westminster-style parliamentary government,
has also accentuated and reinforced the tendency to regionalism, increasing
the need for political élites to devise means of intergovernmental cooperation and the coordination of a range of state activities and expenditures.
Over time the pressures of finding ways to effectively integrate the regions
into the heart of the cabinet's decision making have strained the only practical mechanism for doing this: the national party system. Parties once
accomplished this through a system of 'ministerialism', which revolved
around the formation and role of federal cabinets in Canada. Reg Whitaker
has described it as a political device that:

> ... places a premium on the regional representativeness of the executive
> [encouraging] the emergence of regional power-brokers as key Cabinet minis-
> ters, who thus play a double role as administrators and as political leaders of the
> regions.... In the absence of strong class bases to national politics [such]
> cadre-ministerialist party organization rests most comfortably on what loosely
> can be called a patron-client model. The regional discontinuities of the coun-
> try lend themselves to a clientelist type of politics in which one sees vertical
> integration of [regional] sub-cultures and horizontal accommodation among
> elites generated by these sub-cultures. So long as politics revolves mainly
> around questions of patronage and regional bargaining, ministerialism fits in
> well with the needs of the party as an organization.[32]

The problem for the practitioners of this mode of regional integration and
representation is that the problems of industrialism and urbanism, depres-
sions and wars, trade and international competition, debts and deficits
demand universalist, bureaucratic, and generally non-partisan solutions.
Under the pressure of these wider forces, *ministerialist* government has ex-
hibited a tendency to become *administrative* government, and regionally
sensitive politics has given way to functionally oriented bureaucracy. This
provides a large part of the explanation for the declining effectiveness of ministerialism as the chief means of politically integrating Canada's regions.[33]

A forced reliance on ministerialism as the primary means of politically integrating the regions suffers from other shortcomings as well. Regional ministers, and in general the role of regional caucuses within governing parties, will vary from government to government due to their numbers, levels of activity, cohesion, and effectiveness. Governing parties in Canada have often been handicapped by having very few or no elected members from a region. And while a regional minister or caucus can enjoy influence disproportionate to the size of the region represented, or the size of the caucus, this depends on the experience, knowledge, articulateness, and persistence of the caucus members, and in particular on the political skills and longevity of the regional minister.[34]

This reveals the serendipity, the sheer luck involved in the quality of representation a region receives from the ministerialist system. Regional electorates may or may not be presented with high-quality political candidates from which to choose; regardless, they may or may not make the 'right' choice for this purpose in terms of the party for which they choose to vote. Moreover, they have little or no control over the quality of candidates with which they are presented. Even if voters in a region are in this sense fortunate and wise enough, they may still lose out if a governing party is not in power long enough to allow regional ministers to exert a noticeable impact on the structure of power relations within the federal government and bureaucracy. In sum, while ministerialism *may* be capable of delivering stable, high-quality regional representation over an extended period of time, it does so less through design than as the result of a fortuitous conjunction of factors, conditions, and personalities.

Others disagree with the notion that Canada's political institutions are central to the problem of regional integration and representation. David Smith, for instance, gives pride of place to the singular importance of Canadian political leaders (particularly prime ministers) as the linchpins of national political integration. He also places greater emphasis on the structures and processes associated with party organization. For Smith, the *policy and organizational choices of leaders and parties* have determined the mode of political incorporation of people and territory in Canada. If regional tensions have been fomented, it is because Canadian prime ministers have consciously chosen to make a pan-Canadian rather than regional appeal. For Smith, the answer to regional alienation is to find a way to extend 'the structuring effect of the pan-Canadian appeal' into the constituency. This will not be achieved through reformist tinkering with national political institutions; it will only be accomplished, Smith argues, with the *nationalization of individual Canadians into a single political community*. Such pan-Canadianism can be combined with localism by diffusing to the local and regional level the political debate over value choices and national policies, transforming political debate at the constituency level into a microcosm of the national political discourse. Parties should concern themselves with this honourable task (thereby thwarting regionalism at its source), rather than further accommodating regionalism through the redesign of national political institutions.[35]

In defence of the advocates of institutional reform, it should be pointed out that the policy choices leaders and parties make and the organizational forms they construct are not immune to the effects produced by the operation of other political institutions. Indeed, one can usefully regard the ensemble of Canada's political institutions as a matrix: a set of interrelated and interdependent institutions. Significant changes to any one of these institutions will alter the structure of political demand and the kind of political incentives that characterize the political system as a whole. Institutional changes, therefore, should not be considered irrelevant to the intensity and quality of regionalism in Canada; they cannot fail to have some effect on the output side of the political ledger (policy and organizational choices, the issues parties choose to politicize, and so on).

Still, what of Smith's recommendation that political parties advance the political integration of the regions by submerging or ignoring local or regional issues and personalities in favour of a nationally generated political discourse and agenda? The appropriate response to this is to question how long such artifice could be sustained, and ultimately at what political cost (in terms of broken voter-party ties and the further alienation of regional electorates) once the 'spell' (if ever successfully cast) was broken? Simply put, the interests and concerns of 'region' are often not congruent with those of 'nation'. Both the advocates of institutional reform and Smith tend to disregard the often antagonistic relationship that exists between centralizing (or globalizing) economic and bureaucratic forces and the material and cultural interests and identities of regions and localities. The project of developing and diffusing to the regions a single national discourse may be consistent with the desire of élites at the centre to control, regulate, and integrate the national polity's disparate regions, but if this does nothing more than impose upon those regions and locales the values and perspectives of national élites, then it accomplishes little more than to temporarily craft a form of legitimized political and bureaucratic domination. In such instances, what may appear to élites at the centre as disintegrative regional or local parochialism can be otherwise understood as regional opposition to centralizing forces that tend to be oblivious (if not hostile) to regional concerns and resistant to regional representations.

It does not seem likely, then, that political regionalism could be submerged for any extended period of time by national political parties simply through the technique of diffusing to (or imposing on) the regions an integrative national political discourse. Conversely, the straightforward political strategy of openly courting the regional vote may be fine for regional parties, but is less available to national party élites than Smith supposes. Whether, when, and in what manner national parties make effective regionalist appeals, and the extent to which regional concerns can be meaningfully addressed by the party in power, are circumscribed by a number of conditioning factors. First, the structure of the economy and the dominant strategy of economic growth might place quite strict parameters on a region's role and prospects, thereby limiting both the willingness and the capacity of political élites at the centre to respond to regional representations and concerns.[36] As well, attempts to make government policies more sensitive to regional needs and concerns will encounter the inertia and stiff resistance of a functionally oriented federal bureaucracy.[37] Finally, regional electorates and representatives will encounter different 'political opportunity structures' at the centre, determined by the balance of political forces at any one time that enhances their leverage or shrinks their political impact and margin of manoeuvre. Parties operate within these parameters, and party strategies, regionalist appeals, and voter responses will vary depending upon economic and political circumstances at both the regional and national level.

Looking to the Future

The deficiencies and biases of Canadian political institutions aside, does a fragmented right and weak left guarantee the centrist Liberals another long period as Canada's governing party? Some of the requisite elements for such a scenario seem to be in place, but a key component of Liberal political hegemony in the past—an unassailable Quebec base—is missing and seems unlikely to be recovered in the near future. Still, as long as it is the Bloc Québécois that attracts the allegiance of francophone voters (and not a party contesting seats in the rest of Canada), continued Liberal dominance may not be difficult. Under these circumstances, a unified and resurgent right would seem a more likely source of electoral threat. Yet even if the major obstacles to this development are somehow overcome, the Liberals' demonstrated prediliction in good brokerage fashion to govern from the right unless threatened from the left will tend to undercut the government's conservative critics. However, should the governing Liberals remain focused on the electoral threat posed by the right, disgruntled left-of-centre support will continue to be siphoned away from the Liberal Party (as the NDP has done in Atlantic Canada). This would force the centrist Liberals to move left in order to stem this leakage, thereby opening space for right-of-centre parties to make a more effective appeal to their traditional electorate. A revival of national party competition encompassing a more polarized and enriched political debate could well ensue.

Finally, there is a lesson for all the parties provided by the Tory débâcle of 1993. It is that no party can ignore the need to maintain its base of core supporters; no party can secure its long-term electoral position by attempting to simultaneously appeal to fundamentally different social and political bases as the Mulroney Tories did. Brokering a national consensus may indeed be the most heroic function our parties can perform, but if done as the centrepiece of a political strategy for winning and holding power, parties can become victims of their own ambition, torn asunder while attempting to span deep and enduring divisions within Canadian society.

Notes

1. Jeffrey Simpson, *Discipline of Power: The Conservative Interlude and the Liberal Restoration* (Toronto: Personal Library, 1980):xiii.
2. For an overview and critique of this model, see J. Brodie and J. Jenson, 'Piercing the Smokescreen: Stability and Change in Brokerage Politics', in *Canadian Parties in Transition*, 2nd edn, edited by A.B. Tanguay and A.-G. Gagnon (Toronto: Nelson Canada, 1996):52–72.
3. H.D. Clarke, J. Jenson, L. Leduc, and J. Pammett, *Absent Mandate: The Politics of Discontent in Canada* (Toronto: Gage, 1984).
4. J. Wearing, *The Ballot and Its Message: Voting in Canada* (Toronto: Copp, Clark, Pitman, 1991):57.
5. J.A. Corry, *Democratic Government and Politics* (Toronto: University of Toronto Press, 1946):221.
6. M. Goldfarb and T. Axworthy, *Marching to a Different Drummer: An Essay on Liberals and Conservatives in Convention* (Toronto: Stoddart, 1988):135.
7. Ibid., 10.
8. R. Johnston, A. Blais, H.E. Brady, and J. Crete, *Letting the People Decide: Dynamics of a Canadian Election* (Montreal and Kingston: McGill-Queen's University Press, 1993):82.
9. R. Johnston, 'The Reproduction of the Religious Cleavage in Canadian Elections', *Canadian Journal of Political Science* 18, no. 1 (1985):PAGES?.
10. M. Stevenson, 'Ideology and Unstable Party Identification in Canada: Limited Rationality in a Brokerage Party System', *Canadian Journal of Political Science* 18, no. 1 (1987):813–50; James Bickerton, 'Creating Atlantic Canada', in *Canadian Politics: An Introduction to the Discipline*, edited by A.-G. Gagnon and James Bickerton (Peterborough: Broadview Press, 1991); Goldfarb and Axworthy, *Marching to a Different Drummer*; C. Campbell and W. Christian, *Parties, Leaders and Ideologies in Canada* (Toronto: McGraw-Hill Ryerson, 1996).
11. J. Brodie and J. Jenson, 'Piercing the Smokescreen: Brokerage Parties and Class Politics', in *Canadian Parties in Transition*, edited by Alain-G. Gagnon and A. Brian Tanguay (Scarborough: Nelson Canada, 1989):39.
12. A. Brian Tanguay, 'The Transformation of Canada's Party System in the 1990's', in *Canadian Politics*, 2nd edn, edited by James P. Bickerton and A.-G. Gagnon (Peterborough: Broadview Press, 1994):122.
13. Robert Laxer, 'Foreign Ownership and Myths About Canadian Development', *Canadian Review of Sociology and Anthropology* 22, no. 3 (1985):311–45; Robert Laxer, 'The Political Economy of Aborted Development: The Canadian Case',

in *The Structure of the Canadian Capitalist Class*, edited by R.J. Brym (Toronto: Garamond, 1985):67–99.

14. Gilles Bourque as quoted in Leo Panitch, 'Elites, Classes and Power in Canada', in *Canadian Politics in the 1990s*, 4th edn (Scarborough: Nelson Canada, 1995):169.

15. Ibid., 170.

16. Ibid. Quoted in the *Toronto Star* (18 October 1975).

17. Ibid.

18. Donald Blake, '1896 and All That: Critical Elections in Canada', *Canadian Journal of Political Science* XII, no. 2 (June 1979):264.

19. Ibid., 278.

20. This is the position clearly articulated and applied in R. Johnston et al., *Letting the People Decide*.

21. See Ken Carty, 'Three Canadian Party Systems: An Interpretation of the Development of National Politics', in *Party Democracy in Canada: The Politics of National Party Conventions*, edited by George Perlin (Scarborough: Prentice-Hall, 1988); Richard Johnston, 'The Electoral Basis of the Canadian Party Systems, 1878–1984', in *Canadian Political Party Systems*, edited by R.K. Carty (Peterborough: Broadview Press, 1992):587–623.

22. R. Johnston et al., *Letting the People Decide*, 37, 45–6.

23. Ibid., 65–6.

24. For instance, over the span of the three party systems identified in the UBC approach, the Liberal Party's Catholic core support base persisted. On the other hand, once Liberal ties with western voters were broken (due to the Liberal government's growing insensitivity to western concerns at a time when the Conservatives were transforming themselves into a more attractive alternative), voters in that region only rarely have shown a willingness to again vote Liberal.

25. Ibid., 72–3.

26. Analysis of the 1993 and 1997 federal elections' results confirm this. See R. Johnston, A. Blais, E. Gidengil, N. Nevitte, and H. Brady, 'The 1993 Canadian General Election: Realignment, Dealignment or something else?' a paper presented to the Annual Meeting of the Canadian Political Science Association, Brock University, St Catharines, Ontario, 2–4 June 1996, p. 8. In this paper the authors present some preliminary results from the 1993 national election study. The authors characterized the partisan changes that occurred outside Quebec as a vote shift within ideological families; in other words, ideological affiliation did matter when partisans defected to another party. Only in Quebec, however, did they discern evidence of a fundamental realignment of voters in terms of party identification. The Bloc Québécois sucked up both Tory and NDP *voters* and also won them over as *identifiers* (i.e., as self-identified party supporters or 'partisans'). Even more significantly, the Bloc mobilized those francophone Quebecers who had previously abstained from voting in federal elections as well as new voters entering the electorate. For a preliminary analysis of the 1997 federal election that confirms the centrality of region to the pattern of partisan support, see E. Gidengil, A. Blais, R. Nadeau, and N. Nevitte, 'Making Sense of the Regional Vote in the 1997 Canadian Election', a paper presented to the Annual Meeting of the Canadian Political Science Association, University of Ottawa, June 1998.

27. This section is drawn from James Bickerton, 'Parties and Regions: Alternative Models of Representation', in *Canadian Parties in Transition*, 2nd edn, edited by

A. Brian Tanguay and Alain-G. Gagnon (Scarborough: Nelson Canada, 1996): 496–502.

28. John Porter, *The Vertical Mosaic: An Analysis of Social Class and Power in Canada* (Toronto: University of Toronto Press, 1965).

29. Janine Brodie and Jane Jenson, *Crisis, Challenge and Change: Party and Class in Canada* (Toronto: Methuen, 1980).

30. Hugh Thorburn, 'Interpretations of the Canadian Party System', in *Party Politics in Canada*, 6th edn, edited by Hugh Thorburn (Scarborough: Prentice-Hall, 1991):114–24.

31. Alan Cairns, 'The Electoral System and the Party System in Canada, 1921–1965', *Canadian Journal of Political Science* 1, no. 1 (1968):55–80; Richard Simeon, 'Regionalism and Canadian Political Institutions', *Queen's Quarterly* 82, no. 4 (1975):499–511; Peter Aucoin, 'Regionalism, Party and National Government', in *Party Government and Regional Representation in Canada*, P. Aucoin, research co-ordinator, volume 36, *Research Studies: Royal Commission on the Economic Union and Development Prospects for Canada* (Toronto: University of Toronto Press, 1985); D. Smiley and R.L. Watts, *Intrastate Federalism in Canada*, volume 39, *Research Studies: Royal Commission on the Economic Union and Development Prospects for Canada* (Toronto: University of Toronto Press, 1986).

32. Reginald Whitaker, *The Government Party: Organizing and Financing the Liberal Party of Canada, 1930–1958* (Toronto: University of Toronto Press, 1977):407.

33. Generally speaking, the greater the extent to which regionally circumscribed and defined interests diverged from the strategies and policies devised by the national government to address wider concerns, the more unlikely it became that a single integrated party system would suffice as the primary mechanism of regional integration and representation. The problems inherent in doing so were clearly evident as early as the period immediately following the First World War when the governing parties' inability to placate both the interests of western farmers and eastern business and industry led to the rise of protest parties on the Prairies. Something similar (if not quite so dramatic) can be said to have occurred in the Atlantic region in the 1997 election.

34. Herman Bakvis, *Regional Ministers: Power and Influence in the Canadian Cabinet* (Toronto: University of Toronto Press, 1991); P.G. Thomas, 'Parties and Regional Representation', in *Represention, Integration and Political Parties in Canada*, volume 14, edited by Herman Bakvis, *Research Studies: Royal Commission on Electoral Reform and Party Financing* (Toronto: Dundurn Press, 1991); P.G. Thomas, 'The Role of National Party Caucuses', in P. Aucoin, research coordinator, volume 36, *Research Studies: Royal Commission on the Economic Union and Development Prospects for Canada* (Toronto: University of Toronto Press, 1985):124.

35. D.E. Smith, 'Party Government, Representation, and National Integration in Canada', in *Party Government and Representation in Canada*, P. Aucoin, research coordinator, volume 36, *Research Studies: Royal Commission on the Economic Union and Development Prospects for Canada* (Toronto: University of Toronto Press, 1985):50–4.

36. In this connection Janine Brodie has examined the role of Canada's regions in what she identifies as three successive post-Confederation national economic strategies (the First, Second, and Third National Policies). Brodie argues that such strategies have been premised on long-term economic-growth models that

require national policy frameworks that inevitably and necessarily benefit the dominant business interests at the centre. Economic structures in this way have been created that are not easily altered and have generally accorded Canada's peripheral regions a rather limited and constrained economic role. The disaffection that springs from the resulting spatial inequalities gives rise to regional protest and regional parties, but it cannot be assumed that fundamental change in the situation and prospects of regions can be easily effected, if at all, regardless of the quality of the region's representation. Janine Brodie, 'Regions and Regionalism', in *Canadian Politics*, 2nd edn, edited by James Bickerton and Alain-G. Gagnon (Peterborough: Broadview Press, 1994):409–25.

37. See James Bickerton, *Nova Scotia, Ottawa and the Politics of Regional Development* (Toronto: University of Toronto Press, 1990).

CHAPTER 2

THE PROGRESSIVE CONSERVATIVES: BROKEN TIES, BROKEN DREAMS

The Conservative Party is Canada's oldest, going back to the pre-Confederation period. The party's first leader, John A. Macdonald, was also Canada's first prime minister, governing from 1867–73 and again from 1878 until his death in 1891. The key to Conservative dominance during this period was Macdonald's skill at brokering a binational coalition of English and French, Catholic and Protestant. This set the pattern for attaining political power in Canada, though it would be close to a century before another Conservative leader would replicate Macdonald's formula as the basis for winning consecutive majority governments. Instead, it would be the Liberal Party that would become the party of English-French reconciliation *par excellence*.

The First Party System, 1867–1917

The Confederation of British North American colonies brought about in 1867 primarily by Macdonald and his Liberal-Conservative Party, as it was then called, contained some key Tory elements. Principal among these was the idea of loyalty to the Crown and membership in the British Empire. Macdonald's 'dominant concern was to keep the British connection unbroken, to follow British institutions, to preserve the spirit of the British Constitution, and to save Canada for a British civilization. Canadians must be either English or American, said Macdonald, and he was determined to be English.'[1] Secondly, Canadian conservatism believed in the importance of privilege; it 'accepted and approved of class, rank and distinctions'.[2] Finally, Macdonald's Conservatives preferred a strong central government entrusted with sufficient powers to build and maintain a transcontinental political unit in North America; government would be the instrument for building a society, not a necessary evil to be strictly limited. Most of the policies identified with Macdonald's long tenure—protective tariffs, building the Canadian Pacific Railway, recognition of trade unions, partial extension of the vote, and a partnership with French Canada—are rooted in this Tory ideology. These elements provided a central core of continuity for Conservative supporters throughout the first and second party systems.

While Toryism gave Macdonald a broader ideological appeal than his Liberal opponents in the early years of Confederation, it was the successful brokering of a French-English alliance that underpinned the Conservative Party's nineteenth-century success. This coalition was premised initially on the inherent compatibility of a tolerant Toryism in English Canada and the deeply entrenched, Church-sponsored conservatism of French Canada. By 1890, however, this partnership was placed under great strain by the hardening and sharpening of attitudes engendered by the Riel rebellion and its aftermath (specifically Riel's execution) and by the rise in Ontario of D'Alton McCarthy's Equal Rights Association, an uncompromising political movement that stood for a single language (English) and a single system of public schools. In combination with Ontario's anti-Catholic Orangeites, the militantly pro-British, Protestant wing of Ontario Conservatism weakened the more tolerant Toryism of an earlier period, and with it the basis of Conservative electoral dominance.[3]

It was in this context that Macdonald fought his last election in 1891. The Liberals, now under the leadership of a French Canadian, Wilfrid Laurier, were advocating a policy of unrestricted reciprocity ('u.r.', the nineteenth-century equivalent of free trade) with the United States as a cure for Canada's economic ills. For Macdonald and his Conservative loyalists, the Liberal platform was a godsend. It allowed them to focus the election on questions of loyalty, patriotism, and identity: 'the principles of British unity, British commerce, and British sympathy as against Continental unity, Continental trade, and Continental sympathy'.[4] Using the slogan, 'the old man, the old flag, the old policy', the Tories were able to play on both the emotional connection many Canadians felt towards both Macdonald the man and Britain the mother country, as well as the self-interests of important economic actors—the banks, railways, and manufacturers—who benefited from the National Policy. This carried the day for the Conservatives, despite the strong attraction free trade held for farmers. The fight against 'u.r.' minimized Tory losses in Ontario and gave them a life-saving margin of twenty-one in Nova Scotia and New Brunswick, where 'above everything else, the loyalty cry was heard and heeded'.[5]

The reprieve for the Tories was temporary. When they lost power in 1896, it heralded a basic realignment in the loyalties of Quebec voters in particular.[6] Underlying this was a number of factors, not the least of which was the fact that the Liberals had chosen an able French Canadian as their leader. But this alone cannot explain the shift of political hegemony from Conservative to Liberal. The Liberals shifted policy ground as well, subduing their historic anticlericalism and accepting key Tory policies that were proven vote-getters, most notably the National Policy of high tariffs to protect

Canadian manufacturers. This shift made the Liberal Party more palatable both to francophone Quebecers and to the manufacturing interests of Central Canada. This demonstrated both the party's growing maturity and its embrace of the fundamental tenets of brokerage politics.

Liberal leaders and policy shifts aside, the well-known maxim that 'Opposition parties don't win elections, governing parties lose them' also quite aptly applies to the Tory defeat of 1896. The strain of holding together a disparate political coalition that included growing numbers of Anglo-Protestant and Franco-Catholic extremists was already beginning to show before Macdonald's death. Macdonald's decision not to commute the death sentence of Louis Riel—the Catholic, French-speaking leader of the Métis uprising of 1885—proved to be a flashpoint for these divisions. Indeed, Quebec's francophone voters' movement away from the Tories began in the very next federal election (1887). The alienation of francophone Catholics was reinforced by the Manitoba schools crisis (the Manitoba government's decision to purge the French language from its schools). Finally, the party's leadership crisis after Macdonald's death—the party had four different leaders over the next five years—did nothing to help Tory electoral prospects.

Now deprived of astute bicultural leadership (the Macdonald-Cartier team), and pressured in Ontario by the rise of Anglo-Protestant extremism and by an upsurge of radical agrarianism (the Patrons of Industry), the Conservatives were neither able to hold onto their Quebec base of Catholic francophone supporters nor offset this loss by consolidating the Anglo-Protestant vote in Ontario. Though the Conservatives would remain strong over the next fifteen years in the bastions of Anglo-Protestantism—Ontario, Manitoba, and British Columbia—it was the Laurier Liberals who would govern Canada on the basis of solid majorities in Quebec, the Catholic areas of the Maritimes, and (after 1905) the rapidly growing and immigrant-filled provinces of Saskatchewan and Alberta. This fundamental division of voter loyalties would remain largely intact until the Diefenbaker revolution of 1957-8.

When the Conservatives next regained power in 1911, they did so on the basis of an electoral strategy that acknowledged the party's weakness in Quebec and their need for an electoral ally in that province capable of appealing to francophone Catholic voters. The main issue over which the 1911 election was fought in English Canada was the Liberal proposal for a free trade agreement with the United States (in natural products only). A popular idea with western farmers and other exporters of staple products, the Liberal embrace of 'reciprocity' marked a return to the party's philosophical roots, but also to their losing program of 1891. Once again, the Conservatives portrayed reciprocity with the United States as an attack on the National Policy and Canada's British ties, rallying their supporters with the slogan 'No Truck or Trade with the Yankees'. This patriotic appeal was supported by commercial interests who were nervous that their protected domestic markets would be endangered by some future extension of the free trade agreement beyond natural products. This dovetailing of economic interest and patriotism gave the Tories an overwhelming victory in Ontario, Manitoba, and British Columbia. In Quebec the Tories' electoral alliance with French-Canadian nationalists led by Henri Bourassa—who was opposed to Laurier's naval policy because it further involved Canada in Britain's imperialist ventures—deprived the Liberals of the majority of Quebec seats to which they had become accustomed and upon which they depended. Though Conservative gains in Ontario and Quebec were sufficient to return the party to power after fifteen years in opposition, this long-awaited victory was achieved through a quite contradictory call to arms in the name of the British connection (in English Canada) and French-Canadian nationalism (in Quebec).

Of course, such an unlikely political alliance could not last. The allies were bound by mutual hostility to Laurier's policies and political style, not by any real commonality of interest; once Laurier was defeated, this became abundantly clear. It is true that both the Tory leader Borden and the nationalist Bourassa rejected the local focus, political patronage, and corruption that fuelled party politics during the Macdonald and Laurier regimes. For them politics was meant to be about loftier goals: defining and pursuing a transcendent national interest. Their respective national and political visions, however, differed dramatically. Borden exemplified the new progressivist, modernizing spirit of his era, which above all valued progress, rationality, and businesslike efficiency in private and public affairs. This made him uncomfortable with the trade-offs, compromises, and petty partisanship that were so deeply rooted in Canada's party and government affairs. Bourassa also disliked and opposed the extensive patronage and corruption of party politics, but his vision of an independent bilingual and bicultural Canadian identity was directly at odds with the Tory embrace of the British Empire and 'Britishness' as the central element of Canadian identity.[7]

It should be remembered that this seemingly odd political alliance of strange bedfellows was not unprecedented, having been first cemented by Macdonald and Cartier. Nor would this be the last time that Quebec nationalists would make common cause with a Tory party rooted in an Anglo-Protestant core support base that was largely unsympathetic with (if not hostile towards) the national vision and political aspirations of Quebec's francophones. The same political dance would be repeated in the 1980s when under Brian Mulroney's leadership the Conservative Party and Quebec nationalists would once again cement an alliance against the Liberal Party, with the same dim prospects for sustaining such a partnership. In both cases, the alliance emerged as the result of an internal quarrel among Quebec francophones that led nationalists to strike a strategic alliance with political enemies of the Liberals. In such instances, Quebec politics is turned on its head, with major consequences for the Canadian party system and the shape of national politics.

For the Conservatives, the collapse of their alliance with Quebec nationalists shortly after the 1911 election likely would have been fatal to their re-election chances had not the First World War intervened. Borden was able to delay the next federal election until 1917 when the horrors and extreme demands of wartime stirred the passions of English and French alike around a crucial issue: conscription. With mounting losses in Europe and sagging voluntary enlistment, Borden's government argued that conscription was necessary to carry on the war effort and support the troops already overseas. This precipitated a split in Liberal ranks, with most English-speaking Liberal MPs joining Borden's Conservatives in a new Unionist government, leaving a rump of mostly French-speaking Liberals in opposition. Borden was convinced the war was remaking Canadian society and politics; that a new party system was taking shape that might well spell the end of the old parties, but all for the greater good of Canada. As noted by historian John English, 'Unionism proposed to abolish party by declaring itself the embodiment of the public interest.'[8] For Borden, winning the war and nurturing the emergence of this new politics took precedence over safeguarding the partisan interests of the old Tory party.[9]

The consequences of the realignment of political loyalties induced by the conscription crisis and Unionism were potentially devastating for both the party system and the country, threatening to divide both along purely ethnic and linguistic lines. And indeed, French-English tensions, mistrust, and misunderstanding were greater at this time than they had ever been. The division, however, was not quite so stark as French versus English. Fortunately, French Canada was not alone in shunning the new bipartisan nationalism associated with Unionism. For the most part, the Maritimes were not won over to it; nor was rural Ontario 'where only a blatant political bribe purchased the loyalty of the Ontario farmer'.[10] This illustrates the resiliency of the party loyalties embraced by regional electorates, even in the midst of upheaval and change. Nor should it be surprising that this resiliency was more apparent in eastern Canada than in the West, where the party system had sunk only shallow roots in the recently formed electorate.

For fifty years the Conservative Party appealed to Canadian voters on the basis of a fairly coherent and consistent Tory ideology and an interrelated and mutually reinforcing set of national policies (trade, tariffs, transportation, and immigration). John A. Macdonald and George Cartier were the embodiment of the founding version of this Canadian Toryism, the appeal of which ran strongly in both the English- and French-speaking communities. However, the delicately brokered English-French alliance at the core of the party's original electoral coalition was gradually eroded by the response of the governing Tories to events (such as the Riel rebellion), the impact on the party of social and religious movements (such as Orangeism), and the adjustments and repositioning undertaken by partisan opponents (in particular the Liberals). After 1896 the core electorate of the Conservative Party had a more pronounced English-speaking and Protestant character as its bicultural appeal waned. This shift became extreme with the conscription crisis of 1917. At the same time, the party's long-held high tariff commercial policy was anathema to western Canada's pro-free trade grain farmers. As a result, by the end of the first party system, the Conservative Party had alienated French Canada almost completely, as well as agrarian interests in the West. Its core electorate in ethnoreligious terms was reduced to Protestant English Canadians, and in regional terms to the commercial and industrial heartland of Ontario.

The Second Party System, 1921–1957

The political phenomenon of Unionism did not long outlast Borden's resignation as prime minister and party leader in 1920. The new prime minister, Arthur Meighen, led a restored Conservative Party into the 1921 election against a reconstituted Liberal Party, which also had a new leader (Mackenzie King), the first to be chosen by convention delegates rather than the parliamentary caucus.[11] Though the old-line parties once again appealed to their traditional supporters in the electorate, 'politics as usual' could not be restored so easily. Instead, the party system was shaken to its foundations by the emergence of a new competitor intent upon smashing the mould of party politics in Canada. The Progressives, the political manifestation of a populist farmers' movement opposed to old-style partyism as practised by the Liberals and Tories, emerged from the confusion and bipartisanship of the 1917–20 period to win sixty-five seats in 1921. This displaced the Conservatives, who managed only fifty seats (thirty-seven of these in Ontario), as the second largest party in Parliament.

The disastrous 1921 result for the Tories, who managed to capture only 30 per cent of the vote, both revealed the foundation of bedrock Conservative support in Canada at this time and presaged the contours of the party's vote during the long period of Liberal rule from 1935 to 1957. The election also heralded a transition from a party system based on classic two-party competition with an intensely local or constituency focus to a system based on regional brokerage featuring Conservative and Liberal parties that were quite different from those of the Macdonald-Laurier era, as well as a variety of third parties that would attempt to break the hold of the traditional parties by making a targeted appeal to specific regions or classes.

It would take some time, however, for this new system of party competition to establish itself. The surging Progressives proved to be a transitory protest movement. During the 1920s they were reabsorbed into the older parties as more familiar patterns of political conflict—regionalism, corruption, tariffs, and appeals to national autonomy versus Empire—reasserted themselves. Rather than being permanently displaced as the second party, the Conservatives rebounded strongly in 1925, winning a total of 116 seats. Most of these additional seats came from former areas of Conservative support in the Maritimes and Ontario. In the former, a deep and prolonged recession was brought on by the closure or downsizing of much of the region's industrial capacity. This stimulated the Maritime Rights Movement, which called for action by Mackenzie King's Liberal government in Ottawa to change national policies that were damaging to the region's interests. Just as the Progressives became the vehicle for western discontent, the recently rejected Conservative Party took up the standard of Maritime Rights, in the process becoming the major political beneficiary of Maritime discontent with the Liberal government's failure to address Maritime grievances.[12] In Ontario, the Tory party's poor 1921 result was shown to be a temporary aberration from the province's traditionally Conservative loyalties. All five Liberal cabinet ministers in Ontario were defeated, including King, whose low-tariff policies and lacklustre image were clearly disliked.[13]

Though Tory strength in Ontario and the Maritimes gave the party the largest parliamentary contingent after the 1925 election, they failed to achieve an outright majority. In the minority Parliament that followed, a constitutional crisis was precipitated when Governor-General Lord Byng refused Prime Minister Mackenzie King's request for a new election; instead Byng called on Meighen's Conservatives to form a government. When Meighen in turn failed to hold the support of a parliamentary majority and was forced to call an election, King used the opportunity to launch a dubious attack on Byng's actions as unconstitutional and undemocratic. Though the Conservative vote share in the ensuing election barely changed from the previous year, their seat total dropped to ninety-one; the Liberals polled only 0.8 per cent more of the vote, but won thirty-seven more seats than the Tories, gaining substantially from the fading Progressives in Ontario, Manitoba, and Saskatchewan.[14] The electoral system had once again imposed its quirky logic, delivering dramatically different seat distributions to the parties on the basis of insignificant changes in the popular vote. This gives the appearance of dramatic reversals in the partisan sentiments of the population when in fact it is nothing more than an electoral system effect. Beneath the changing political fortunes of the parties lay a basic continuity in the partisan allegiances of Canadian voters.

Meighen's second electoral defeat as Conservative leader was followed by his resignation and, for the first time in Conservative Party history, a leadership convention. In 1927 R.B. Bennett, a New Brunswick-born Albertan, was chosen on the second ballot and in 1930 he led his party back into government. As in 1926, this reversal occurred despite virtually no change in the governing party's national vote totals. It happened because the Conservatives managed to partially break the Liberal stranglehold on the sympathies of francophone Quebec voters while substantially improving their seats-to-votes ratio on the Prairies.

A number of factors combined to produce the surprising if modest turnaround of Tory fortunes in Quebec: the economic situation and particularly growing unemployment after the stock market crash of 1929, the declining salience of the conscription issue in Quebec (especially since Meighen, its arch-proponent, was no longer Conservative leader), and in particular the growing economic difficulties and fears of Quebec's dairy farming regions (where the Tories made their Quebec gains). Growing unemployment was also a problem on the Prairies. Combined with the recent defeat of an influential provincial Liberal administration in Saskatchewan and the fickleness of the electoral system, the Prairie results become somewhat more comprehensible.[15] Still, the 1930 election proved to be an anomaly; it would take the Tories another twenty-eight years to duplicate the feat.

In retrospect, losing power in 1930 was a fortuitous event for the Liberals; winning power was nothing short of disastrous for the Conservative Party. When after five years of economic depression Bennett finally decided to follow US President Roosevelt's lead and proposed a program of radical reforms (the so-called Bennett New Deal), it came too late for his party to stave off the wrath of Canadian voters and a resounding electoral defeat. With three new protest parties (CCF, Social Credit, and Reconstruction) siphoning off voter support, the Tories were pushed back to the same 30 per cent of the vote they had tallied in 1921. The party's poor result in Quebec and the Prairies, where they won a grand total of eight seats, was particularly alarming, reaffirming with special emphasis the alienation of these regions from the Conservative Party. With Ontario providing twenty-five of the party's forty seats, the Conservatives in Parliament were reduced to little more than a regional party.

Through the next two decades of Liberal dominance, the Conservative Party struggled to survive as a national party, averaging 30 per cent of the votes and forty to fifty seats. Following Bennett, who resigned in 1938, the party had six leaders in the next ten years: Robert J. Manion, Richard Hanson, Arthur Meighen (again), John Bracken, and George Drew. The party also struggled to find its way ideologically. Subject since the Borden years to the contending influences of the Tory philosophy, which had been dominant in the Macdonald era, and a more recent 'business liberal' outlook that was more individualist and antistatist, from the mid-1930s onward the party moved uncertainly towards embracing a more welfare liberal orientation as manifested in the Bennett New Deal and the party's change of name (at Bracken's urging) to Progressive Conservative in 1942. The ideological tenor of the times and the growing popularity of the socialist CCF no doubt helped to account for this movement to the left, which nevertheless produced no discernible electoral benefit for the Tories at a time when all parties seemed to be moving in this direction, and others somewhat more credibly.[16]

The Conservatives' reformist repositioning in search of a larger constituency was reversed for a time after George Drew assumed the leadership in 1948.[17] John Bracken, Drew's predecessor, had been a left-leaning former Progressive premier of Manitoba before taking over as Tory leader. Drew, however, had won a majority in Ontario by launching an all-out assault on the socialist threat posed by the CCF. As Ontario premier, he was a staunch defender of provincial autonomy against the centralizing thrust of Ottawa's tax regime and social programs, a campaign he continued as federal Conservative leader. Conservative strategists hoped that Drew's stance against the federal government's invasion of provincial jurisdiction would appeal to Quebecers who were equally wary of the implications of Ottawa's postwar role. Any potential appeal to Quebecers on this score was blunted, however, by Drew's own Anglophile and anti-French past and by the stark personal contrast between this representative of Protestant, Anglo-Saxon Ontario and the new Liberal leader, Louis St Laurent (a native francophone Quebecer to whom the leadership had been passed in 1948).[18] Nor did Drew's big business, urban Ontario image go down well in the Maritimes or on the Prairies, where regional resentment against the country's economic power centre ran deep. In the postwar elections of 1949 and 1953, the Conservatives remained mired at forty to fifty (mainly Ontario) seats.

When Drew stepped down as leader in 1956, expectations for his successor were low. The national economy continued to hum along under the watchful eye of its competent Liberal managers, but cracks had begun to appear in what previously had seemed an impenetrable Liberal facade. With the end of the Korean War and a widening gap in regional growth rates, it was becoming apparent that not all were benefiting equally in the national prosperity. In particular, the Maritime provinces were beginning to clamour for federal intervention to address structural problems that were plaguing their economies. Their displeasure was expressed first by electing Conservative provincial governments in New Brunswick and Nova Scotia, the first in over two decades. The Prairies, too, were feeling the effects of a prolonged slump in wheat prices. Still, with arguably the best economic record in the democratic world, the Liberals felt fairly certain that 'nobody was going to shoot Santa Claus'.[19]

Not only did the Liberal government show insufficient concern about the economic problems of the peripheries, they seemed increasingly arrogant in their general exercise of power, a perception driven home by the 1956 pipeline debate in Parliament and Liberal measures to override parliamentary traditions and bring the debate to an end. The pipeline debate also raised concerns about the growing extent of American control over Canadian resources and industry. Both issues would come back to haunt the Liberals in the coming election.

Wittingly or not, in 1956 the Conservatives chose a leader who was ideally suited to capitalize on these various Liberal weaknesses. John Diefenbaker, who had failed to win the leadership on two previous occasions, was in many ways the opposite of Drew: a small-town Saskatchewan lawyer of non-British heritage and a populist who liked to defend 'the little guy' against the big interests. Diefenbaker was popular with the rank-and-file of the Conservative Party, but not with its Toronto-centred establishment. A highly effective orator and enthusiastic campaigner, Diefenbaker's sympathy for the problems of farmers, peripheral regions, and the less advantaged in society, and his strong sense of traditional Anglo-Canadian patriotism (with its wariness of the United States), changed both the complexion of Tory policy proposals and voter perceptions of the party.[20]

> Where formerly the Conservative Party had stood for balanced budgets and restricted economic intervention by government, it now, under the leadership of Diefenbaker, appeared to be favouring a welfare-statism that places it to the left of the Liberals. . . . its six-year period of rule featured such items as increased old age pensions, extended and enlarged unemployment insurance benefits, and heavy financial assistance to the provinces, most notably the Prairies and the Maritimes.[21]

In the 1957 election, Diefenbaker's appeal in Atlantic Canada and Ontario was sufficient to give the Tories more seats (though not more votes) than the Liberals. The continuing strength of third parties in the West (where the CCF and Social Credit together won forty-four seats) barred the way to a Tory majority. Nevertheless, it soon became clear that Diefenbaker's growing appeal in English-speaking Canada would enable him to accomplish that without Quebec. Within a year a new election delivered the biggest landslide in Canadian history; Diefenbaker swept aside the Social Credit and CCF in the West and, with the support of Quebec Premier Maurice Duplessis and his Union Nationale Party, took fifty of Quebec's seventy-five seats, winning a Tory majority in that province for the first time since 1887.

The Diefenbaker victories of 1957–8 decisively brought the second party system to an end. As Johnston et al. argued, the pattern of party support associated with this era of party politics was shaped primarily by two dimensions of Canadian politics. Its ethnoreligious basis, whereby the Liberal Party counted disproportionately on the support of francophones and Catholics and the Tories on Anglo-Protestants, was less a function of the issues of language and religion *per se* than it was a reflection of the division between these groups over the moral and symbolic claims of the British connection. The Tories wished to preserve and enhance Canada's ties to the British Empire; the Liberals resisted its pull. This division between the parties and their supporters was a major element of continuity linking the first and second party systems. With the further passage of time and continued change in the ethnocultural make-up of Canada, the British connection would continue to fade in significance for Canadians, precipitating a bitter internal struggle within the Progressive Conservative Party over its basic orientation to questions of language and nationality. During the third party system, this would become a key point of weakness in party solidarity and competitive positioning *vis-à-vis* the Liberals, the equivalent of a Tory 'glass jaw'.

The other dimension of Canadian politics that shaped party loyalties before 1957–8 was a rural-urban one, and in particular the political association of farmers. Generally opposed to the National Policy's high tariffs (which were supported by both labour and capital), export-oriented farmers were antagonistic to the Conservatives, the party that had consistently championed that policy. The Liberal Party benefited from this, as did third parties in the West. However, with the gradual disappearance of Empire connections and the subsequent detachment of Canada's commercial policy from such considerations, the Conservatives ceased to associate the National Policy with the primal question of Canadian identity and nationality. Their acceptance of the lower tariff regime associated with the postwar General Agreement on Tariffs and Trade (GATT) meant that farmers in the West and elsewhere were free to become part of the Conservative electoral coalition, which they did in large numbers once there was sufficient incentive for them to do so.[22]

The Third Party System, 1962–1984

Appearances to the contrary, the lopsided 1958 election result did not herald the onset of another Macdonald-style era of Tory dominance based on the elimination of third party competitors in the West and a Conservative revival in Quebec. In retrospect, however, it did mark a crucial turning-point in Canadian party politics. Diefenbaker's assumption of power precisely at the beginning of the first postwar recession, his profound inability to understand Quebec, the evident weakness of his large parliamentary contingent from that province, and finally his own headstrong personality and paranoid leadership style all contributed to the party's disappointing electoral performance in 1962. The party lost sixty-eight of its seats in Quebec and Ontario, and ninety-two in total. While the Liberals picked up the majority of these seats, forty-one went to third parties: the NDP, which added eleven additional seats to the CCF's meagre 1958 total, and the Social Credit with thirty seats, twenty-six of these from rural and small-town Quebec. Clearly, many small 'c' conservatives in rural and small-town Quebec were less impressed by Diefenbaker and his party than were their counterparts in English-speaking Canada. At the same time, their disillusionment with the Liberals created an unprecedented opportunity for a virtually unknown third party—the Créditistes (the Quebec branch of the Social Credit)—who offered their own brand of conservative populism.

The elections of 1963 and 1965 confirmed and reinforced the shift made evident in 1962. The results pushed the Conservatives back into opposition while denying the Liberals an outright majority. While Diefenbaker gave the Tories a new lease on life by extending the party's appeal beyond its Ontario base and dramatically altering its Toronto-centred, big business image, by the same token he became a serious liability in French and urban Canada. A movement to remove him, led by party president Dalton Camp, culminated in a 1967 leadership convention that chose Nova Scotia Premier Robert Stanfield as the new party leader. However, the drawn-out internal struggle to depose Diefenbaker, who continued to be supported by a majority of his parliamentary caucus, left scars on the party that would handicap subsequent leaders for years to come. The conflicts it triggered were both personal and policy based. Prominent Conservatives were labelled as either Diefenbaker loyalists or opponents, proponents of the British connection and Diefenbaker's 'one Canada' vision or those who were willing to reach out to French Canadians by accepting bilingualism and reaching an agreement with Quebec.[23]

During Robert Stanfield's tenure as party leader, which lasted until 1976, the party lost three elections, though it came within two seats of forming a minority government in 1972 when the Tories won 107 seats to the Liberals' 109.[24] Respected for his integrity, judgement, and moderation, Stanfield has sometimes been referred to as 'the best Prime Minister Canadians never had'. His misfortune was to face an opponent in Pierre Trudeau whose intelligence, magnetic television persona, and force and clarity of vision, especially on the question of French-English relations, made him a formidable political opponent. Stanfield, however, did much to modernize Conservative Party organization and policy while consolidating Diefenbaker's gains in western and Atlantic Canada. Despite almost continuous harassment from within by Diefenbaker loyalists and minority caucus dissension on the question of support for bilingualism, Stanfield was able to win broad acceptance within his caucus and party for the policy of official bilingualism (enacted by the Liberals in 1969). Still, Quebec remained an electoral wasteland for the Conservatives where all his well-intentioned efforts came to naught. In the increasingly polarized terrain of Quebec politics, fought over by nationalist and federalist forces led by their respective home-grown champions (René Lévesque and Pierre Trudeau), there seemed to be no room for a second federalist party. The Conservatives were not so much disliked as merely redundant.

The 1976 convention to replace Stanfield revealed a shift rightward in the attitudes of party activists, evinced less by the party's choice of leader on that occasion than by delegate opinions on a range of issues. Perlin's comparison of the 1967 and 1976 conventions indicates a growing concern among Conservatives about the rapid growth of the federal bureaucracy and what they perceived as 'Liberal statism'.[25] Moreover, despite Stanfield's best efforts, divisions within the party involving the social and cultural differences between French and English Canadians continued to have a disruptive effect on party unity.[26] The convention chose as its new leader Joe Clark, a young, ideologically moderate MP from Alberta. Third on the first ballot, Clark was the compromise candidate between the two Quebec-based front runners: Claude Wagner, a Stanfield recruit lured away from the provincial Liberals in Quebec, and young, bilingual labour lawyer Brian Mulroney, who was well-connected within the party but whose lavish spending in the campaign raised the hackles and suspicions of some delegates.

Joe Clark's leadership was handicapped by his youth (thirty-six when elected leader), his relative anonymity (headlines the day after his convention victory read 'Joe Who?'), and, in the age of television, his physical awkwardness and pompous-sounding speaking style. Nevertheless, he demonstrated a capacity for organization building and performed well in Parliament. Most notably, Clark continued Stanfield's work of changing the party's image within Quebec and building a viable organization there. He also sought through the appointment of key personnel and through policy development to balance the 'democratic tory' and 'business liberal' elements within the party, a task made increasingly necessary (and difficult) by the growing strength within the party of the business liberal perspective. According to Christian and Campbell, Clark, despite these efforts, 'clearly failed to develop a coherent ideological synthesis that would provide the basis for a long-term reconciliation. . . . Only on some policy issues, such as the Constitution debate of 1981, was the party under Clark able to put its internal ideological conflicts aside in a common determination to attain a goal on which both Tories and business liberals could agree.'[27]

Clark's chance to govern came in 1979. After sixteen years of uninterrupted Liberal government, voters in English Canada appeared to have had enough. The economy was stagnant and unemployment and inflation were high. Under these conditions, Clark's Conservatives were able to replicate Diefenbaker's 1957 feat of unseating a Liberal government on the strength of support from English Canada alone. With nothing more than an additional 1 per cent of the vote compared to 1974, the Conservatives picked up forty-one seats for a total of 136, only two of which were in Quebec. With a balanced Atlantic contest, a Liberal Quebec, and a Tory West, it was Ontario that determined the outcome, providing 78 per cent of the Conservative seat gains. But alas for Joe Clark, history was not to repeat itself. Nine months after taking power, a new election was forced on Clark's inexperienced and unpopular government. The result this time was a restored Liberal majority and the second coming of Pierre Elliot Trudeau.[28]

The Liberals' 1980 election win did not alter the basic divisions within the Canadian electorate. The Conservative support bases had widened to the point where they had become the dominant party outside Quebec. Diefenbaker's appeal to distinct elements in English-speaking Canada had reshaped the support base of the Conservative Party: as in the second party system, the Tory constituency was still an ethnically and religiously narrow one (primarily British, northern European and Protestant), but after Diefenbaker it was more rural, agrarian, and populist than previously. Overall support levels for the party were higher in the third party system than in the second, and greatest in the Prairie and Maritime regions, while the party remained very competitive in Ontario. This was the Diefenbaker legacy.[29]

Thus, even though the Tories lost the 1980 election, outside Quebec they won 102 seats to the Liberals' seventy-three. The Liberals remained the party strongly favoured by francophones, immigrants, and Catholic Canada; the Conservatives were the preferred choice of Protestant Anglos and northern Europeans. Regional support bases were also fairly well defined: the Conservatives were the dominant party in Nova Scotia, PEI, and the four western provinces, while remaining competitive and occasionally dominant in Ontario; the Liberals controlled Newfoundland, New Brunswick, Quebec, and parts of Ontario (particularly where immigrant or Catholic numbers were high). There was no truly national party, with the NDP tending to bar the Liberals' way in Ontario and the West, and Liberal hegemony in Quebec continually frustrating the Tories.

Throughout his tenure as leader, Joe Clark had been on the defensive against elements within the party who did not fully accept his leadership: old Diefenbaker loyalists who saw him as a part of the anti-Diefenbaker alliance; right-wing ideologues who saw him as a wishy-washy moderate who blurred the distinction between Conservatives and the governing 'Liberal-socialists'; and those who simply viewed him as an electoral liability, unable to change the public's image of him as a weak, fumbling leader. The latter charge against Clark was given greater credibility by his failure to hold onto power in 1979–80. As a result, many in the party were determined, come what may, to unseat him as leader before the next general election.[30] Ironically, in true catch-22 fashion, it was this very internal divisiveness and infighting that fed the public's negative perception of Clark as a weak leader unable even to master his own party, let alone the country. What Perlin has termed 'the minority party syndrome'—an internal fractiousness focused on the leader that brings electoral defeat, which in turn breeds further discontent and internal fractiousness—was once again at work within the Conservative Party.[31] Under such circumstances, would the Tories ever again be the majority party in Canada?

The Mulroney Interlude

By 1983, at the tail end of Canada's worst recession since the 1930s, the popularity of the Trudeau Liberals had sunk to new lows. Yet despite their big lead in the polls, many Conservatives remained convinced that Clark had to go, that he was vulnerable should the Liberals replace Trudeau (by his own admission in his last term as prime minister) with former Liberal Finance

Minister John Turner. Waiting on the sidelines since his resignation in 1975, Turner was thought to have (especially by the media) both the charisma and business liberal credentials needed to attract disenchanted centre-right voters back to the Liberal Party. Among those seeking to depose Clark were ardent supporters of Brian Mulroney, who remained a leading candidate (like Turner, from the sidelines) for the leadership of his party. Goaded by a less-than-favourable leadership review vote (he received 66 per cent) into calling a convention to once and for all 'clear the air', Clark narrowly lost to his arch-rival on the fourth ballot.

Brian Mulroney won the 1983 leadership convention for a number of reasons. His business background and use of right-wing symbols made him acceptable to the growing business liberal element within the party. This was crucially important in a party that was increasingly small 'c' conservative (to use another term, 'neo-conservative') in its ideological predisposition. At the convention in 1983, fully 57 per cent of delegates placed themselves on the right; 75 per cent of these chose Mulroney on the last ballot.[32] Other factors were equally important: Mulroney's strong organization and extensive network within the party; his attraction for the party's 'social outsiders' to whom Mulroney stressed his own humble origins (an electrician's son from Baie-Comeau) and his consistent loyalty to their icon, Diefenbaker; perhaps most of all, because Mulroney successfully portrayed himself as a 'winner', the complete bilingual candidate who could capture Quebec and bring the Tories back to power.[33]

With a deeply unpopular Liberal government that Canadians seemed finally to have turned against irrevocably, and with their first fluently bilingual Quebec leader, the Conservative Party in 1984 was poised to repeat Diefenbaker's momentous 1958 landslide. Mulroney suggested as much, but promised his party that in one sense this time around would be different. He would overcome the historic obstacle that previously had cut short the party's hold on power: the need to resolve the conundrum of Quebec. Mulroney would appeal to an alienated Quebec by promising the province a better constitutional deal; at the same time, he would strive to keep his party close to the ideological centre by embracing Liberal-implemented universal social programs as a 'cornerstone of our party's philosophy' and 'a sacred trust'.[34] In effect, the Conservatives under Mulroney would seek to replicate the political success of their arch-rivals by adopting for themselves the basic elements of the Liberal Party's formula for success. They would have to resist the temptation to join lock-step the Thatcherite-Reaganite march to the right; even more important, they would have to move their party into position to bridge the French-English divide and in doing so storm the Liberal ramparts of 'Fortress Quebec'. In this way, the Progressive Conservatives would become Canada's new 'Government Party'.

The 1984 election result represented a dramatic change from the previous century in that the Liberal Party's strongholds in the Catholic areas of eastern Canada collapsed. Particularly devastating for the Liberals was the loss of Quebec, where the Tories won fifty-eight seats. This can be attributed primarily to the Conservatives' choice of Mulroney as leader and to the party's less centrist orientation compared to the governing Liberals, which created an opening for an alliance between the Mulroney-led Tories and Quebec nationalists (and disenchanted federalists) on economic and constitutional issues. This set the stage for the recreation of the original nineteenth-century élite-brokered Tory coalition of francophones and francophobes (replicated later with the Borden-Bourassa pact) with the same incoherence and insta- bility that would have to be overcome.[35] After 1984 tensions inherent to this coalition were clearly evident.

Mulroney's leadership win in 1983 was also a victory for right-wing business liberals within the party and a defeat of the 'moderate establishment'. Since the convention in 1976 that chose Joe Clark as leader, the Conservative Party had become increasingly more antistatist, decentralist, pro-American, and socially conservative.[36] This was not an accurate description, however, of either the party's Quebec wing or the Quebec electorate. As Goldfarb and Axworthy noted in 1988 with reference to national delegates at Conservative Party conventions:

> French-speaking Conservatives were far more inclined to adopt moderate positions on social and foreign policy issues than their English-speaking colleagues. . . . If there is any Red Tory element left at all in the Progressive Conservative party, it is to be found in Quebec. . . . The only group registering a significant dissent from the overall right-of-centre consensus in the Conser- vative Party were French-speaking Tories.[37]

The more centre-left orientation of Quebec party members was a reflec- tion of the prevailing ethos within the Quebec electorate, which was clearly to the left of English-speaking Canada.[38] This ethnocultural difference of ideological orientation was also apparent on the national question. Bernard notes that Quebec Tories were sympathetic to the Parti Québécois and that 'The Quebec contingent [in the caucus] was at odds with the remainder of the Conservative caucus, composed mainly of persons . . . who were not very willing to grant Quebec any special status.'[39] It did not take long for signs of alienation in the party's English-Canadian base to appear. 'By mid-1986 it had become clear that many Conservatives were outraged by Mulroney's efforts to mollify Quebec [and] with the government's conciliatory attitude toward the liberal and progressive wing of the party (which included many of its Quebec members). . . .'[40]

Despite these indications of serious rifts that could destroy the party from within, the Tories skilfully used the 1988 campaign to cement the social and regional bases—western populists, farmers, business liberals, and Quebec nationalists—of the fragile Mulroney coalition. This was accomplished through two key policy initiatives: the Meech Lake Accord and the Free Trade

Agreement (FTA). With none of the three major parties willing to risk Quebec support by opposing Meech Lake, the election became a virtual referendum on the FTA. An election fought over the issue of commercial policy allowed the Conservatives to pull together its Quebec and non-Quebec supporters, who otherwise tended to diverge dramatically in their public policy preferences. It would also produce a polarization in the government's favour, since they alone occupied one side of the national divide over the FTA.

In 1988, then, the need to make the widest possible appeal—the *raison d'être* of brokerage parties—was somewhat less in evidence than usual as the parties sought to mobilize core supporters and polarize the electorate on a key question of public policy. That the result favoured the Conservatives was due primarily to a major realignment of the groups with a stake in tariff protection (with the cleavages of 1878 reversed) and to the reinforcement of the Conservative hold on Quebec, thanks largely to the constitutional accord of 1987 and to a lessening of Quebec's traditional concern for its tariff-protected industries. In fact, Quebec was the only province where the Tories did better than they did in 1984, increasing both their share of the popular vote and their seat total (from fifty-eight to sixty-three).

An analysis of the 1988 election result outside Quebec reveals that this election marked a return to third party system norms. The strategy of polarization enabled each party to recruit most of its traditional electorate. In 'Canada outside Quebec', the Tory vote dropped below 40 per cent and the party lost forty-seven of the 153 seats it had won in 1984.[41] A regional analysis of the vote indicates that for the most part, those constituencies that had historically favoured the Tories were returned to the party in 1988.

In Atlantic Canada traditionally Tory seats in the more Protestant areas of anglophone New Brunswick and Nova Scotia (and St John's, Newfoundland) remained so. Prince Edward Island 'bucked the trend' by returning four Liberals in 1988. In Ontario the Conservatives did well in their areas of traditional strength: in rural areas and in affluent, white-collar suburban ridings. West of Ontario the Conservatives remained dominant in Alberta and in rural areas of the region generally, its main competitors in British Columbia and Saskatchewan were not the Liberals but the NDP. The results outside Quebec in 1988 (106 Conservatives, seventy-one Liberals) were in accord with the seat shares each party commanded throughout the third party system. In sum, outside Quebec there was a very strong element of continuity in the pattern of voter support for the Conservative Party. In the case of the West, this continuity stretched back to the Diefenbaker revolution thirty years earlier; in eastern Canada, it went all the way back to the first party system.

Clearly, then, it was the transfer of francophone loyalties in Quebec to the Tories that explains the reversal of Liberal-Conservative fortunes in the 1980s compared to the 1963–80 norm. The overture to Quebec nationalists had paid off handsomely for Mulroney's party. It allowed the party to break out of its social base in Protestant English Canada to become the majority party once again, as it had been in the nineteenth century. But there was a tectonic rift in the base of Mulroney's new Tory party: deep ethnocultural differences in ideological orientation and on Canada's primal national question. This created a vexing and threatening problem on the one hand for the party's rapprochement strategy vis-à-vis Quebec and, on the other, for maintenance of the party's core electorate outside Quebec. There was a political price for brokering this alliance, which in 1988 had yet to be paid. And when the foundations of the Mulroney coalition did crumble in the early 1990s, so did the foundations of the Tory party, not only in Quebec but in English-speaking Canada as well.

The Fourth Party System

The Conservatives' victory in 1988 was certainly an atypical one for modern Canadian elections. It was based not on the usual rhetorical struggle for the high ground on a wide range of issues in order to broker the support of the median voter but rather one in which the parties actively sought to polarize the electorate along the economic-social dimension over an issue of commercial policy. The Free Trade Agreement inked by the Conservative government was linked by its partisan opponents (in a fashion reminiscent of turn-of-the-century Tory tactics) to questions of national sovereignty and identity. In contrast, the oft-central ethnocultural dimension was neutralized in 1988 by an all-party agreement on the Meech Lake Accord. This collusion to suppress the national question would come back to haunt the traditional parties. It left the field open for new protest parties closer to the position of the median voter in francophone Quebec and English-speaking Canada respectively. The traditional parties after 1987 (including the NDP) attempted to move Canadians and Quebecers towards a consensus position on the Constitution (one arrived at by the parties). However, when the 'bottled up' discontent over the national question could no longer be contained, 'it shattered the foundations of party choice'.[42]

This was not the only problem faced by the Conservatives going into the election of 1993. Besides bearing ultimate responsibility for two failed constitutional accords (Meech Lake and Charlottetown), and the widespread rancour these generated, the economy had plunged into a severe recession after 1990, one that was especially hard on the industrial heartland of central Canada. All other things being equal (which they were not), any government would have had a difficult time retaining popular support under these conditions. Facing such daunting re-election prospects, a key change in personnel was made. The resignation of Prime Minister Brian Mulroney and his replacement by cabinet minister Kim Campbell early in 1993 was widely viewed as the removal of one of the major obstacles to a third term for the Conservatives. Campbell's attributes—her gender, relative youth, intelligence, bilingualism, and western origins (MP for Vancouver)—were meant to put a fresh face on a government that had become associated with some highly unpopular policies (such as the GST) and personalities (the prime minister himself); they were also meant to assuage the party's angry western supporters, while at the same time addressing the need to present the party as open and sensitive to women's issues.

In the 1993 election campaign, both the Conservatives and the Liberals returned to form by pitching themselves as moderate, centrist brokerage parties. They found that the old rules of the game no longer seemed to apply. The broad centre, which previously had been a bountiful provider for parties willing to troll for votes in its waters, had been seriously diminished by new parties siphoning off disenchanted and radicalized voters. Though pre-election polls suggested the possibility that both brokerage parties would suffer electorally as a result of this development, it was the governing Progressive Conservative Party that foundered due to its lack of credibility on key economic-social issues (the deficit and job creation), but even more importantly because the median Conservative voter shifted towards the polar position on both the major dimensions of electoral competition (economic-social and ethnocultural) into the waiting arms of the Reform Party in English-speaking Canada and the Bloc Québécois in Quebec. With its baseline support draining away, the Tories were facing disaster should their campaign to attract weakly committed centrist support fail, as it did.

The Tories sought vainly to differentiate themselves from the Liberals while still hugging the centre by portraying themselves as offering a 'middle way' between the spendthrift Liberals and the overzealous Reformers.[43] 'The governing Conservatives, caught between the gradualist and cut-now visions of change offered by the challengers, tried to have it both ways, arguing that the Liberals were too timid about the economy and that Reform was too radical.'[44] In a similar vein, the Tories sought to occupy the compromising middle ground in Quebec between the Liberals, typecast as hardline federalists, and the separatist Bloc Québécois.

At the same time, it must be noted that the Conservative campaign in 1993 did not always follow the classic brokerage script well. For better or worse, it was decided that the campaign would revolve principally around the new leader's image and personality rather than defence of the government's record or a new set of policy proposals.[45] One former senior Tory strategist and adviser sees Kim Campbell as a victim of circumstances beyond her capacity to understand or control, 'swept up by the forces of expediency that ... put regaining power ahead of convictions, and ultimately crushed her and the party'.[46] This suggests that the inherent difficulty of sustaining a campaign focus on little more than image and personality throughout a federal election campaign was magnified by the new Tory leader's inexperience. Not only did Campbell acquiesce to this dubious strategy, she committed some major gaffes in its execution; her ill-considered statements that nothing could be done about unemployment for the rest of the century, and that an election campaign was an inappropriate time to discuss reform of social policy, sent the wrong message to voters about the party's concerns (or more precisely, the lack thereof).[47] This must be set against the background of the economic and constitutional setbacks of 1990–3 that had already hardened public opinion against the Conservatives. This left the party with precious little credibility on these questions, even with their own previously loyal supporters.[48]

In the 1993 election the Conservatives were reduced to two seats and 16 per cent of the vote, the most devastating reversal for a governing party anywhere in the democratic world. Still, amid the ruins of this momentous defeat, there were indications of continuity and the remnants of an electoral base. In Atlantic Canada, where they finished second in every constituency (save the one they won) in 1993, they remained the clear alternative to the Liberals. Throughout the region their strongest showings were also the constituencies in which Reform did best, and these invariably were areas of traditional Conservative Party strength. In Quebec, the recently constructed Tory base, precariously balanced on Mulroney's overture to nationalist Quebecers, simply dissolved into the Bloc Québécois, a less compromising (and compromised) vehicle for nationalist aspirations. The fact that the BQ vote almost exactly tracked the No vote in the 1992 Charlottetown referendum suggests the close link in Quebec between the national question and support for the new nationalist party. The Conservatives retained only one of their sixty-three seats, with their popular vote declining from 52.7 per cent to 13.5 per cent, a level comparable to their worst showings in pre-1984 elections.[49]

While the Conservatives could find some consolation in their Atlantic Canadian numbers, and perhaps reconcile themselves to the loss of francophone Quebec (at least the Liberals were not the beneficiaries), it was the results in Ontario and points west that were truly devastating. In Ontario the popular vote for the Conservatives fell by more than twenty points (to 17.6 per cent), almost exactly matching the 20 per cent of votes gathered by Reform, which won one seat and finished second in many traditionally Conservative constituencies in rural southern and eastern Ontario and in the middle-class suburban areas of the province's cities. In twenty-five ridings, the gains made by Reform were enough to tip the balance between Liberals and Tories.

In Manitoba and Saskatchewan, the rural base of Conservative political power was shattered by the desertion of its voters to Reform. Where this was insufficient to elect the Reform candidate (Reform won in five rural ridings), it was enough to get a Liberal elected in previously unfriendly territory. With only 11 to 12 per cent of the Midwest vote in 1993 compared to 22 to 27 per cent for Reform, and no second place finishes, even the Ontario results were relatively good by comparison. Though the Liberals won close to two-thirds of the seats, their popular vote totals indicated their lukewarm appeal in this region. And Liberal results farther west were downright disappointing. This was of no benefit to the Tories, however, who managed only 13.5 per cent and 14.6 per cent of the vote in Alberta and British Columbia respectively. In 1993 Reform became the party of choice for bedrock conservatives and others disenchanted with the mainstream alternatives.[50]

In the aftermath of their 1993 débâcle, the Progressive Conservative Party was faced with extremely difficult and unsavoury strategic choices. The adjustments the party made to win over and retain Quebec francophone support also prevented the party from effectively responding to the challenge posed by the rise of the Reform Party, which was clearly intent on poaching traditional Conservative supporters. Adapting party strategy in response to this new reality, however, would not be easy, nor would it guarantee political success. The 25 March 1996 federal by-elections, in which Reform finished a strong second to the Liberals in two of the three contests outside Quebec, were discouraging for Conservatives looking for some rebound in voter support, or for some indication that Reform's 1993 performance was simply a one-time protest vote. At the same time, the politically unseasoned Reform caucus suffered from outbreaks of internal dissension that led to the censuring and expulsion of sitting members. This highlighted the ongoing difficulties faced by an avowedly populist party espousing a plebiscitarian view of their role in Ottawa (whereby MPs are expected to represent constituent views regardless of their fit with party policy), and attempting to operate within a parliamentary system that demands relatively strict party discipline. The Tories could only hope to benefit over time from the political fallout Reform would likely continue to suffer as a result of these contradictory impulses.[51]

With the Liberals continuing to occupy the centre-right during their first mandate and the NDP showing no signs of imminent revival, the Conservatives were faced with three strategic options. The first and most natural was to try to recapture the core support lost to the Reform Party and hope that their rivals (rather than they themselves) would self-destruct during the course of the ensuing war of attrition for the hearts and minds of conservative voters. The alternative to this—a negotiated merger or alliance of the two parties—was promoted by the Tory premiers of Alberta and Ontario.[52] Both these strategic options implied a consolidation of the Conservative Party's position on the right and would mean conceding the centre to the Liberals and abandoning any aspiration to once again become Canada's pre-eminent national brokerage party.[53]

The third strategic option for the Tories was to take advantage of the Liberals then current incarnation as a right-of-centre party by leap-frogging to their left. Such a strategy, advocated by respected former Conservative Party president Dalton Camp, had its own risks: it would sharply reverse the party's gradual drift to the right since the 1970s and also go against the grain of recent Conservative successes at the provincial level (notably Alberta and

Ontario). Moreover, what core support the party retained might be sacrificed in the process without the party being 'believed' by an electorate justifiably sceptical of a deathbed ideological conversion. Still, this strategy would replicate a path of resuscitation previously pursued (the Diefenbaker revolution in 1957–8). Moreover, with new leader Jean Charest at the helm (a popular francophone leader), the Tories might dream of once again appealing to centre-left francophone voters in Quebec.

The lesson to be derived from the Progressive Conservative Party's misfortune in 1993 is *not* that the Canadian electorate is notoriously volatile and unstable in its partisan attachments, though at first blush the election result appears to confirm this well-established model of Canadian voter behaviour. Rather, traditional Conservative supporters were deserted by their own party élites intent upon playing brokerage politics by clinging to the centre and gambling that nationalist support in Quebec could be won over by accommodating Quebec élites on the national question. It was, in fact, the underlying *continuities* in the Canadian electorate that made this high-stakes courting of Quebec both a vital part of a winning formula for the Conservatives and a dangerous gambit that risked giving deep offence to the partisan sensibilities of long-term supporters. The reaction of voters to this party behaviour can best be understood if the beliefs, values, and rationality of each party's core supporters are presumed to have remained fairly constant and consistent. Viewed from this perspective, the instability in voter choice in 1993 that shattered the party system was party-induced; it was party manoeuvring in search of strategic advantage and the support of the weakly committed median voter that eroded the commitment of core supporters and therefore the stability of historic party vote shares. Indeed, the elections of 1984 and 1988 were not indicative of massive voter instability, only Quebec's switch of allegiance. Otherwise, the results were within the bounds of the parties' traditional vote share, resting on long-established core electorates.

Many voters, it appears, used the 1993 election to cast judgement upon the political élites who engaged in an extreme form of brokerage politics.

> Brokerage . . . seems to have been a major underlying issue in the campaign, rivalling or even overshadowing jobs and the deficit. The winners were those who most clearly identified with it or who most clearly opposed it. . . . Those who practiced it half-heartedly or with a bold new twist—the Conservatives and the NDP—were the big losers.[54]

Forbes's argument—that the 1993 election result represented a 'backlash against brokerage'—is insightful. The Tories bore the brunt of voter backlash first and foremost because it was they who had governed for the previous nine years, and also because they so obviously relied on an image-driven brokerage strategy in the 1993 campaign without due regard for the need to uphold the principles and priorities of the party's core clientele.

As one study by a Tory insider of the Conservatives' 1993 election campaign concludes: 'The overriding lesson from the election is simple: ideas do count. Standing for something does matter . . . [If the Progressive Conservative Party does not understand this] there is no role for it in Canada's political firmament and few should mourn its passing.'[55]

At the centre of this pattern of brokerage party behaviour in Canada was Quebec. Winning a national mandate and getting broad parliamentary representation required parties to seek a voter base in Quebec, which in turn required them to broker compromises on questions of national identity and unity as well as on social and economic policy. They were compelled to reach across the chasm between their median English-speaking supporter and the median voter in francophone Quebec, a task the Tories finally accomplished in 1984 and 1988 after the Liberals had provided an historic opening for them to do so. This accomplishment for the Conservatives, however, proved temporary and largely illusory. Its social base outside Quebec had always been further from the median Quebec voter than was ever the case for the Liberals. In effect, the Mulroney Conservatives had to engage in a form of *imperial overstretch* in order to win over and continuously accommodate Quebec.[56] Even so, their connection with Québécois voters was tenuous at best. Thus, only a year after their 1984 election victory, the party suffered an 88 per cent decline in its Quebec membership.[57] Moreover, their Quebec caucus, membership, and voter base was distinctly to the left of the rest of the party on social policy and had a starkly different understanding of the character of the national identity and Quebec's place within Confederation. In the end, the effort to bridge these yawning differences created the agents of the Conservative Party's demise (in the guise of Reform and the Bloc), and prevented the Tories from making the necessary adjustments once it was clear that the new protest parties were stealing away the Conservative Party's support base.

A further problem was the closed, élitist nature of Conservative Party organization, which left the party as little more than 'a vehicle for the leader, devoid of much latitude or capacity to provide for its own preservation and survival'.[58] This type of organization, so reminiscent of descriptions of the Liberal Party during its long years of power, is a virtual prerequisite for the leader-centred brokering that has been typical of the Liberal and Conservative parties.[59] It insulates party leaders from party members and allows them wide leeway to make and alter party policy, regardless of what the policy preferences and core values of the majority of party members may be. Alienated from policy determination and strategic decision making, and rarely if ever consulted by party élites, members become disillusioned and cynical. In the 1990s the Reform Party appeared to offer the opportunity for greater member participation while pledging to respect grassroot opinion. On this count alone, Reform became an attractive alternative for Conservative Party members who felt ignored or excluded from party decision making.

The construction of the Mulroney coalition was a superb demonstration of the intricacies of Canadian brokerage politics and its capacity on occasion to produce the most amazing and ungainly of creations. But such things also have a certain Frankenstein dimension: their creators may come to rue the day they brought them to life. Such is the price of arrogance when mere mortals attempt to trump the forces of nature, or political leaders the beliefs, values, and basic inclinations of their party's core supporters.

The 1997 Election

In the 1997 election campaign that culminated on 2 June with the re-election of a majority Liberal government, Tory leader Jean Charest attempted to recreate a broad, centre-right, English-French brokerage party that would be the natural (and national) alternative to the governing Liberals. That he failed to do so is hardly surprising. Despite the Tory election pledge to cut taxes, fiscal and social conservatives in western Canada had no compelling reason to opt for the 'reasonable facsimile' version of Reform offered by Charest. Even if they had considered doing so, Charest's dogged and principled adherence to the strategy of resolving Canada's constitutional impasse by finding a way to accommodate Quebec was sure to drive western conservatives—who tended to take a hard line on this question—back to Reform. In any event, Charest's Conservatives won a paltry share of the vote in the West and only one Manitoba seat.[60]

In Quebec the Conservative Party's accommodative stance on the national question, attractively pitched by Charest, harkened back to Mulroney's strategy of presenting the Conservatives as a 'middle way' between the separatists and the more hardline federalist Liberals. While appealing to soft nationalists and sufficient to win a respectable share of the vote (22 per cent), the strategy secured only five seats and failed to dislodge the Bloc from their dominant position among francophone voters. This left open the question of whether Conservative Party gains in 1997—attributable primarily to Charest's popularity with Quebec voters—would be sustainable under a different leader.[61]

In Atlantic Canada, where the Conservative support base was most intact after 1993, the party repatriated virtually all their traditional core electorate by capitalizing on voter disenchantment with Liberal cuts to social programs and the Liberal government's failure to address high unemployment levels. In this region, in this election, the Conservatives presented themselves as defenders of social programs against slash-and-burn Liberals. By continuing to present their party as a moderate alternative to the Liberals, but one more in tune and responsive to the concerns of rural dwellers, the Tory strategy in the Atlantic region became the one advocated by Dalton Camp: revive the party by positioning it to the left of the program-cutting Liberals.[62]

It also seems likely that the Tory votes garnered in Ontario, where the Conservatives and Reform each took a 20 per cent share, was based less on the party's attempt in this region to match Reform's call for tax cuts or the repeal of federal gun control legislation than the sharp contrast between the two parties' stance towards Quebec and the national question. Still, as in the West, only one Conservative was elected, leaving the twenty-person Conservative caucus dominated by Quebec and Atlantic Canada, regions where Reform's more ideologically driven conservatism and hard line on Quebec's distinct society have found little or no resonance.

While the overall results indicate that neither the Conservative Party under Charest nor the Reform Party under Manning can hope to challenge successfully for national power without the support base now held by the other, the same results would seem to make the prospect of merger or coalition impossible since it would require one of the parties to adopt positions that seem sure to alienate the core electorates they have at present. As noted by political party specialist John Courtney, 'If they [the Reform Party] are going to continue to attack Quebec, they're never going to win Ontario. That puts them on the horns of a dilemma—for if they moderate their message on Quebec, they run the risk of losing their core support in Alberta and British Columbia.'[63] The same claim, of course, can be made about the future of the Progressive Conservatives, only in reverse. In the aftermath of the 1997 election, with a Conservative caucus dominated by its Atlantic Canadian contingent, the Tory platform will be tilted somewhat to the left and towards the East. This would be in line with the inclinations of the present Tory caucus who want a government that is favourable towards progressive social policies.[64] Yet this seems an unlikely way to win back the support of western conservatives who have an affinity for Reform's more ideologically driven, right-wing populism. As long as Canada as presently constituted continues, the Conservative Party seems likely to be stymied in its attempts to construct an electoral coalition sufficiently broad to win national power.

As the dust settled from the 1997 election result and the Progressive Conservative caucus slipped back into its role as Canada's fifth party (in terms of the size of its parliamentary contingent), events elsewhere in the Canadian political firmament were conspiring to throw a wrench into the party's rebuilding efforts. The resignation of the leader of the Quebec Liberal Party had been followed by a growing chorus of Quebec and Canadian voices urging Conservative leader Jean Charest (according to polls at the time Quebec's most popular politician) to switch allegiances and assume the leadership of the provincial Liberals 'for the good of Canada'. After an intense period of political courting of Charest, he finally relented and stepped down as national leader of one party in order to become the provincial leader of another, but also to assume the leadership of the federalist forces within Quebec in their ongoing battle with Lucien Bouchard's referendum-wielding sovereigntists.

This sudden and unexpected turn of events left Charest's old party, the Progressive Conservatives, with a serious problem. Charest's youth, personal popularity, demonstrable political skills, and bicultural appeal were key assets for a party attempting to return from political oblivion. Now these assets were lost to the party and an alternative foundation for the rebuilding effort would have to be found. Consistent with brokerage party behaviour, the once-powerful Tories reacted to the stinging rebuke of the electorate by opting to replace Charest using an innovative method of leader selection that (it was hoped) would present the party as a progressive and democratic organization, while simultaneously contributing to party renewal by expanding member involvement in the leadership selection process.[65] There were several candidates, only one of whom had an established national profile and reputation: former leader Joe Clark. Clark came close to winning an outright majority on the first ballot, and easily won on the second. Fifteen years after he had lost the leadership, Joe Clark was once again leader of the Progressive Conservatives. His first statements as leader were to reaffirm the moderate, centrist character of his party and to reject outright any notion of merging with the Reform Party to create a 'united alternative' on the right. On the Quebec issue, he castigated both Preston Manning and Jean Chrétien for their hard line against changing the Constitution to accommodate Quebec's demands, promising that he would handle the Quebec issue differently.[66]

There can be no doubt that the elections of 1993 and 1997 mark a new era of party politics in Canada. The main loser in this new pattern of party competition has been the Progressive Conservative Party. A large component of its core electorate from the third party system—western conservatives and populists won over during the Diefenbaker years—has been lost. As well, the Ontario base of support that has sustained the party since Confederation has been severely reduced. The party is now engaged in something akin to a search for its soul, resolutely turning back to its past in order to find its way forward into the future.

Notes

1. As quoted in C. Campbell and W. Christian, *Parties, Leaders and Ideologies in Canada* (Toronto: McGraw-Hill Ryerson, 1996):27–8.
2. Ibid., 28.
3. J.M. Beck, *Pendulum of Power: Canada's Federal Elections* (Scarborough: Prentice-Hall, 1968):58–9.
4. Ibid., 57.
5. Ibid., 63–8.
6. In some parts of the country, the election of 1896 was only a temporary aberration from established support patterns (as in Ontario and Manitoba); elsewhere, as in the Maritimes, there was barely a ripple of change. It was primarily

in Quebec where a fundamental shift occurred, the culmination of a period of change beginning with the election of 1887. See Donald Blake, '1896 and All That: Critical Elections in Canada', *Canadian Journal of Political Science* XII, no. 2 (June 1979):268–9.

7. John English, *The Decline of Politics: The Conservatives and the Party System 1901–1920* (Toronto: University of Toronto Press, 1977):Chapter 3.

8. John English, 'The End of the Great Party Era', in *Canadian Political Party Systems*, edited by R.K. Carty (Peterborough: Broadview Press, 1993):153.

9. Ibid., 141.

10. Ibid., 148.

11. Going into the 1921 election, not one provincial government remained that was Conservative, a major factor during an era when federal and provincial parties were much more integrated and mutually supportive than they are today.

12. See E.R. Forbes, *The Maritime Rights Movement, 1919–1927* (Montreal: McGill-Queen's University Press, 1979).

13. Beck, *Pendulum of Power*, 169. The Tories piled up huge majorities in Ontario's cities, winning sixty-eight of eighty-two seats in the province.

14. Ibid., 183.

15. Ibid., 197–203. In 1930 the Tories picked up eleven seats in Manitoba on 48 per cent of the popular vote, whereas they won no seats in 1926 with 42 per cent of the vote.

16. See J.L. Granatstein, *The Politics of Survival: The Conservative Party of Canada 1939–1945* (Toronto: University of Toronto Press, 1967).

17. Campbell and Christian, *Parties, Leaders and Ideologies*, 38.

18. George Perlin, *The Tory Syndrome: Leadership Politics in the Progressive Conservative Party* (Montreal: McGill-Queen's University Press, 1980):53.

19. Beck, *Pendulum of Power*, 300.

20. Campbell and Christian, *Parties, Leaders and Ideologies*, 38–42.

21. Peter Regenstreif, *The Diefenbaker Interlude: Parties and Voting in Canada* (Toronto: Longmans Canada, 1965):52.

22. R. Johnston, A. Blais, H.E. Brady, and J. Crete, *Letting the People Decide: Dynamics of a Canadian Election* (Montreal: McGill-Queen's University Press, 1992):52–9. As noted by Brodie and Jenson, the minority Diefenbaker government of 1957 was quick to consolidate its image as a government friendly to Prairie farmers and farmers generally. It did so through a series of measures that indicated its willingness to act on farmers' concerns. 'All told, there was good reason for the farmer to support Diefenbaker's Conservatives.' J. Brodie and J. Jenson, *Crisis, Challenge and Change: Party and Class in Canada* (Toronto: Methuen, 1980):247.

23. Perlin, *The Tory Syndrome*, passim.

24. In the 1972 election the Tories took 105 of the seats outside Quebec to the Liberals' fifty-six; in 1974 this advantage was reduced to ninety-four versus eighty-one; in 1979 it would increase to a margin of 134 to forty-seven. With the exception of 1968, the Conservatives after 1957 were the dominant party outside Quebec.

25. Perlin, *The Tory Syndrome*, 188.

26. Ibid., 191.

27. Campbell and Christian, *Parties, Leaders and Ideologies*, 47.

28. See Jeffrey Simpson, *Discipline of Power: The Conservative Interlude and Liberal Restoration* (Toronto: Personal Library, 1980).

29. Johnston et al., *Letting the People Decide*, 65.
30. P. Martin, A. Gregg, and G. Perlin, 'The Tory Quest for Power', *Party Politics in Canada*, 5th edn, edited by H. Thorburn (Scarborough: Prentice-Hall, 1985): 172–5.
31. Perlin, 'The Progressive Conservative Party', 169–71.
32. Martin, Gregg, and Perlin, 'The Tory Quest for Power', 176.
33. Ibid., 176–80.
34. Campbell and Christian, *Parties, Leaders and Ideologies*, 52, 54.
35. Johnston et al., *Letting the People Decide*, 72–3. Indeed, during Macdonald's time, at least there was a strong Quebec Bleus tradition that was ideologically compatible with English Canadian Toryism; in the 1980s what passed for conservatism among Quebec francophones was a pale remnant of its former self.
36. M. Goldfarb and T. Axworthy, *Marching to a Different Drummer: An Essay on Liberals and Conservatives in Convention* (Toronto: Stoddart, 1988):30–5.
37. Ibid., 75.
38. M.D. Ornstein, 'Regionalism and Canadian Political Ideology', in *Regionalism in Canada*, edited by R.J. Brym (Richmond Hill: Irwin, 1986); R. Gibbins and N. Nevitte, 'Canadian Political Ideology: A Comparative Analysis', *Canadian Journal of Political Science* 18, no. 3 (1985):577–98.
39. A. Bernard, 'Liberals and Conservatives in the 1990s', in *Canadian Parties in Transition*, 2nd edn, edited by A.B. Tanguay and A.-G. Gagnon (Toronto: Nelson, 1996):77.
40. Ibid., 77.
41. Ibid., 78.
42. Johnston et al., *Letting the People Decide*, 254.
43. P. Woolstencroft, 'Doing Politics Differently: The Conservative Party and the Campaign of 1993', in *The Canadian General Election of 1993*, edited by A. Frizzell, J.H. Pammett, and A. Westell (Ottawa: Carleton University Press, 1994):17.
44. J. Pammett, 'Analyzing Voting Behaviour in Canada: The Case of the 1993 Election', in *Party Politics in Canada*, 7th edn, edited by H. Thorburn (Scarborough: Prentice-Hall, 1996):591.
45. Woolstencroft, 'Doing Politics Differently', 15–17; see also Hugh Segal, *No Surrender: Reflections of a Happy Warrior in the Tory Crusade* (Toronto: Harper-Collins, 1996). Segal suggests that the outgoing Mulroney government and the senior civil service had left behind an elaborate assemblage of policies that could have been used as an election platform, but that Campbell and her advisers chose to ignore it.
46. Segal, *No Surrender*, 205–6.
47. Campbell and Christian, *Parties, Leaders and Ideologies*, 60.
48. In 1993 the only socio-economic and ethnoreligious variables that produced positive coefficients for the Tories were the presence of university graduates and Protestants. The Maritimes were the only region where their performance was better than the party's Ontario performance. The coefficient measuring continuity in Tory support represents the single most statistically robust and strong determinant of its vote in 1993. As with the Liberals, there was a negative association between support for the Conservatives at the riding level and the per cent rejecting the Charlottetown Accord. M. Eagles, J. Bickerton, A. Gagnon, and P. Smith, 'Continuity in Electoral Change: Patterns of Support for Canadian Parties,

1988 and 1993', a paper presented to the 1995 Biennial Meeting of the Association for Canadian Studies in the United States, Seattle, WA, 18 November 1995, 14.

49. Ibid., 3–5. As one would expect, in 1993 the Bloc preyed on Tory seats almost exclusively, but not so with regard to Tory voters. The Bloc also found votes among former supporters of the NDP and Liberals, with a further significant portion coming from 'outside recruitment' (i.e., former abstainers or alienated fringe party voters in federal elections). R. Johnston, E. Gidengil, N. Nevitte, and H. Brady, 'The 1993 Canadian Election: Realignment, Dealignment or Something Else?' a paper presented to the Annual Meeting of the Canadian Political Science Association, Brock University, St Catharines, Ontario, 2–4 June 1996, 8.

50. While Reform's attraction for right-wing voters in BC is understandable, a shift to Reform from the left-wing NDP is illogical in ideological terms since the centrist Liberals should have been the party of choice for voters switching from the NDP. This phenomenon may be explainable, however, by the sharp reaction in BC to the Charlottetown Accord (68.3 per cent voted No to Charlottetown). This may have thrown support to Reform, which occupied a polar position on the ethnocultural dimension of Canadian politics and was the only party to oppose the Accord. This stand likely drew additional support that otherwise would have stayed with the NDP or gone to the Liberals. M. Eagles, J. Bickerton, A. Gagnon, and P. Smith, The Almanac of Canadian Politics, 2nd edn (Toronto: Oxford University Press, 1995):513–17, 575–80.

51. Susan Delacourt, 'Tories See Chance to Gain from Rivals', The Globe and Mail (9 May 1996):A1; Jeffrey Simpson, 'Reform Must Decide Whether It Is a Populist or Democratic Party', The Globe and Mail (9 May 1996):A20.

52. B. Laghi, 'Klein Warns Federal Tories Not to Count on Support', The Globe and Mail (Toronto) (3 April 1996):A4.

53. For example, the May 1996 'Winds of Change' conference in Calgary, attended by sixty-five conservative intellectuals and politicians, was billed as an attempt to figure out how to unite the right in Canada by bridging the gap between the Conservatives and Reform. See James McCarten, 'Tories, Reformers Ponder Strategies to Avoid Splitting Right-wing Vote', The Chronicle-Herald (Halifax) (27 May 1996):C16.

54. H.D. Forbes, 'Interpreting the 1993 Election', in Party Politics in Canada, 7th edn, edited by H. Thorburn (Scarborough: Prentice-Hall, 1996):566.

55. D. McLaughlin, Poisoned Chalice: The Last Campaign of the Progressive Conservative Party? (Toronto: Dundurn Press, 1994):304.

56. The term is Harvard historian Paul Kennedy's, who used it as a general explanation for the decline of great empires. See Paul Kennedy, The Rise and Fall of the Great Powers: Economic Change and Military Conflict from 1500–2000 (New York: Random House, 1987).

57. P. Woolstencroft, 'The Progressive Conservative Party 1984–1993: Government, Party, Members', in Party Politics, 7th edn, edited by H. Thorburn (Scarborough: Prentice-Hall, 1996):293.

58. Ibid., 299.

59. See R. Whitaker, The Government Party: Organizing and Financing the Liberal Party of Canada (Toronto: University of Toronto Press, 1977); Joseph Wearing, The L-Shaped Party: The Liberal Party of Canada 1958–1980 (Toronto: McGraw-Hill Ryerson, 1981).

60. At 34 per cent, 'support for granting Quebec distinct society status is very limp in the rest of Canada' outside Quebec; this proportion is likely lower in western Canada. In the 1997 election, the Reform Party took sixty of the West's eighty-eight seats. See Andre Blais, Elisabeth Gidengil, Richard Nadeau, and Neil Nevitte 'The Fickle Finger of Folk', *The Globe and Mail* (7 June 1997):D1, D9.

61. In a preliminary analysis of their data, the national election survey research team (Blais, Gidengil, Nadeau, and Nevitte) found support for sovereignty in Quebec during the 1997 campaign remained strong at 44 per cent and belief that the Bloc was the party best able to defend Quebec's interests at 64 per cent. Those Bloc voters who planned to switch to the Conservatives decided to do so primarily because of the higher approval rating on average they gave to Conservative leader Charest (sixty-seven on a 100-point scale) as opposed to Bloc leader Gilles Duceppe (thirty-eight). The Bloc Québécois recaptured forty-four of the fifty-four seats they held on 38 per cent of the vote; the Liberals took twenty-six seats and 36 per cent of the vote. Ibid., D1.

62. John Gray, 'Defiant Region Awaits Its Fate', *The Globe and Mail* (7 June 1997): A1, A8. The PCs won thirteen of the region's thirty-two seats, the Liberals eleven, and the NDP eight. Liberal support in the region was further whittled down by the NDP, which made significant gains in Liberal strongholds like francophone New Brunswick and Cape Breton after the Chrétien Liberal government had turned its back on the policies and principles that had long made these areas a Liberal stronghold. True to form, Newfoundland diverged from the pattern in the Maritimes, returning Conservatives in the urban St John's seats and Liberals in the rural 'around the bay' seats.

63. As quoted in Graham Fraser, 'New Parliament Won't Be Run Same Old Way', *The Globe and Mail* (4 June 1997):A6.

64. Anne McIlroy, 'Tories Tilt Platform to Left, Toward East', *The Globe and Mail* (20 June 1997):A4.

65. The leadership selection process chosen by the Tories was a complicated, hybrid system meant to ensure a national rebuilding process. However, the new system generally confused onlookers accustomed to the delegate convention model and robbed the party of the excitement and media attention of a national convention. The new system worked as follows. On the first ballot, each party member in each constituency was given the opportunity to vote directly for the new leader. However, constituencies rather than individuals were granted an equal weight in determining the outcome by allocating 100 points to each constituency, with the individual vote totals for each leadership candidate prorated at the constituency level as a proportion of 100. If no candidate received a majority of these prorated votes on the first ballot, a second ballot would be held three weeks later. If there were more than two contestants on the second ballot, a preferential ballot would be used, one that allowed voters to rank their choices. If no candidate secured a majority of first choices on this preferential ballot, then second choices would be counted and so on until one candidate had accumulated an overall majority.

66. Brian Laghi, 'Clark Blasts Manning for Fuelling PQ Fires', *The Globe and Mail* (16 November 1998):A7.

CHAPTER 3

THE LIBERALS:
CANADA'S 'GOVERNMENT PARTY'

The Liberal Party dominated Canadian politics in the twentieth century. At the end of the century, they had governed Canada at the national level for seventy-five of the previous 105 years. In the nineteenth century, however, the Liberals and their predecessors were much more likely to be in opposition than in government. It is even questionable whether the Liberals constituted a national party at all during the first couple of decades following Confederation. The party operated more as a loose coalition of interests comprised of several factions: George Brown's antiestablishment 'Grits' from western Ontario, the anticlerical Rouges from Quebec, and anticonfederates and Independents from the Maritimes. As simultaneous elections and the secret ballot became the norm, and as the demands of parliamentary democracy with its adversarial dynamic gradually took hold, those opposed to or alienated from John A. Macdonald's grand coalition were fused into a single national party. This process was undoubtedly aided by the emergence and success of Liberal parties at the provincial level; indeed, by the time Wilfrid Laurier finally led the federal Liberals to national victory in 1896, his provincial counterparts were ensconced in power in every province. This was the beginning of a now-familiar pattern in Canadian politics, whereby a party entrenched in power at the national level is systematically ousted at the provincial level prior to its final defeat federally.

The key to Liberal success in the twentieth century, at least prior to 1984, was the party's popularity with francophone voters in Quebec. It took some time for this affinity between Quebecers and the Liberals to develop. Prior to Confederation and for most of the first three decades afterwards, the Liberal Party (and its antecedents) were denounced by the Catholic Church hierarchy in Quebec either for their anticlerical and republican views (as with the Rouges in Quebec) or for their anti-French and anti-Catholic attitudes and rhetoric (as was the case with the Grits of western Ontario). Liberal leaders after Confederation struggled to divorce their party from this legacy and hence make it more acceptable to the Church and to francophone Quebec voters.[1] Once they had done so, the French Catholic voter would become the most prominent and consistent element of the Liberal coalition, the key to Liberal electoral success in the twentieth century.

In the nineteenth century, however, it was the Macdonald-Cartier coalition of English-Canadian Conservatives and French-Canadian Bleus that were dominant. Prior to 1896, if the anomalous election of 1874 is set aside —its outcome was wholly determined by negative public reaction to the Pacific Scandal—the Macdonald-led Liberal-Conservative Party secured a majority of Quebec seats on five of the six occasions they formed a government.[2] However, as argued in Chapter 2, the French-English, Catholic-Protestant coalition that had been forged around a nation-building agenda and maintained through skilful political leadership was beginning to disintegrate even before Macdonald's death shortly after his last election victory in 1891. This political alliance had been premised on the shared conservatism of Ontario Tories and Quebec Bleus, a partnership made possible by the constitutional relegation of language and cultural issues to the provincial level of government (where they would not threaten the fragile basis of the federal coalition).[3]

Besides the nineteenth-century Liberal Party's suspect position on Catholicism and the role of the Church, there was another factor that hindered the breadth of its appeal to Canadian voters: the party's stubborn philosophical adherence to the principle of free trade.[4] The origins of this philosophical orientation lay at the heart of nineteenth-century liberalism. The Upper Canadian 'Reformers' and 'Clear Grits', who were the historical forerunners of the Liberal Party in English Canada, 'opposed the tendency of the Conservatives to meddle in economic matters which, by orthodox liberal economic doctrine, ought to be left to the natural laws of economics'.[5] On principle, nineteenth-century liberals (and Liberals) were committed to laissez-faire and to the idea of close economic ties to the United States as the natural market for Canada. The 1867 platform of the Reform Party (which quickly thereafter adopted the name Liberal Party) asserted that it was the 'duty' of Canadians to cultivate friendly relations with the United States, 'and especially to offer every facility for the extension of trade and commerce between the two countries'.[6] The first two leaders of this new party, Alexander Mackenzie and Edward Blake, 'maintained an unyielding opposition to protective tariffs as an unjust restriction on individual liberty'.[7] These deeply held convictions led the Liberal Party to oppose Macdonald's National Policy. Even later, when the Laurier-led Liberals accepted the essentials of the National Policy out of political necessity, a preference for lower tariffs and freer trade—and a positive view of the Canada–US relationship as naturally and inevitably close—continued to be a defining characteristic of the Liberals and an important element of continuity in the party's appeal to its core electorate.

If Liberal advocacy of free trade with the United States in 1891 handed the Conservatives the issue they needed to mobilize the electorate in English

Canada behind Macdonald one more time, the altered balance of power between the two parties occasioned by the arrival of the new Liberal leader, Wilfrid Laurier, was also apparent. Laurier sought a rapprochement between the Liberals and Quebec by disavowing the anticlericalism of the old Quebec Rouges. And whereas previous party leaders Mackenzie and Blake 'had been remote figures who tended to express an Ontarian rather than a Canadian viewpoint', Laurier was a Catholic French Canadian with the charismatic qualities and national vision of Macdonald.[8] Unlike the latter, Laurier was also a champion of provincial rights, a position that drew an increasingly favourable reception in Quebec as the limitations of its influence in Parliament became clearer.[9] Laurier's appeal may not have been enough to lead his party to national victory in 1891, but his skilful brokering of Canada's cultural divide did win his party a clear majority of Quebec's seats in that election. It also laid the basis for a series of Liberal election victories premised on a strongly Liberal Quebec that could counterbalance the entrenched Conservative leanings of Anglo-Protestant Ontario. Support for provincial rights—also a key element in the electoral success of provincial Liberals such as Ontario's Oliver Mowat, Nova Scotia's William Fielding, and Quebec's Honoré Mercier—fit easily into the 'limited government' philosophy of nineteenth-century liberals. It also came naturally to a party in opposition at the national level for most of the first thirty years of Confederation, facing a governing party (Macdonald's Conservatives) who were implacably centrist if not imperialist in their attitude towards the provinces.

The final step that helped to bring the party to power in Ottawa was Laurier's pragmatic acceptance of Macdonald's National Policy. The vexing question of the tariff (or, more specifically, Liberal attacks upon it) was virtually absent as an election issue in 1896. In the Maritimes, with popular Liberal premiers ensconced in power and no loyalty cry to move the voters, the Liberals were able to come close to the Tories in seats. In Ontario the two parties were even, with the Tories retaining a slight advantage in Manitoba. Overall in English Canada, the Conservatives collected seventy-two seats to the Liberals' sixty-nine. It was in Quebec where the tide was turned, with the once-mighty Conservatives taking a mere sixteen seats to the Liberals' forty-nine. As the core of Ontario Conservatism was increasingly influenced by a militant Protestantism and Anglo-Saxon racialism, and (after the death of Macdonald) as there was no English-speaking Conservative leader in whom French Canada could put its trust, francophone Quebecers turned decisively to Laurier.[10]

The Liberals' pragmatic acceptance of the National Policy in 1896 was not the same as principled commitment, and the issue would be revisited by the party in 1911. In the interim, a long period of economic growth and national prosperity helped return the Liberals to power in 1900, 1904, and 1908. The latter election represents perhaps the quintessence of Canadian federal elections during the first party system: 'two bourgeois parties pitted against each other, with no differences but scandals between them. The electorate, of necessity, had to fall back on traditional loyalties to make a choice.'[11] The main division this election revealed was an ethnic and religious one, with constituencies with large Anglo-Protestant populations aligning with the Conservative Party and those with large numbers of French, Catholic, or non-British ethnic minorities with the Liberal Party. In the West this pattern of partisan support also prevailed, indicating that the party system developed in the East had been successfully exported to the West, despite the latter's recently settled population and its much larger contingent of voters who were neither French nor British (27 per cent in 1911).[12]

While the Liberal embrace of the National Policy after 1896 helped to mute ideological and policy differences between themselves and the Tories, there was at least one remaining difference in political orientation that helps to explain the continuing and persistent differentiation of core support bases from which each party brokered for further support. This was the question of Canada's relationship to the British Empire. Whereas the Tories 'sought to promote greater and more equal Canadian participation in imperial and world affairs' while revelling in Canada's role within the Empire, the Liberals leaned towards a more isolationist and autonomist policy, based on a distaste for imperialism and colonial subordination. This attitude was particularly strong within the Quebec wing of the Liberal Party; English-speaking Liberals with personal and emotional ties and loyalties to Britain were more ambivalent in their attitude towards the Empire. Laurier's fundamental attitude was demonstrated in the naval bill of 1910, which provided for the establishment of a separate Canadian Navy rather than an immediate contribution to the British Royal Navy as advocated by the Conservatives.[13]

In the election of 1911, the Liberal Party's fundamental predisposition towards free trade and its ambivalence towards Canada's role and place within the Empire combined to topple the party after fifteen years of uninterrupted power at the national level. Its platform of Reciprocity (limited free trade) with the United States cost the party dearly in the bastions of pro-British English Canada—Ontario, Manitoba, and British Columbia—while its naval policy was seized on by Quebec nationalists led by Henri Bourassa, who attacked Laurier for ignoring the interests and sentiments of French Canada and seeking to 'pitchfork French Canadians into Imperialism'.[14] In Ontario big business lined up against the proposed Reciprocity Agreement, with eighteen prominent Toronto Liberals issuing a manifesto calling the proposals 'the worst blow ever to threaten Canadian nationality'.[15] In a case of truly strange bedfellows, an 'unholy alliance' of the pro-imperialist Conservatives in English Canada and anti-imperialist nationalists in French Canada produced a massive victory for the Tories in Ontario and a sharply reduced Liberal majority in Quebec, the latter in particular sealing the Liberals' fate. In any event, the nationalists' third party strategy failed: Bourassa had hoped his group would hold the balance of power in Ottawa; instead, they were marginalized by a Conservative government that didn't need them.[16] Both the Liberal Party and francophone Quebec voters learned a hard lesson in 1911: never again would the Liberals stand for election on a platform of free trade with the United States; and it would be eighty-two years before a plurality of Quebec voters would again be convinced to support a nationalist third party as an alternative to a strong Quebec contingent firmly within the governing party's caucus.

The election of 1911 was the last of the old two-party system that has been referred to as the first party system. The wartime election of 1917 was a virtual referendum on conscription, with most English-speaking Liberals joining Robert Borden's Conservatives to form the Unionist Party. Leaving nothing to chance, the government also passed legislation that enfranchised close female relatives of servicemen overseas and disenfranchised citizens of alien birth or mother tongue naturalized after 1902. The latter measure was crucial to the re-election of Borden's government. It deprived the Liberals of many of their supporters in the West, where they won only two of the region's fifty-seven seats. The other regions of the country were true to form: Ontario demonstrated a predictable patriotism, sending seventy-four Unionists to Parliament and only eight Liberals; Quebec francophones voted overwhelmingly for the anticonscription Liberals, giving Laurier sixty-two of its sixty-five seats. In the Maritimes, the Liberal Party remained intact, taking 45 per cent and 50 per cent of the vote in Nova Scotia and PEI respectively, while New Brunswick—a microcosm of the country as a whole—clearly divided its support along ethnic lines, with the Anglo-Protestant majority voting Unionist and the French-Catholic minority voting Liberal. Never was the ethnoreligious divide in Canada so clearly reflected in regional and party terms, nor so ominously for national unity. The aftershocks of this wartime election would continue to shape party strategies and voter alignments for decades to come.

The first fifty years of Confederation were a time of evolution and consolidation for the Liberal Party. For the first half of this period, the party struggled to define itself and to develop a successful electoral strategy in its competition with the Conservatives. In this fashion, an assemblage of fragmented and disparate factions, who for one reason or another were opposed to Macdonald's governing coalition, was transformed into a coherent political party. It took a number of elections for this loose coalition to transform itself into a coherent political party. In response to the major issues and conflicts of the day, a number of key elements of ideology, program, and orientation were developed and articulated by party leaders.

Simultaneously, the major components of a core support base within the Canadian electorate were assembled: French Canadians, Catholics, ethnic-minority communities, and free-trading primary producers. Some elements of this voter support base were acquired because of the Liberal Party's favourable disposition towards free trade and provincial rights, or its ambiguity towards (rather than enthusiastic embrace of) the British Empire.

Others were won over through calculated leadership and policy changes. In regional terms, the party established strongholds in Quebec, the Prairies, and the more Catholic and French-speaking areas of Ontario and the Maritimes.

The Second Party System

During the second party system, the Liberal Party remained in power for all but six years. Their leader for most of this period was William Lyon Mackenzie King, the longest-serving prime minister in Canadian history. King (the grandson of the infamous Reform politician who led the 1837 rebellion in Upper Canada) won the Liberal leadership convention that followed Laurier's death in 1919. His first and principal task was to use his considerable skills in political reconciliation and brokering in order to reunite a Liberal Party divided into its French and English components by the conscription issue. Secondly, he was faced with the need to adapt nineteenth-century Canadian liberalism to the urban, industrial society that Canada was rapidly becoming. King was well suited to meet both challenges: he was one of the few English-speaking Liberals in Ontario to reject Unionism and remain within the Liberal Party throughout the war; he also had been a labour relations specialist who wrote a book, *Industry and Humanity*, which recognized the need for labour unions and a new role for the state as an arbiter and promoter of cooperation between business and labour.

As prime minister, King was extremely careful not to alienate Quebec, giving its provincial government wide leeway to run its own affairs and avoiding issues that could precipitate the kind of cultural and political conflict that had come to a head during the First World War. He would also appeal to Quebec with his commitment to Canadian independence along isolationist lines; for King, Canada's future lay with its continental, not its European, connections. Each of these fundamentals underlying King's tenure as party leader and prime minister was firmly rooted in the basic appeal that had been made continuously at least since the beginnings of Laurier's leadership in the late 1880s. The party had always been a defender of provincial rights and the autonomy of provinces within their constitutionally defined spheres of jurisdiction; sensitivity towards the concerns of French Canadians and particularly Quebec was virtually guaranteed by Laurier's long tenure as party leader (1887–1919) and the strong (sometimes dominant) contingent of Quebec francophone MPs within the parliamentary caucus. And the long history of the party's more continentalist orientation (compared to the Tories)—stemming from a philosophical preference for limited government and the operation of economic forces unhindered by the distortions introduced by high tariffs, and a disinclination towards Empire—made King's pursuit of complete autonomy from Britain a natural and logical extension of liberal thought and previous Liberal policy.

On the other hand, King's sensitivity to the divide between capital and labour in modern industrial society, and the class conflict it could engender, led him to nudge Canadian Liberalism away from its commitment to nineteenth-century ideals and towards a more positive liberalism that accepted the need for government intervention in the economic and social realms in order to promote individual welfare and opportunity and reduce industrial strife.[17] As Reg Whitaker noted, 'That the party never rejected support of the vested capitalist interests, while at the same time never entirely losing its credibility with the voters as a party of democratic reform, left it precisely the flexibility and freedom of action to "wheel and deal" in the centre of the political spectrum and to make the kind of practical accommodations necessary to maintain its hold on power.'[18]

King's ideological leanings were often as not submerged from view by this 'wheeling and dealing' in the centre, betraying a more dominant characteristic of King the politician: he was first and foremost a cautious pragmatist and a political tactician, as captured in Frank Scott's poetic imagery: 'Doing nothing by halves, that could be done by quarters. We had no shape, because he never allowed us to take sides. And no sides, because he never allowed them to take shape.'[19]

The Liberal Party's ideological ambivalence and the personal qualities of its leader served the party well in the context of Canadian politics in the interwar period. Where 46 per cent of Canada's population had been involved in agriculture in 1891, only 33 per cent were so engaged in 1921, dropping to 29 per cent in 1931. The growth of an urban, industrial working class and a white-collar tertiary or service sector had fundamentally altered Canada's class structure and population distribution. Industrial workers, however, were internally divided along lines of craft and industrial unionism, as well as radical and moderate factions. They were further divided by language and ethnicity, with Quebec workers generally organized by the Church into Catholic unions that were opposed to socialism (in all its variants) and committed to the maintenance of industrial peace. Finally, with the federal government forced to retreat from the labour scene by judicial interpretations of the Constitution that awarded jurisdiction over this area to the provinces, the labour movement became further regionalized in its focus and demands. All these factors contributed to the weakness of organized labour (and its spokespersons and allies) as a national political force.[20]

While urbanism and industrialism, then, introduced a new dynamic of class-based politics that politicians could not ignore, it was the enduring regional and cultural dimensions of Canadian politics that continued to shape party competition. In the election of 1921, it was not the growing numbers of industrial workers who fundamentally challenged the traditional parties but the declining agrarian class, and in particular the western grain farmers who were still the most significant societal group on the Canadian Prairies in terms of numbers and organizational strength. Their arrival on the party scene in the form of the Progressives was dramatic, but ultimately short-lived. As the decade wore on and the traditional themes of Canadian politics reasserted themselves, King—aided by an improvement in farmers' economic fortunes—was able to woo many Progressive MPs and supporters back to the Liberal Party. This was less difficult than it might have been had the Progressives been united on strategy and a common vision of their goals and objectives; instead they were divided between adherents to a more or less conventional understanding of party politics and the Albertan followers of Henry Wise Wood and his populist, antiparty concept of group government. After winning sixty-five seats and 23 per cent of the popular vote in 1921, by mid-decade the Progressives were reduced to twenty seats and 5 per cent of the vote. It was King's Liberal Party that was the prime beneficiary of this rapid decline, 'repatriating' much of the support that had gone to the Progressives in Ontario, Manitoba, and Saskatchewan.[21]

King's manoeuvring to bring Progressives back to their former Liberal home came at a price. His reluctance to act on the demands of the struggling Maritimes in the early 1920s (because these demands generally conflicted with those of the western-based Progressives) helped the Conservatives win a near sweep of the region's seats in 1925 and a strong majority there in 1926. This was counterbalanced, however, by Liberal gains in Manitoba and Saskatchewan. With the Tories now shut out of French Quebec, a national majority for the Liberals could be secured with only a fair performance in Ontario, something King failed to accomplish in 1925 but managed in 1926.[22]

The 1920s produced a decade of Liberal government, but it was an unconvincing display of Liberal dominance. Two of the three Liberal governments during this period were minorities, and the Conservatives had recovered by mid-decade to a position of clear supremacy in English Canada. Mackenzie King may have orchestrated a Liberal recovery on the Prairies, but it was only the complete alienation of French Canada from the Tories that kept him in power. This overreliance on a solid Liberal Quebec left the Liberals vulnerable to even a minor shift of voter alignments in that province. Thus in 1930, when a combination of political and economic factors gave the Conservatives their first minor breakthrough in Quebec since their alliance with the nationalists in 1911, the Liberals were sent—fortuitously as things turned out—into opposition.[23]

After the Conservatives' disastrous experience in government during the Depression, King would win three consecutive majorities (in 1935, 1940, and 1945) before stepping down in 1948 in favour of his handpicked successor, Louis St Laurent, who would lead the party to two additional majority victories (in 1949 and 1953). The Liberal Party during this era was truly dominant, winning elections with relative ease, unopposed by any effective national opponent. It held sway in Quebec, Manitoba, and throughout most of Atlantic Canada, while facing different regional opponents in other parts of the country: the Conservatives in Ontario and British Columbia, the CCF in Saskatchewan and British Columbia, and the Social Credit in Alberta. While not strictly the party of Catholics during this period, there was a strong association between the Catholicity of a constituency and its propensity to vote Liberal; this relationship was even stronger if the population happened to be largely French Canadian.

In the election of 1935, in the midst of the Depression, the Liberals made no sweeping campaign promises, nor proposed any radical solutions to the economic crisis; instead they used the slogan 'It's King or Chaos' to attract voters alienated from the enormously unpopular Conservative government of R.B. Bennett. Though the Liberal popular vote fell slightly, the party made gains almost everywhere, taking twenty-five of twenty-six seats in the Maritimes, sixty of sixty-five in Quebec, fifty-six of eighty-two in Ontario, fourteen of seventeen in Manitoba, and sixteen of twenty-one in Saskatchewan. Only in Alberta and British Columbia did the Liberals lose ground to two new parties (the Social Credit and the CCF) offering voters a more radical alternative than the Liberals. Still, with 173 of 245 seats, this was the greatest political victory in Canadian history to that point in time.[24] That is, until the election of 1940. With Canada at war and his political opponents fragmented and ill-prepared, King appealed to Canadians for a popular mandate to conduct the war effort. In any event, the Liberals outdid their 1935 performance, piling up 181 seats while substantially improving their weak position in Alberta and British Columbia.

For the most part, the Liberal Party during the Depression remained quite conservative in its response to the economic crisis. Wedded to the idea of limited government and provincial autonomy, and chary of provoking a backlash in Quebec against any federal intrusion into provincial jurisdiction, King neither advocated in opposition nor pursued in power any equivalent to Roosevelt's New Deal. This changed with the enormous demands on the federal government created by the 1939–45 war. Under such circumstances, adherence to the principles of laissez-faire liberalism and classical federalism was bound to give way. Moreover, by this time the Keynesian revolution had arrived, and 'while King was apparently never personally convinced, Keynesian economic thinking soon came to dominate the thinking of senior civil servants in the Department of Finance'.[25] With the federal government completely overshadowing the provinces in taxing and spending power by 1945, and the government politically committed to economic management and the creation of national social programs as the centrepiece of its postwar plans, Liberal Party ideology shifted notably further in the direction of welfare liberalism. This effectively transformed the federal Liberals from champions of provincial rights to protagonists for strong central government.

It was not just the needs of wartime or the development of a new economic theory or the growing influence of senior bureaucrats that explains this ideology and policy (though these are all relevant). It was due also, perhaps even primarily, to the growing strength of the political left in Canada during the war, particularly the CCF. King's government was forced to adjust, to steal the socialists' thunder by passing or proposing to pass progressive labour and social legislation.[26] Even so, the results of the 1945 election indicate that the Liberals would have lost their majority if not for their continued dominance of Quebec.[27] The Conservatives came back strongly in Ontario; the CCF and Social Credit did well in the West. Many commentators were unhappy with the outcome, which they felt demonstrated a pronounced lack of national unity. One American observer 'compared Quebec to the "solid South" in his country's politics, and saw it as operating as a brake on the dominant Liberal Party, and preventing it from giving the other parts of the country—and particularly western Canada—the bolder policies they wanted'.[28] This was not the first, nor would it be the last such interpretation of Canadian electoral outcomes. It represents yet another thematic element running through the history of Canadian politics.

Concerns about national unity were effectively submerged for the next decade, however, by economic prosperity and Liberal political hegemony. The close and quiet cooperation between political, bureaucratic, and corporate élites that had been a hallmark of the war years was extended virtually without a hiccup into the postwar era. This managerial approach emphasizing efficient administration and 'Liberal identification with the Canadian corporate establishment' reached its high point between 1948 and 1957 during the prime ministership of Louis St Laurent.[29] With national economic prosperity continuing, it seemed as if the Liberals would govern forever. A certain 'greyness' and predictability descended over Canadian political life during these years, which was reflected in increased voter apathy: voter turnout fell from 74 to 67 per cent.[30] Canadians also continued to exhibit little in the way of class voting, while partisan allegiance on the basis of ethnicity, religion, and region remained strongly pronounced.[31]

A new factor in these postwar elections was the addition of a fourth province east of Quebec. In a 1949 referendum, Newfoundland voted 52 per cent in favour of joining Canadian Confederation. It was quickly established that the island would follow its own distinctive pattern of politics and voting. The successful leader of the pro-Confederation forces in Newfoundland, Joseph Smallwood, who drew his support from the outports, became premier and provincial leader of the Liberal Party in Newfoundland. Newfoundland's anti-Confederates, rallied by the business interests of the capital city, attached themselves to the Conservatives. This established a tradition in federal politics whereby the two St John's constituencies would more often than not return Conservatives, and the five 'outport' seats Liberals. In a reverse of the general Canadian pattern, the Tory ridings in Newfoundland tended to be populated in the majority by Catholics, while the Liberal outport ridings were predominantly Protestant.

Of course, the perception of Liberal invincibility generated by the large majority wins of 1949 and 1953 was not wholly accurate. The efficiency of the Liberal system of governance from the point of view of bureaucratic administration was beginning to exhibit certain negative consequences for the party as a partisan political organization. Moreover, prognostications of continued Liberal dominance were premised in part on the assumption of a stand pat opposition that was unlikely to do anything dramatic to change the nature and character of their appeal to voters. Both factors played a role in the Liberals' fall from grace in 1957.

Under St Laurent, the Liberal Party's transformation into the government party reached its logical culmination 'with the virtual fusion of party and state ... the Liberal Party, as a political party, was growing less distinct— the party was more a vehicle for elite accommodation, involving not only the elite of the two linguistic and cultural groups in Canada but the bureaucratic and corporate elite as well'.[32] Paradoxically, this became an impediment to the political health of the party. An increasingly complacent, élitist, and technocratic government was vulnerable to populist critics who charged it with being undemocratic, unresponsive, and arrogant. And in 1956–7 the most effective critic of all was the new Tory leader, John George Diefenbaker.

In the 1957 election campaign and the famous pipeline debate that preceded it, Diefenbaker positioned his party as the defender of democratic values against an arrogant government, of Canadianism against 'American millionaires', of the 'little man' against the big interests, and the hinterlands whose concerns the Liberal government ignored or considered secondary. By outflanking the Liberals on the left, Diefenbaker would break their hold on the Maritimes and the Prairies, regions with troubled economies that by the mid-1950s had ceased to reap the benefits of postwar economic prosperity.

In Atlantic Canada the Liberal seat total fell from twenty-seven to twelve, while on the Prairies—where grain prices were no higher than they had been in the hungry 1930s—the Liberals lost eleven of their seventeen seats. Diefenbaker's passionate eloquence regarding his Anglophilic conception of a British-inspired and British-centred Canadianism had its greatest appeal in British Columbia and Ontario. In Ontario the Liberals lost thirty seats and were confined for the most part to peripheral areas of the province: eastern and northern Ontario where the French Canadian population was substantial, the Windsor area, and the Niagara Peninsula. In total, the Liberals won only forty-three of the 190 seats outside Quebec; only continued Liberal dominance in Quebec prevented the Conservatives from winning an outright majority.[33] Conservative strategists had explicitly designed a campaign that would bring them to power without significant representation from Quebec; the results in 1957 can be read either as a vindication of this approach or simply as a self-fulfilling prophecy.[34]

The 1958 election rendered the Liberal Party a shadow of its former formidable self. The party's new, inexperienced leader, Lester Pearson (a career civil servant for most of his adult life), rashly and unwisely 'launched a scathing attack on the [new] government and concluded with a pusillanimous demand that it resign'.[35] When Diefenbaker happily obliged him and called a general election for 31 March 1958, none of the defeated Liberal cabinet ministers chose to reoffer; even nineteen of the Liberals who were elected in 1957 declined to run again. The Liberals made a further strategic error by running on Pearson's diplomatic record and his Nobel Peace Prize (for his role in ending the Suez crisis). Canadians, however, were more concerned about domestic matters.[36] Precampaign polls had clearly indicated a considerable Conservative victory and the campaign itself only served to swell the Conservative tide.[37] Even Quebec voted so as not to isolate itself from the inevitable winner: the Liberals won only twenty-five of the province's seventy-five seats; the Conservatives took the rest. In total the Liberals won only forty-nine seats and one-third of the popular vote, the worst showing in the party's history. In two of the Maritime and all four western provinces, they won no seats at all. The second party system—characterized by Liberal dominance and a Tory party whose strength was confined to Ontario—was brought to a sudden, tumultuous (and somewhat unexpected) end.

The Third Party System

Looking back on Liberal Party success prior to 1958, it was clear that their core support was rooted in the country's Catholic population, especially in Quebec and the Maritimes. Religious differences, it seems, had translated into differences over 'the moral and symbolic claims of the British connection', with the Tories supported by Anglo-Protestants championing imperialism and the British connection, and the Liberals supported by Catholics and ethnic minorities inclined to resist the pull of Empire.[38]

It was upon this Catholic core that the Liberal Party rebuilt its political hegemony in the third party system, enjoying another long period of political dominance from 1963 to 1984. During this latter period, however, the Liberals relied on a more centre-left urban appeal and a made-in-Canada national unity/national identity strategy that reinforced the party's traditional support base among French Canadians and ethnic minorities. Diefenbaker's populist appeal—especially in rural and small-town Canada —had allowed the Conservatives to break out of the narrow Ontario base to which they had been relegated in the second party system and to displace populist third parties in the West, as well as the Liberals (who had been prime beneficiaries of the four-party competition that characterized politics in the West during most of the second party system). Thereafter, the Liberals, with a secure Quebec base but virtually shut out of western Canada, had to pursue parliamentary majorities in urban Ontario. It typically held pluralities in only four provinces: Newfoundland, New Brunswick, Quebec, and Ontario. In contrast to the second party system, the dominant characteristic of the party system between 1962 and 1984 was that there was *no truly national party*, making minority governments an ever-present possibility.

The third party system also featured two new-old political forces. The right-wing, populist Social Credit Party had been devastated in its Alberta base in 1958, but recovered in 1962 thanks largely to Quebec, where the party's Quebec wing won twenty-six seats (see Chapter 6). From the mid-1960s onward, however, this party was in inexorable decline, and by 1980 was wiped off the federal electoral map. In contrast, the New Democratic Party (successor to the CCF) after its creation in 1961 showed limited but resilient electoral strength. With a consistent 16 to 20 per cent of the vote, it threatened the Liberal Party from the left, wielding considerable influence in times of minority government and making it difficult for the Liberals in power to 'cheat' too far right-of-centre without paying with a slippage of voter support to their left-wing rival. This strategic positioning and 'keep the Liberals honest' role made the NDP a significant player in the third party system and a serious long-term threat to the Liberals (see Chapter 4).

Underlying these changes in the pattern of party competition were changes in Canada's economy and society. Urbanization proceeded apace and the service and public sectors grew exponentially. Thus, between 1946 and 1971, the percentage of the labour force on government payrolls expanded from 9 per cent to 22 per cent. And these public sector workers were the focus of a new wave of unionization.[39] The burgeoning public sector and other white-collar workers in the rapidly expanding service sector became the focus of party competition; Canada's urban middle classes were swelling the electorate, and all of Canada's major political parties were forced in one fashion or another to seek their support. More than any other party, however, it was the Liberal Party that succeeded in doing so.

For the Liberals, the trauma of losing control over state power in 1957–8 was made all the more complete by the dramatic shrinkage of the party's political support base and the ranks of its elected members. The Liberals clearly had been outflanked by the Diefenbaker Conservatives, beached in terms of their strategic positioning and political appeal by a shift in the discourse and policy orientation of late-1950s Progressive Conservatism, and the public's altered perception of that party and its leadership. The completeness of the defeat did have one beneficial effect for the Liberals. It purged the party, not only in the sense of removing the overweening influence that extended years in power had granted the aging, élitist, small 'c' conservative party establishment but in actual physical terms as well. Between 1958 and 1962, a generational change of personnel occurred, opening up both ideological and physical space within the party. The result was greatly increased influence for the younger, more progressive, left-of-centre elements: those more strongly Keynesian and welfarist in their policy predilictions, more favourably disposed towards state intervention in the economy and technocratic planning, and, in strategic terms, covetous of the electoral support of Canada's growing urban middle class.

The need for a major overhaul and reconstruction of the party had both an ideological-policy dimension and an organizational dimension. The revamping and redirection of party ideology and policy began with the Kingston Thinkers Conference in 1960. The progressive, left-leaning policy prescriptions advocated there by younger, emergent figures within the party—condemned by some as an embrace of socialism—was, in fact, something more closely approximating a commitment to put in place a comprehensive welfare state in Canada. Pearson allowed the policy balance to swing towards welfare liberalism, and somewhat fitfully over the next decade, the welfare state in Canada was completed under the guidance of Liberal governments. Pearson, was, however, distinctly cool to economic nationalism, even that of close cabinet colleagues such as Walter Gordon. A believer in international integration, Pearson placed a high priority on restoring the closest possible trade and diplomatic relations with the United States after 1963, and displayed traditional Liberal openness to a political and economic partnership with the Americans, further integrating Canada into an American-dominated continental economy.[40]

It would be easy to overstate the predominance at this time of the left-leaning, social democratic element of the Liberal Party. Under Pearson there was a marriage of old guard and new guard Liberals, clearly expressed in right-left factional splits within Liberal cabinets.[41] The party's electoral strategy of courting the urban middle class—and its calculated flirtation with the NDP—gave impetus and substance to moderately leftish, moderately nationalist minority Liberal governments after the elections of 1963 and 1965. But it also produced a backlash from more conservative-minded business liberals within the party and cabinet.

> The Liberal Party [in the 1960s] has continued to speak the language of King: ambiguous and ambivalent, presenting first its radical face and then its conservative face, urging reform and warning against hasty, ill-considered change, calling for increased state responsibility but stopping short of socialism openly, speaking for the common people but preaching the solidarity of classes.[42]

Pearson was prime minister for five years, but never managed to lead his party to a majority. Though the Diefenbaker government had self-destructed, support levels for the Tories remained high enough in the West, the Maritimes, and parts of Ontario to hold the Liberals to a minority, especially given the fragmentation of votes and seats resulting from the moderate electoral successes of the NDP and Créditistes. In addition to the continuing differences in the way Catholics and Protestants voted, Canadians during this period tended to be split along urban-rural lines, with the Liberals predominantly an urban party (distinctly unpopular with farmers) that also drew disproportionately upon the votes of immigrants, French-speakers, and younger Canadians. The Tories, reduced to their former position of weakness in Quebec, were primarily a party of rural and small-town English Canada. No party seemed capable of making a truly national appeal, however, until the election in 1968 of Pierre Elliott Trudeau as Liberal leader and prime minister.

Trudeau came to Ottawa in 1965 as one of Quebec's 'Three Wise Men', recruited by the Liberals to help stem the rising tide of nationalism in Quebec. That province was in the throes of its Quiet Revolution, and its demands on Ottawa had begun to preoccupy the government and the country more than any other issue. Between 1963 and 1968, the Royal Commission on Bilingualism and Biculturalism worked to fulfil its mandate of advising government on the future of ethnocultural relations in Canada. In April 1967 Trudeau entered the federal cabinet as justice minister, and soon thereafter caught the attention of English Canada with his proposal to broaden the divorce law and his bill to liberalize the Criminal Code with respect to homosexuality and abortion. But it was at the constitutional conference of February 1968 when Trudeau 'burst upon the consciousness of tired, discouraged federalists as a leader to defend the citadel of eroding federal power'.[43] Trudeau stressed the lack of logic in a 'two nations' concept of Canada, rejecting both the 'biculturalism' advocated by the Royal Commission as well as the notion of 'two peoples' found in the 1968 platform of the Conservative Party.[44] He also ridiculed the idea of 'special status' for Quebec, the core demand of Quebec's provincial parties and an idea endorsed by the federal New Democrats.[45]

> Even in a sociological sense the former would lead to two nation-states, while the latter would reduce Quebec's influence in Ottawa and limit the French fact, juridically and politically, to Quebec. His theme of 'one Canada' and 'one nation' evoked such a favourable response that it became his chief stock-in-trade. Conservatives said that he was catering to the Anglo-Saxon backlash, and so he was. But he was saying the same thing in French Canada. . . .[46]

It is undoubtedly true that Trudeau's appeal was clearly tied to his position on Quebec; his willingness to confront Quebec politicians 'catered to the Anglo-Saxon backlash everywhere: here was a Frenchman who could put the trouble-making Frenchmen in their place'.[47] For French Canada, Trudeau's arguments implied a greater representation of francophones in Ottawa. At the same time, the source of his popularity initially and throughout his political career went well beyond this to more intangible qualities of charisma and style.

On 6 April 1968, just one short year after assuming his first cabinet post and despite the aversion of a good part of the Liberal establishment, Trudeau was elected as Liberal leader. He wasted no time in calling a general election and then proceeded to pursue a 'love-in' with the media and public. 'Trudeau-mania' afflicted all ages and categories of citizens, but especially women and the young. And what was the source of this enthusiasm? There seems to have been a fair bit of agreement that it had to do with the mood of the country and the image of the leader. One year after centennial celebrations, people were 'charisma-hungry' and wanted a positive, reassuring leader-symbol to match their new, confident image of themselves as a country.[48]

In the election, Trudeau's campaign themes—'the just society' and 'parti-cipatory democracy'—were tailor-made for the times. Campaign coverage, however, was affected less by debate about the achievement of these high-minded ideas than by the media's fascination with Trudeau's personality. Only Atlantic Canada proved immune, entrusting most of their votes and seats to favourite son Robert Stanfield (the former premier of Nova Scotia) and his Progressive Conservatives. In Quebec Trudeau increased the Liberal popular vote, but failed to add to the party's total of fifty-six seats. Ontario, on the other hand, was a Liberal rout. The Liberals took sixty-four of eighty-eight seats, reducing the Conservatives (who won seventeen seats) to their worst Ontario showing since 1874! On the Prairies, Trudeau managed to im-prove appreciably upon Pearson's dreadful 1965 seat total (one Manitoba seat) by winning eleven of the region's forty-five seats, while both urban and rural BC succumbed to Trudeaumania, returning sixteen Liberals to Ottawa.[49]

The honeymoon with Trudeau was not to last. Besides passage of the Offi-cial Languages Act and movement towards bilingualization of the federal civil service, the first Liberal majority government in over a decade accom-plished remarkably little. A political *Wunderkind* in 1968, Trudeau, the apos-tle of rationalism in politics, had each area of government reexamined, 'with the end result that little change was made from previous patterns. . . . Far more damaging politically was Trudeau's personal feat of offending almost every major group in the population outside Quebec.'[50] In 1972, with unem-ployment high and a growing English backlash against the government's attempts to establish the 'French fact' in Ottawa, the Liberals ran on the complacent theme of 'The Land Is Strong' and came within a hair's breadth of losing office. The Liberals held onto 109 seats, while the Conservatives increased their total to 107, with the NDP holding the balance of power. Only Quebec again kept the Liberals in office by returning fifty-six Liberals for the third election in a row; in Atlantic Canada the Liberals did marginally better, while elsewhere Liberal support and seat totals fell off badly. The end result roughly divided the country into two camps, one predominantly franco-phone, the other anglophone. 'The politics of national unity once again had been made manifest as entrenched national division.'[51]

The Trudeau government performed much better during the subsequent two years of minority government. As there was a need to court NDP support to stay in power, important legislation was brought in and passed in a number of areas, including a number of left-nationalist initiatives such as the creation of Petro-Canada and the Foreign Investment Review Agency. The nationalist thrust of government policy in these years was somewhat unfamiliar ground for the Liberals, but was spurred by parliamentary and electoral pressure from the more left-nationalist NDP, which strengthened the hand of economic nationalists within the Liberal Party. While Trudeau himself was hostile to nationalism on principle, paradoxically '[this] contributed to the party's modest nationalist inclination, for the alternative to Canadian nationalism was seen to be not internationalism but the powerful nationalism of the American empire ... [This] allowed some Liberals to justify nationalist measures as a means of achieving autonomy, a goal which has been a fixture of Liberal policy since the time of Laurier.'[52] As well, nationalist initiatives emanating from Ottawa had the salutary effect (in Trudeau's eyes) of acting as a counterbalance to Quebec nationalism and more broadly to the expanding demands and assertiveness of the provinces.

When the Liberals engineered their own defeat in Parliament in 1974, they were able to run against the Conservative platform of wage and price controls as a means of controlling the high level of inflation Canada was experiencing without offering any solutions of their own. As well, a number of left-leaning policies were announced, 'aimed at appealing to the floating vote that campaign strategists guessed was hovering to the left of the Liberals'[53] At the same time, leader images played a large role in the outcome, with the Liberal campaign exploiting Trudeau's dynamism compared with Stanfield's rather stodgy, negative image. The Liberals' image-driven campaign required that journalists be kept at a distance from Trudeau, and no appearances were made except under controlled and favourable circumstances.[54] The subsequent majority gained by the Liberals in 1974 was not a landslide; only marginal gains were made in Atlantic Canada and Quebec, with the West nearly as Tory as before. Ontario, once again, was the decisive battleground and the key to Liberal fortunes, with the party adding nineteen new seats there. But it was close: a swing of 5 per cent to the Conservatives at the expense of the Liberals would have meant the loss of seventeen of these new Liberal seats.[55]

The 1974 election campaign is instructive on the nature of brokerage politics as practised in Canada. Coherent policies endangered electoral success, so they were to be avoided. The Conservatives were pinned down on an important policy in 1974, for which they paid an electoral price. In the passage that follows, Senator Keith Davey, Liberal campaign manager and chief strategist during the Trudeau years, outlines the traditional wisdom of a winning party strategy in Canada.

The traditional strength of the Liberal Party has been that we spanned so much of the centre of the stage, that we forced the Tories way out to our right and we forced the New Democrats away out to our left, and so this is a party that at one and the same time can contain [small 'c' conservative] Ross Thatcher and [left-nationalist] Walter Gordon; we've managed, to some extent, to make the cities think we are for them and to make the country think we are for them and even to be the party of labour and big business at the same time—that's been a neat trick.[56]

While the Liberals were busy performing this trick, with varying degrees of success, in five consecutive elections (1963, 1965, 1968, 1972, and 1974), the other parties were virtually barred from power. The NDP was confined to western Canada and a small base of support in Ontario, while the Conservatives were crippled by their weakness in Quebec. In both cases, the formula for Liberal electoral success pre-empted the rise of their opponents: the quasi-social democratic and mildly nationalist policy agenda pursued by the Liberals during this period siphoned off potential support for the NDP, while French Canada and the issue of English-French relations were well staked out by the Liberals, especially after the ascension of Pierre Trudeau to the leadership. With the Quebec electorate increasingly polarized by the federalist-nationalist struggle, the Liberals succeeded in all but monopolizing the federalist side of the debate, in the process becoming synonymous with the notion of 'French power' in Ottawa. The NDP was never able to register with the unions or left-leaning voters in Quebec (most of whom had become supporters of Quebec independence) and the Conservatives struggled to win two seats there in 1972 and three in 1974.

So the Liberals were destined to remain in power throughout this period, and on certain issues the party did manage to piece together a distinct party strategy and construct a viable political alliance supportive of its position. This was certainly true with regard to French-English relations and related constitutional issues, but no similar process occurred with regard to the development of new strategies and options for other key areas, such as the economy or social policy. Instead, by the end of the decade continuing internal division among state and party élites on these matters produced only inertia, indecision, and paralysis.

Undoubtedly, the mid- to late 1970s were troubled years for the economy. Wage and price controls were imposed by the Liberal government in 1975 (after Trudeau had ridiculed Stanfield in 1974 for proposing controls) in a desperate attempt to halt rising inflation; economic growth and productivity were at a virtual standstill; and unemployment remained high. The federal government seemed unable to do much of anything to alter these general conditions. To make matters worse for Trudeau and his cabinet colleagues, René Lévesque's Parti Québécois had been elected as the government of Quebec in November 1976, promising to hold a referendum on sovereignty before the end of their mandate.

Within the Liberal Party itself, the reformist thrust of the 1960s—when modernization and democratization of the party were the watchwords of the day—had all but dissipated.

> On paper, [the party] had been democratized. It now had a more open formal structure. A national executive, elected by the party membership rather than appointed by the leader, met regularly.... Despite these changes, and others of their ilk, despite the rhetoric of participation and leader accountability, of membership renewal and policy consultation ... the party was in essential ways no more powerful than it had been under King and St Laurent. In fact, some political scientists argued it was slightly less so.... Now that the party's elites were dependent on the leader's abilities to swing the electorate's votes rather than the other way around [as in earlier times] ... the party was often described by both its adherents and its opponents as little more than a leader's machine driven by a small cadre on his behalf, with policy made by government bureau-cracy far from the party's sight. To many Canadians, it seemed as though the Liberal Party had gone from oligarchy to oligarchy in one generation.[57]

In the run-up to the 1979 election, party strategists fretted over the atti-tude of the undecided and uncommitted voters. The party's geographic base had become too narrow, with large gaps in the West and parts of Ontario. The fate of the government's re-election chances relied almost completely on the disposition of the floating vote in urban Ontario. All the party's hard-learned professional campaigning techniques were applied towards winning over this portion of the electorate.

> ... the expensive opinion polling and the even more expensive television and print advertising, the superlative speeches written by the high-priced help to be delivered by the leader at the huge rallies with the orchestrated crowds, the massive efforts to get the right headlines in the press and the right stories in the television news—the purpose of all that was to win the floating vote.... It was the uncommitted voters that the [party] insiders talked about with so much anxiety in the winter of 1979.[58]

In the election itself, general public dissatisfaction with the state of things and weariness with a Liberal government that seemed long in the tooth and bereft of new ideas could not be overcome by all the machinations of the professional insiders. Although the government sustained minimal losses in the Atlantic provinces and actually increased their seat total in Quebec, it lost twenty-three seats in the crucial province of Ontario. 'The West, where the party's standings fell from 13 to 3, was little short of disaster.'[59] Joe Clark's Progressive Conservatives had taken 136 seats and won a minority victory on just 36 per cent of the vote; Diefenbaker's 1957 feat of winning a Canadian election without support from Quebec had been repeated.

The internal reform process that inevitably seemed to follow on the heels of electoral defeat had just begun within the Liberal Party when an astonishing turn of events brought Trudeau and the Liberals back to power just nine short months after having lost it. Clark brought in a 'hard' budget to deal with a rising government deficit and escalating energy costs, with little fear of defeat in Parliament because the Liberals were leaderless (Trudeau had announced his retirement). With the Liberals leading in the public opinion polls, the ever-opportunistic Liberal strategists saw an opportunity. The Conservatives were caught off guard and defeated in the House on the budget vote; Trudeau was persuaded to reverse his decision to resign and lead the Liberals in the subsequent election. With striking continuity, the campaign was once again shaped along regional lines. In Central Canada, Clark's Conservatives were branded as sell-outs to Alberta for proposing to allow energy prices to rise sharply; in contrast, the Liberals presented themselves as protectors of the 'national interest'. In this way, the politics of energy were presented as a contest between the national interest and the selfish demands of regionalism. This also pitted the populous energy-consuming provinces against the energy-producing provinces of the West. Even the provincial Conservative government of Ontario was forced to line up against their federal cousins. The Liberals, for their part, ran on an explicitly nationalist centre-left platform, promising strong federal intervention to address the energy crisis. The Liberals made gains in Atlantic Canada and Quebec (giving them seventy-four of the province's seventy-five seats). The real key to victory, though, was that urban Ontario flipped once again, giving back to the Liberals twenty of the twenty-three seats the party had lost only nine months earlier. The Liberals were back in power with a majority, though their elimination as a major party in western Canada was confirmed and reinforced.

The last Trudeau government moved quickly on the economic and constitutional fronts after returning to power in 1980. In both cases, its initiatives met with dubious success, or outright failure. On the constitutional front, the federalist forces won the Quebec referendum by a sixty to forty margin. This left Trudeau free to pursue his vision of renewed federalism. He had shelved the recommendations of the Task Force on Canadian Unity (the Trudeau-appointed Pepin-Robarts Commission), which released its report in 1979. The task force recommendations had promoted the concepts of dualism and regionalism as the basis for a renewed constitutional deal, and suggested some decentralization of powers to the provinces as well as a recognition of Quebec's distinct society and the possibility of further asymmetry in the division of powers.[60] Instead, Trudeau pushed aggressively to repatriate and reform the Constitution by adding a Charter of Rights and Freedoms and an amending formula while not conceding any new powers to the provinces.[61] That he succeeded in doing so in 1982 against considerable odds is a testament to his political will and strong vision on this issue; that it was accomplished only by excluding the government of Quebec from the final agreement did not bode well for the future. On the economic front, a strongly nationalist and centrist energy policy—the National Energy Program —generated a rush of new exploration and development activities, but also further alienated the West (because it sharply reduced potential provincial royalties from oil and gas) and the United States (which strongly protested its negative impact on American oil and gas companies). The federal government's new national industrial strategy was tied to its plan for a series of energy megaprojects. When a severe economic recession led to the collapse of energy prices in the early 1980s, so did the Liberal government's proposed energy megaprojects and its national industrial strategy. By 1983, stymied by the recession, unemployment, inflation, and a sharply rising fiscal deficit, the Trudeau government was forced to shelve its ambitious economic plans. In its last year in office, it seemed adrift and without direction.

The Liberal Party since the time of Mackenzie King had been a centrist party that sought and clung to power by brokering a broad ideological and ethnocultural coalition between business and welfare liberals, as well as among French, English, and ethnic minorities. The third party system marked the onset of modern elections in Canada, with the growing influence of television, pollsters, centrally devised ad campaigns, and the careful creation of leader images. The electorate was increasingly urban and middle class. All the major parties recognized the importance of these changes for electoral politics and attempted to adapt to them by making organizational, leadership, and program changes. Still, along with such significant and substantial change was a notable degree of continuity in both the essentials of partisan appeals to the electorate and the fundamental characteristics of the core support bases in the electorate upon which each party had come to rely.

The Liberal Party struggled throughout the 1960s to redefine itself and its core electorate, and to devise a strategic and programmatic response to the political challenges posed by the changes in Canadian (and particularly Quebec) society. On the whole, the party became more social democratic and nationalist in its orientation, though the shift remained moderate and was continually subject to hedging and reversals depending upon political or economic circumstances. This reflected the balance within the Liberal Party itself, where business liberals and welfare liberals continued their tug-of-war over their party's ideological orientation and political agenda.[62]

Nonetheless, by the end of the Trudeau era the party had become identified with a clearly left-of-centre agenda and a coalition made up of older and newer elements. Regionally, it was strong in the poorer, northern half of Atlantic Canada, in Quebec, and in its traditional areas of support in Ontario; socially, its traditional appeal to Catholics, francophones, and the ethnic population remained, to which women, youth, and the economically less fortunate had been added. At least two-thirds of delegates to the 1984 leadership convention held to replace Pierre Trudeau (who had decided not to contest another election) could be categorized as welfare liberals in their attitudes, opposed to cutting social benefits or services in order to reduce the deficit. On the national question, the party clearly stood for individual rights, provincial equality, and maintenance of a strong central government. Herein lay the ideological, regional, and social foundations of the Liberal Party at the end of the Trudeau era.[63]

The Mulroney Interlude

During Pierre Trudeau's last term as prime minister, federal Liberals endured a barrage of criticism from American politicians, the Canadian business community, and the provinces, all of whom reacted sharply to what they perceived as the excessively nationalist and centrist direction of government policy. Trudeau was succeeded as leader and prime minister in 1984 by John Turner, a former finance minister who sported impeccable business liberal credentials. Turner attempted to lead the party in a more centre-right business liberal direction, to moderate (if not abandon) its centrism, and to sanction constitutional changes designed to accommodate Quebec nationalism. His intent was to rebuild the party's ties to what once had been an important component of their core support base: those well disposed to freer trade, less government intervention in the economy, and a close, mutually beneficial relationship with the United States. His efforts succeeded only in creating dissension and confusion within a party that had been significantly made over during the Trudeau years.[64]

The general election Turner called a few short months after assuming the Liberal leadership resulted in a dramatic change from the voting patterns of the previous century. The Liberal Party's stranglehold on the French-Catholic areas of eastern Canada collapsed. Particularly devastating for the Liberals was the loss of Quebec, where the Tories won fifty-eight of seventy-five seats. Turner's Liberal caucus was reduced to a forty-seat rump, with representation from traditional Liberal strongholds in Atlantic Canada, Quebec, and Ontario. Their vote share (28 per cent) was the lowest they had ever experienced.[65]

John Turner had called the election in the wake of a postleadership convention blip in the public opinion polls that appeared to augur well for the party's election chances. But his own rusty and oddly dated performance (he had been out of politics for almost ten years) and the accumulated grievances that had built up against the government party over two decades produced a downward spiral in support during the campaign. Particularly devastating was a spate of patronage appointments recommended by Trudeau and made by Turner just before the election call, an invitation to popular outrage and partisan criticism.[66]

For the next four years as Opposition leader, Turner struggled with a party and caucus deeply divided over his leadership and policy direction. A 1986 policy convention had clearly indicated the party's desire to move in a left-of-centre direction, by implication telling Turner to 'forget what he learned in his eight years on Bay Street'.[67] Though the Conservative performance in office created opportunities for partisan attacks (the Mulroney government suffered through several scandals involving cabinet ministers), the internally divided Liberals were unable to consolidate their position as the logical alternative to the government. Indeed, public opinion polls suggested that the NDP was positioned to supplant the Liberals in the next election. Moreover, Mulroney had reinforced his hold on francophone Quebec by reaching a tentative agreement with all ten provinces on changes to the Constitution (the Meech Lake Accord). When that election came in 1988, therefore, it was not fought on the question of national unity, since all three parties had given their support to the recent constitutional deal. Instead the issue was the Free Trade Agreement between Canada and the United States, and John Turner's Liberals entered the campaign facing the possibility of their historical demise as one of Canada's two national parties.

The Liberals and NDP went into the 1988 campaign locked in a struggle for the mantle of official Opposition. Viewed from this perspective, the election result—the Tories were re-elected with a majority government and the Liberals finished second—was also a victory for John Turner and the Liberal Party. Turner's spirited opposition to the 'Mulroney trade deal' was not enough to convince the majority of Canadians that the Liberals had a viable alternative to the deal, but it did stave off the NDP challenge by reconstituting and reinforcing the traditional Liberal vote on the centre-left of the Canadian political spectrum.[68]

As argued by the authors of Letting the People Decide, the Liberal decision to choose an extreme position in opposition to the free trade deal with the United States allowed them to mobilize Liberal identifiers and non-partisans while ensuring the NDP would not undercut them.[69] All three parties cooperated in suppressing division on other issues, in particular (as noted earlier) the question of Quebec's place within the larger Canadian political community. Thus liberated from the complications introduced by the ethnocultural division, the parties were free to differentiate themselves on another, less explosive dimension—commercial policy. They could safely prime voters 'to consider the deep-seated values which motivate their choice of party'.[70] By choosing historically rooted cleavages as the basis for their appeals, old coalitions could be rebuilt and each party's traditional electorate consolidated.

An analysis of the 1988 election result outside Quebec reveals that this election marked a return to third party system patterns. The strategy of polarizing the electorate on a time-worn issue enabled each party to recruit most of its traditional support. The Liberals saw their support base in English-speaking Canada repatriated, even though the party was uncomfortably at odds with itself over both free trade and the Meech Lake Accord. Consistent with traditional patterns, Liberal members were returned from the poorer and more Catholic areas of the Maritimes and the 'around-the-bay' seats in Newfoundland, while traditionally Tory seats in the more Protestant areas of anglophone New Brunswick and Nova Scotia (and St John's, Newfoundland) remained so. In Ontario the Liberals won forty-three seats to the Tories' forty-six and slightly more of the popular vote. The party did well in areas of traditional strength: northern Ontario and Ottawa, and in constituencies where there was a significant Catholic or ethnic vote. In the West the party made a comeback in Winnipeg and its environs, again helped by Catholic, francophone, and ethnic voters.[71] The three western-most provinces remained barren ground for the party; only John Turner in his Vancouver seat was elected. In the polarization over free trade, it was the NDP that benefited in Saskatchewan and British Columbia, while Alberta went completely Tory for the sixth consecutive election (save for one Independent Conservative).

The real difference in 1988 were the results in Quebec, where the Conservatives added to their 1984 seat and vote totals while the Liberals were reduced to a paltry twelve seats and 30 per cent of the vote, the worst showing in that province in the history of the party. In effect, with its stranglehold on francophone Quebec, the Mulroney Conservatives were enjoying the same huge advantage over their opponents that had for so long accrued to the Liberals. In its essentials, surprisingly little had really changed in Canadian party politics, yet the effect on electoral outcomes was profound.

The Fourth Party System

For reasons previously discussed, the strategic advantage that gave the Conservatives their historic victory in 1988 could not be repeated in the federal election of 1993. For their part, the Liberals were able to retain the core supporters that had been repatriated in 1988 while augmenting this voter base with other left-of-centre voters deserting the collapsing NDP. In addition, the party's hopeful if somewhat contradictory pitch to voters that stimulative job creation and defence of social programs could be combined with a prudent approach to deficit reduction won over many weakly committed voters who were both wearied and worried by high unemployment and three years of economic recession. This balanced and nuanced approach stands in sharp relief to the party's 1988 campaign and is attributable to a careful repositioning of the party under the leadership of Jean Chrétien. Finishing second to Turner in 1984, Chrétien easily won the leadership convention that followed Turner's resignation in 1990. A year later at the Liberal Party's Aylmer Conference, party ideology was redefined in order to reassure business interests scared off by the party's left-nationalist positioning during the 1980s. Chrétien summed up the results of Aylmer as a rejection of the old ideas of *nationalism* and *welfare-statism* and an embrace of the new realities of *globalism* and *free trade*. Though Liberal delegates at the 1992 biennial conference were 'cut from the same Left-Liberal cloth as their predecessors', Chrétien continued leaning towards the centre-right business liberal position, a shift that was confirmed in the Liberal Red Book that constituted the party's 1993 election platform.[72] The collapse of support for the NDP in the year leading up to the 1993 election made this ideological repositioning less costly for the Liberals (in terms of foregone left-of-centre support) than it otherwise would have been at any time since the early 1960s.[73] Having shored up their left-of-centre core support in 1988 and then carefully moved the party to a more centrist policy position prior to the 1993 election, the Liberals were well placed strategically to win the lion's share of available mainstream voters.

In Atlantic Canada the Liberals were able to build on their strong showing in 1988 when they swept the poorer, northern part of the region. In 1993 they took thirty-one of thirty-two seats, with a vote share ranging from 52 per cent to 67 per cent. Even core Tory seats in the Protestant, rural constituencies of mainland Nova Scotia and anglophone New Brunswick were lost, though in several of these contests the presence of a Reform Party candidate was crucial to the Liberal victory. As might be expected in the country's poorest and most dependent region, where government investment has traditionally been expected to supplement a weak private sector, the Liberals' promise of job creation through infrastructure projects was well received. Three provincial Liberal victories just months prior to the election demoralized Conservative Party activists and were a further boost to the federal Liberal campaign.[74]

In Quebec the Liberals increased their seat total from twelve to nineteen, but did not improve their standing with francophone voters. There was a strong negative correlation between support levels for the Liberals and the predominance of francophones in the riding. Indeed, support for the party in francophone constituencies dropped from approximately 25 per cent in 1988 to around 20 per cent of the vote in 1993. This contrasts sharply with the strong support for Liberals in francophone areas outside Quebec and can be attributed almost entirely to negative reaction within Quebec to the party's role in the constitutional wars of 1980–92. Liberal leader Chrétien, closely associated with the events of those years, suffered from a very low popularity rating in most of the province. On the other hand, and perhaps for similar reasons, the Liberals continued to win overwhelming support from the anglophone and allophone (other minority language) communities, winning perhaps 90 per cent of this vote. The party also did well in ridings bordering on other jurisdictions. With 33 per cent of the provincial vote, the Liberals continue to have a considerable base in Quebec, but the ethnolinguistic narrowness of its appeal in an overwhelmingly French-speaking province did not bode well for the prospect of future growth.[75]

In Ontario, where voter turnout was its lowest since 1953, the Liberals increased their popular vote from 39 per cent to 53 per cent and won ninety-eight of the province's ninety-nine seats. The Liberals clearly benefited from the split of conservatively inclined voters between the Tories and the Reform Party, which made the difference in twenty-five ridings. The Liberals also benefited from the collapse of the NDP in the province due in no small measure to the extreme unpopularity of Bob Rae's provincial NDP government during a period of economic recession and fiscal austerity. It was no coincidence that the NDP's vote decline of 14 per cent over 1988 exactly matched the Liberal vote increase in Ontario. It seems reasonable to suggest that many of these voters migrated to the Liberals, the party closest to the NDP ideologically.[76]

Though the Liberals won close to two-thirds of the Midwest region's seats, their popular vote total in Saskatchewan (32 per cent) was unimpressive. This was even more true in Alberta, where the Liberals received only 25 per cent of the vote and four seats (a marginal improvement over historic levels) and British Columbia, where a 28 per cent vote share produced six Liberal seats. In 1993 Reform was the dominant party in the West. The lack of Conservative and Liberal appeal in the two westernmost provinces was no doubt linked to the sharp reaction of voters there to the 1992 Charlottetown Accord, supported by the Conservatives, Liberals, and NDP but opposed by Reform; 60.2 per cent of Albertans and 68.3 per cent of British Columbians voted No to Charlottetown. This may have thrown support to Reform, which claimed for itself the 'no special status for Quebec' position. This hardline stand on the national question likely drew additional support to it that otherwise may have gone to the New Democrats or the Liberals.[77]

Three and one-half years after taking office, characterized by a full-blown assault on the deficit that featured large reductions in federal transfers to the provinces for social programs and a sizeable cut in the size of the federal government, the Chrétien government sought the public's approval for its policies in an election called for 2 June 1997. The Liberals had made good on their 1993 promise to reduce the federal government's annual deficit to manageable proportions—and then some—but at considerable cost to services and programs. Moreover, despite its job creation promises in 1993, unemployment levels remained stubbornly high. On the constitutional front, the federal government in 1995 had barely survived another Quebec referendum and was subject to severe criticism of its handling of the separatist threat. Chrétien's own unpopularity among francophone Quebecers seemed a serious liability for federalist forces in the province. In sum, the government could boast about its efficient handling of the country's financial crisis, but on other fronts its record was distinctly mixed.

In 1993 the Liberals had presented themselves as a moderate, centrist party that promised to take a balanced approach to the country's economic and social problems. In 1997 the same party ran a complacent campaign that stressed its competent handling of the fiscal crisis and pointed to the positive signals indicating a healthy Canadian economy that was in for a sustained period of growth. Little was offered in the way of a program for the next four years, during which there were likely to be budget surpluses to decide what to do with and yet another Quebec referendum. In going to the polls well before it had to, when it was comfortably ahead in the polls, the government was being opportunistic; its implicit message to voters was to trust the government based on its performance in its first mandate.

The electorate in different regions of the country responded in dramatically different ways to this appeal. Overall, the Liberals won a majority of seats, the first time since Louis St Laurent that a Liberal government had won two consecutive majorities. However, their 1993 total was reduced by twenty-two seats to 155, even though the total available had been expanded from 295 to 301. As well, the geographic dispersion of Liberal support was highly uneven. The 1997 result suggests that what formerly had been the party of Quebec now had become the party of Ontario. Though the Liberal share of the popular vote there declined somewhat (from 53 per cent to 48 per cent), the party still won 101 of the province's 103 seats. The general consensus among analysts was that Ontarians, having experienced two tumultuous years of dramatic policy changes under the radically conservative provincial government of Premier Mike Harris, voted for calmness and stability. Though not enthusiastic about Chrétien and the Liberals, they were both a familiar and a safe choice. Once again, as in 1993, the Liberals were helped greatly by the Reform-Tory even split of the right-of-centre vote. As in 1993, their combined total would have been enough to beat Liberal candidates in twenty-five constituencies.[78]

In contrast to their strikingly similar performance in Ontario, the Liberals suffered major losses in Atlantic Canada, where the party was reduced from thirty-one seats to eleven (with only PEI remaining solidly Liberal). Some of the losses were dramatic and unexpected, such as the defeat of cabinet ministers Dave Dingwall in Cape Breton and Doug Young in Acadian New Brunswick, both previously bedrock Liberal seats. Even more surprising was to whom these powerful ministers lost. In both cases the giant-killers belonged to the NDP, who previously commanded an anaemic share of the vote in these ridings. (In total, the NDP took eight of the region's thirty-two seats, six of these in Nova Scotia where the Liberals were shut out.) While part of the credit for this dramatic surge in NDP support surely must go to party leader Alexa McDonough (formerly the leader of the Nova Scotia New Democrats), it was federal Liberal policies that were most important in the turnaround. These policies incited a regional protest over lost jobs, cuts in health, and cuts in unemployment insurance. The Conservatives benefited from this protest as well, picking up thirteen seats in the region, all of them in ridings that were traditionally Tory. In these constituencies the reaction against Liberal cuts was registered by a return to voting Conservative, a choice made easier by Tory leader Jean Charest's championing of the protest against social program cuts. That the NDP and Conservatives could credibly and effectively pose as defenders of the welfare state in Atlantic Canada against a Liberal government seeking to undermine and destroy it indicates just how far the Chrétien Liberals had moved from their traditional ideological and policy stance. Liberals in Atlantic Canada could feel with some justification that their party had abandoned them, justifying the sharp rebuke dealt to the party on voting day.

In Quebec the Liberals made only slight headway against the Bloc Québécois, adding six new seats to the twenty they already had and winning 36 per cent of the vote. The Bloc's hegemony over francophone Quebec was only slightly dented, however, as that party held onto forty-four of its fifty-four seats. Given the tepid reception Quebecers gave to new Bloc leader Gilles Duceppe (see Chapter 6), the Liberals might have expected to do better. Some of the votes shaken loose from the Bloc, however, went to Jean Charest's Conservatives, a more acceptable alternative for soft nationalists than the federal Liberal Party, which, despite its gains, remained primarily a party of anglophone and allophone Quebec.

Perhaps the most disappointing results for the Liberals were in the West, where the party managed to take only fifteen of the region's eighty-eight ridings. Whereas in the Midwest region in 1993 the Liberals had won two-thirds of Manitoba and Saskatchewan's twenty-eight seats, they were reduced to one-quarter of this total in 1997. In Manitoba, where the Liberals were criticized for calling the election in the midst of the worst flood in the province's history (but were helped by a three-way split of the opposition vote), the party held onto six seats and 35 per cent of the vote. However, they were not so fortunate in Saskatchewan, where both the NDP and Reform were stronger this time around. Squeezed between strong opponents on the left and right, only one Liberal survived. In Alberta the situation was no better. In the province where 55 per cent of the electorate voted for the Reform Party, only two of the four sitting Liberal MPs were returned to Ottawa, one of which (Anne McLellan) had to await a judicial recount before she could take her place in Chrétien's new cabinet. In British Columbia Liberals were elected in only six of the thirty-four ridings. It seems that little had changed for the Liberals in the three westernmost provinces since 1993 despite their efforts to win plaudits for their deficit cutting and the strong performance of the western provinces' economies. It was perhaps precisely the latter, however, that allowed voters in these provinces to focus on other matters, such as Reform's hard-hitting critique of Liberal constitutional strategy vis-à-vis Quebec and the government's unpopular gun control legislation.

The 1997 election result clearly consolidated and reinforced the pattern of party support established in 1993. Despite the obvious electoral weaknesses of the Chrétien Liberals—they won only 38 per cent of the vote in 1997 and were driven back by their opponents into a central Canadian (predominantly Ontario) support base—this still provided them with almost twice as many votes as their nearest rivals. Indeed, there was never any doubt that they would win the election; it was only a question of whether they would secure a majority. That the Liberals managed to achieve this, in the context of a highly fragmented electorate with five major parties from which to choose, is no mean feat. To accomplish this, they were willing and able to command the centre of the political spectrum, even if this meant moving sharply right once in government and sacrificing Atlantic region MPs for the greater good of the party. In other words, the centre of gravity of the Canadian electorate, now more than ever, lies in Ontario. Throughout the third party system, the Liberal Party sought out majorities here; with the political right in the province hopelessly divided between Conservatives and Reform, and no NDP resurgence yet in sight, the Liberals might govern Canada indefinitely simply by paying close attention to the mood of the median Ontario voter. Under the leadership of Jean Chrétien, the party once again profits from competent and cautious centrist politics, aided by the political fragmentation of its many critics, a situation strongly reminiscent of Liberal domination during the second party system. For the time being, only one national brokerage party survives in this new fourth party system: the Liberal Party, restored to its traditional role as the government party. For the foreseeable future, only the break-up of Canada itself would appear to threaten its continued political hegemony.

Notes

1. J.M. Beck, *Pendulum of Power: Canada's Federal Elections* (Scarborough: Prentice-Hall, 1968):58.
2. Ibid., Chapter 3. The Pacific Scandal, which dragged down the Conservative government, centred on charges of corruption and influence peddling involving John A. Macdonald, his cabinet, and Hugh Allan's Canadian Pacific Railway.
3. As previously discussed, this attempt to insulate federal politics from the divisive and volatile issues surrounding language, ethnicity, and religion ultimately foundered on the government's handling of the Riel rebellion in Canada's West and the polarization of English and French that it incited.
4. This was nowhere so clear as in the election of 1891 when Macdonald was able to portray the Liberal platform of unrestricted reciprocity ('u.r.') with the United States as disloyal, even treasonous, and a threat to all those Canadian industries that were protected by the Conservatives' National Policy tariffs.
5. C. Campbell and W. Christian, *Parties, Leaders and Ideologies in Canada* (Toronto: McGraw-Hill Ryerson, 1996):70.
6. Ibid., 71.
7. Ibid.
8. Beck, *Pendulum of Power*, 72.
9. Campbell and Christian, *Parties, Leaders and Ideologies*, 75. Support among Quebec voters for Laurier's provincial rights stand held even when he angered

the province's Catholic bishops by refusing to sanction or use Dominion powers to protect French-language and religious rights that were being restricted by a number of provincial governments.

10. Beck, *Pendulum of Power*, 80–1.
11. M.J. Brodie and J. Jenson, *Crisis, Challenge and Change: Party and Class in Canada* (Toronto: Methuen, 1980):70.
12. Ibid., 70–2. Though the Laurier Liberals had expected the West to become a 'Gibraltar of Liberalism', the region was divided in its partisan leanings on much the same basis as the East. Only two of ten Manitoba seats and two of seven BC seats went to the Liberals in 1908.
13. Campbell and Christian, *Parties, Leaders and Ideologies*, 76–7.
14. Beck, *Pendulum of Power*, 121.
15. Ibid., 123.
16. Ibid., 132–3.
17. Campbell and Christian, *Parties, Leaders and Ideologies*, 78–80.
18. Reg Whitaker, 'Party and State in the Liberal Era' in *Party Politics in Canada*, 7th edn, edited by Hugh Thorburn (Scarborough: Prentice-Hall, 1996):250.
19. F.R. Scott, 'W.L.M.K.', in *The Blasted Pine*, edited by F.R. Scott and A.J.M. Smith (Toronto: Macmillan, 1962):27–8.
20. Brodie and Jenson, *Crisis, Challenge and Change*, 130–6.
21. Beck, *Pendulum of Power*, 183.
22. Ibid., chapters 15 and 16. The Liberals won a mere eleven seats from their traditional strongholds along the Quebec border and in northern and western Ontario in 1925; twenty-six Ontario Liberals were elected in 1926.
23. Economic difficulties in rural Quebec and the replacement of the hated Meighen (the architect of conscription) with Bennett as Conservative leader swung a number of seats to the party. As well, Church leaders in Quebec apparently decided it was desirable to have a French-Canadian component within the Conservative Party and adopted a position of 'benevolent neutrality and more often practical assistance' towards Conservative candidates. Ibid., 198–9.
24. Ibid., 217.
25. Campbell and Christian, *Parties, Leaders and Ideologies*, 81.
26. The CCF became the official Opposition in Ontario in 1943 and the government in Saskatchewan in 1944; they led both old-line parties in a national public opinion poll in 1943. As well, the union movement was growing in strength and militancy, forcing the federal government to concede union rights. Brodie and Jenson, *Crisis, Challenge and Change*, 193–4, 202, 204–6.
27. Outside of Quebec in 1945, the Liberals finished with seventy-two seats compared to a combined opposition total of 106.
28. Beck, *Pendulum of Power*, 254.
29. Campbell and Christian, *Parties, Leaders and Ideologies*, 82.
30. Beck, *Pendulum of Power*, 288.
31. Ibid. During these years constituencies with large Catholic populations almost invariably returned Liberals. Noted political sociologist Robert Alford noted that the association between social class and voting behaviour in Canada was notably less (indeed non-existent) than in other Anglo-American countries. Robert Alford, *Party and Society* (Chicago: Rand McNally, 1963).

32. Ibid., 254, 257.
33. Beck, *Pendulum of Power*, 291–309. In 1957 the Conservatives improved their vote-share position in all but three isolated Newfoundland seats, while the Liberals lost in all four Prince Edward Island seats (the first time since Confederation) and won only two in Nova Scotia (seats where the Acadian vote was substantial), with New Brunswick divided more or less along ethnic lines as usual. On the Prairies, seven of eight Liberal seats in Manitoba were lost (saving only St Boni-face with its heavy French population), as well as one of their five Saskatchewan seats (where their popular vote fell to 30 per cent) and three of four in Alberta. In British Columbia the Liberals lost six of their eight seats and saw their vote share plunge from 31 per cent to 20 per cent.
34. Ibid., 300.
35. Ibid., 312.
36. Ibid., 312–13.
37. Ibid., 317.
38. R. Johnston, A. Blais, H.E. Brady, and J. Crete, *Letting the People Decide: Dynamics of a Canadian Election* (Montreal and Kingston: McGill-Queen's University Press, 1993):37, 45–6.
39. Brodie and Jenson, *Crisis, Challenge and Change*, 268. In 1967 14 per cent of Canadians under major collective agreements belonged to the public sector, but by 1977 the number was close to 55 per cent.
40. Campbell and Christian, *Parties, Leaders and Ideologies*, 84.
41. David Smith, *The Regional Decline of a National Party: Liberals on the Prairies* (Toronto: University of Toronto Press, 1981):93.
42. Gad Horowitz, as quoted in Stephen Clarkson, 'Pierre Trudeau and the Liberal Party: The Jockey and the Horse', in *Canada at the Polls: The General Election of 1974*, edited by H.R. Penniman (Washington: American Enterprise Institute, 1975):60.
43. Beck, *Pendulum of Power*, 400.
44. Campbell and Christian, *Parties, Leaders and Ideologies*, 44.
45. Desmond Morton, *The New Democrats 1961–1986: The Politics of Change* (Toronto: Copp Clark Pitman, 1986):77.
46. Beck, *Pendulum of Power*, 409.
47. Ibid.
48. Ibid., 406.
49. Ibid., 410–19.
50. Clarkson, 'Pierre Trudeau', 77.
51. Brodie and Jenson, *Crisis, Challenge and Change*, 292.
52. Campbell and Christian, *Parties, Leaders and Ideologies*, 92.
53. Clarkson, 'Pierre Trudeau', 83.
54. Ibid., 83–4.
55. Ibid., 92–3.
56. George Radwanski, *Trudeau* (Toronto: Macmillan, 1978):95.
57. Christina McCall-Newman, 'Power in Trudeau's Liberal Party', in *Party Politics in Canada*, 5th edn, edited by Hugh Thorburn (Scarborough: Prentice-Hall, 1985):158.
58. Ibid., 160.

59. Joseph Wearing, 'The Liberal Party: Reform Pre-empted (1979–80)', in *Party Politics in Canada*, 5th edn, edited by Hugh Thorburn (Scarborough: Prentice-Hall, 1985):163.

60. Task Force on Canadian Unity, *A Future Together: Observations and Recommendations* (Ottawa: Minister of Supply and Services, 1979).

61. This was with the sole exception of Section 92A, which gave the provinces some additional leverage in developing and managing their natural resources, though it also confirmed the federal government's right to legislate and regulate interprovincial and international trade in natural resource commodities. The inclusion of Section 92A was one of the concessions won by the NDP in return for its support of the federal Liberals' constitutional package.

62. Campbell and Christian, *Parties, Leaders and Ideologies*, 83–5; Brodie and Jenson, *Crisis, Challenge and Change*, Chapter 9.

63. Martin Goldfarb and Thomas Axworthy, *Marching to a Different Drummer: An Essay on Liberals and Conservatives in Convention* (Toronto: Stoddart, 1988):15, 76–8, 91.

64. Ibid., 8.

65. Thomas Axworthy, 'The Government Party in Opposition: Is the Liberal Century Over?', in *Party Politics in Canada*, 6th edn, edited by Hugh Thorburn (Scarborough: Prentice-Hall, 1991):286.

66. See Alan Frizzell and Anthony Westell, *The Canadian General Election of 1984* (Ottawa: Carleton University Press, 1985).

67. Joseph Wearing, 'Can an Old Dog Teach Itself New Tricks? The Liberal Party Attempts Reform', in *Canadian Parties in Transition*, edited by Alain Gagnon and Brian Tanguay (Scarborough: Nelson Canada, 1989):285.

68. Thomas Axworthy, 'The Government Party in Opposition: Is the Liberal Century Over?', in *Party Politics in Canada*, 6th edn, edited by Hugh Thorburn (Scarborough: Prentice-Hall, 1991):293.

69. Johnston et al., *Letting the People Decide*, 108.

70. Ibid., 8.

71. M. Eagles, J. Bickerton, A. Gagnon, and P. Smith, *The Almanac of Canadian Politics* (Peterborough: Broadview Press, 1991). Tory support in 1988 was higher in ridings with larger proportions of managers and administrators, higher average family incomes, farmers, and francophones (due to Quebec). In contrast, Liberal support did not seem to be structured by socio-economic or urban-rural variables; party support was negatively correlated with the presence of francophones (again due to Quebec) and positively so with concentrations of immigrants. Coefficients measuring continuity in Tory and Liberal support indicate that a vote for each of these parties in 1984 was the strongest determinant of that party's vote in 1988. M. Eagles et al., 'Continuity in Electoral Change: Patterns of Support for Canadian Parties, 1988 & 1993', a paper presented to the 1995 Biennial Meeting of the Association for Canadian Studies in the United States, Seattle, Washington, 18 November 1995.

72. S. Clarkson, 'The Liberal Party of Canada: Pragmatism Versus Principle', in *Party Politics in Canada*, 7th edn, edited by Hugh Thorburn (Scarborough: Prentice-Hall, 1995):30–1.

73. In 1993 Protestantism and the presence of francophones (due to Quebec) had a negative effect on Liberal vote. So did referendum voting: a high No vote hurt Liberal electoral fortunes in 1993, suggesting the Liberals were tarnished by

voter dissatisfaction with either the substance or process of constitutional reform. There was also strong evidence of riding-level continuity between 1988 and 1993: each percentage increase in the Liberals' 1988 vote produced between .83 and .75 of a vote in 1993. Eagles et al., 'Continuity in Electoral Change', 9.

74. M. Eagles, J. Bickerton, A. Gagnon, and P. Smith, *The Almanac of Canadian Politics*, 2nd edn (Toronto: Oxford University Press, 1995):3–7.
75. Ibid., 77–9.
76. Ibid., 238–9.
77. Ibid., 513–17, 575–80.
78. Murray Campbell, 'Ontario's Support for Grits a Vote for Calm Sailing', *The Globe and Mail* (4 June 1997):A6.

CHAPTER 4

THE NEW DEMOCRATIC PARTY:
THE LEFT TRADITION IN CANADA

While the elections of 1988, 1993, and 1997 produced some dramatic electoral changes, particularly when the focus was on parliamentary seats, it also obscured some important continuities in Canadian party politics. For the New Democratic Party (NDP), the legislative totals suggest a roller-coaster electoral ride. In 1984, at the advent of the Mulroney interlude, the NDP had achieved a kind of political homeostasis: in the eight general elections since 1962 and its formation as successor to the Co-operative Commonwealth Federation (CCF), the NDP had achieved a fairly predictable voter support of up to (though usually just under) 20 per cent.[1] For that, it had been able to elect somewhere between seventeen and thirty-two members of Parliament in particular elections. Between 1965 and 1984, the electoral results had only once fallen below twenty seats—in 1974 when party support dipped to 15 per cent nationally. In 1984 the NDP elected thirty MPs, its second highest total, with 19 per cent of the votes in Canada.[2]

In 1988, with party leader Ed Broadbent topping the polls in voter esteem, the NDP achieved its greatest success, winning forty-three seats and 20.4 per cent of the votes in Canada. The story five years later was very different: along with the virtual disappearance of the governing Progressive Conservative Party, the New Democrats, with a new leader (Audrey McLaughlin from the Yukon), lost almost two-thirds of its voter support, falling to just nine seats and losing official party status in Parliament. Potentially more important was the fact that the party fell from third to fourth place in a Parliament with two new regional protest parties ahead of them: the nationalist Bloc Québécois from Quebec and, just behind the Bloc in seats, the right-wing Reform Party from the West.[3] The 1997 federal election was thus crucial to the NDP. In that election, Canada's social democrats managed to recapture only some of their traditional vote (up to 11 per cent), again finishing in fourth place in the parliamentary sweepstakes with twenty-one seats, one seat ahead of the Tories, who took a considerably higher 18.9 per cent of the national vote.

This chapter examines continuities and discontinuities in voter support for the Co-operative Commonwealth Federation (CCF)/New Democratic Party. Its focus is on the New Democratic Party, and particularly that party's performance in the federal elections of 1988, 1993, and 1997.[4] As the only third party with organizational roots in the first and second party system that has persisted into the present, the development of the CCF/NDP represents a particularly important element in understanding party systems and electoral behaviour in Canada. As a third party of protest with strong regional roots as well, the relationship between success at the provincial level and performance in federal elections, especially in settings such as Saskatchewan, must be considered. As with provincial Social Credit in Alberta and federal Social Credit/Reform (discussed in Chapter 5), these provincial-federal links in the CCF-NDP provided a measure of credibility and support for a third party seeking to play a national role. Indeed, provincial parties provided the basic building-blocks of the federal NDP.

Retrospective: Leftist Politics in the First Party System

The antecedents of leftist politics in Canada coincide with the era of the first party system (1867–1917). There were several seeds from which leftist political action in this country grew, and many of these had British or American sources. Though it had little significant political impact on governance, leftist politics did find *some* party expression during the first party era; for example, in the Canadian general election of 1900, 10 per cent of all votes cast in British Columbia were for Labour candidates. In the contests of 1904, 1908, and 1911, Socialists in BC won between 3 per cent and 7 per cent support, and Labour/Independents up to 10 per cent.[5]

More usually, during this initial period of traditional two-party dominance, leftist perspectives found expression, not so much in party terms but in other organizational forms such as organizations inspired by the Social Gospel, in independent socialist groups formed in the last decades of the nineteenth century, in elements of the suffrage, health, and temperance movements, in agrarian organizations, and often in the links of these organizations and the emerging trade union movement.

Major leftist expression in party terms emerged only during the second party era (1921–57). Federally this first occurred in the 1920s in elements of the Progressive Party and in the efforts of independent labour candidates, and provincially in some United Farmers settings. With the demise of the Progressives by 1930, many of these leftist elements began to coalesce in the founding of the CCF. Not all of these elements were rooted in western protest: for example, in the 1883 Ontario general election, a Labour candidate won 23.4 per cent of the votes in a close three-way race in Hamilton; in 1902 the Socialist Party ran candidates in Hamilton East and Hamilton West; in a 1906 by-election, Labour actually won the provincial Hamilton East riding with over 61 per cent support[6]; and in 1914 an Independent-Temperance candidate won 44 per cent of the vote in Toronto-Parkdale.[7] In its initial party expression, however, both with Progressives and with the Co-operative Commonwealth Federation, political discontent in western Canada figured prominently.[8]

There were a number of separate (at times related) roots to what became the CCF; each reflected a definitional challenge to brokerage notions of Canadian parties and politics. These sectoral/class roots included elements from, among others: (1) trade unions; (2) socialism and socialist/labour parties; (3) agrarian protest; (4) the Social Gospel; and (5) ideas from the early women's movement.

Some of the roots of leftist political/party development in Canada actually predate Confederation. In the early Canadian women's movement (for example, in women's efforts to gain access to Canadian medical schools in the 1850s), there were calls for both the enfranchisement of women and better health care through early forms of Medicare.[9] In the same pre-Confederation period, utopian socialist ideas, such as those espoused by Robert Owen, had gained some attention in Canada as in the US.[10] This is hardly surprising. As Avakumovic has argued:

> ... socialism, like other causes which found support in Canada, came from abroad.... This applied particularly in the formative period of the Canadian socialist movement. Therefore, it is not surprising that socialist ideas ... [like] Robert Owen's brand of socialism ... which were fashionable in the United Kingdom should have made an impact in Canada.... [It] was associated with the establishment of rural communities in which like-minded individuals would live and work together.[11]

Like Owen's early cooperatives in Rochdale, Lancashire, and throughout northern England and Scotland, and his subsequent idealized socialist communes in Britain and the United States, similar socialist/cooperative community experiments were tried in Ontario and elsewhere in Canada in the 1850s.[12]

These influences by the women's movement on political ideas, such as public health and voting rights, continued into the post-Confederation era, exemplified by the efforts of activists such as Emily Stowe, the country's first female medical practitioner. Having led the fight for women's access to medical training and the licence to practice, Stowe also organized the Women's Medical College in 1883 and established the first suffrage group, in Toronto, in 1876. The group, which was initially called the Toronto Women's Literary Club to help disguise its intentions, was subsequently broadened with Stowe as founder/president of the Dominion Women's Enfranchisement Association in 1889.[13] In this latter political effort—to extend voting rights to women—many in the National Council of Women of Canada[14] and the Woman's Christian Temperance Union (which was more active on Canada's Prairies and included activists such as Nellie McClung) were involved from the early 1890s until suffrage was granted between 1916 and 1921.[15] Many of these same activists were involved in the late 1920s 'Persons Case'—which was first lost at the Supreme Court of Canada and overturned by the Judicial Committee of the Privy Council—all part of eighty years of agitation for political rights for, and by, women in Canada.[16] The farmers' movement also produced important contributions by women such as Agnes Macphail; Macphail pushed for reforms of the banks and the economic system.[17]

During the immediate post-Confederation era, trade union organizations were also forming: in 1873, for example, the Canadian Labor Union was formed; in 1883–6, it became the Trades and Labor Congress of Canada (TLC). Distance and isolation meant that much trade union-based political activity was confined to municipal and provincial settings in the early years. Most of the trade union affiliates to organizations like the TLC had connections with the American Federation of Labor (AFL). This AFL connection and debates about moderate versus more radical approaches to both labour negotiations and partisan politics created various tensions. These led to the creation of counterorganizations such as the National Trades and Labour Congress (founded in 1903) and the more radical Industrial Workers of the World (IWW or Wobblies). It also led to more direct political action such as general strikes—for example, at Winnipeg in 1919.[18] These were given political expression in a variety of party forms during the first party system.

During the first party era, there were Labour and Socialist party intrusions into the electoral game. These efforts—such as with the Canadian offspring of the US Socialist Labor Party (1876)[19] and a less doctrinaire splinter group, the Canadian Socialist League (which became the Socialist Party of Canada [SPC] in 1905)—produced little in the way of involvement or support across much of the Canadian working class because of the long hours, poor wages, and tough, physical work. Socialist/workers groupings and the Socialist Party itself managed to develop concentrated pockets of support during this early period in places like Halifax, Montreal, Winnipeg, Vancouver, Hamilton, and in mining centres on Cape Breton and Vancouver Island.[20] They also managed to occasionally send representatives to provincial legislatures (as in Nova Scotia, Ontario, and British Columbia), as well as to municipal offices in various jurisdictions.[21] These provincial and local successes, limited though they were, did represent more class and ideologically based definitions of electoral politics. As discussed earlier, however, such reconceptualizations remained at the fringes of the first party system, which was dominated by ethnocultural and brokerage definitions of party politics and the two main political parties.

The post-Confederation debates about industrial and political action within socialist circles were dominated by Marxist versus earlier utopian ideas. These produced further ongoing splits, such as the split in the SPC, which created the less radical Social Democratic Party (SDP) of Canada in 1910. In much of Quebec, the Church played a major role in the type of unions that developed. That religious divide (noted in chapters 1 and 6)—

as well as the factors of distance, resources, and the various pre-First World War waves of immigration—all had an impact on the role socialist ideas played in the formation of leftist organizations and parties in Canada during the first party system.[22]

During this period, apart from organizing unions, groups like the TLC also agitated for electoral fairness and other reforms: in 1897, for example, the TLC issued *Fair Play in Elections*, calling for more proportional forms of election to ensure a political voice for labour in Canada.[23] It was a cause taken up subsequently by United Farmers and Progressives towards the end of the first party era. In the 1919 *Farmers' Platform*, for example, which was adopted by the Canadian Council of Agriculture and was a central component of Progressive ideas in the 1921 general election, was a call for 'Democratic Reforms': these included proportional representation, initiative, referendum and recall, abolition of the patronage system, reform of the Senate, information on media ownership and control, opening parliamentary seats for women, and election expenses legislation.[24] Some of these issues were to return in the 1960s and 1970s as part of the NDP's early successes in promoting institutional reforms and again in the late 1980s and 1990s as part of the Reform Party's populist protest.

Agrarian protesters, who were mainly but not exclusively from the West, were also important elements in the development of leftist political perspectives in Canada. As outlined in more detail in Chapter 5, four particular strains of 'Prairie populism' contributed to western Canadian political protest. Two of these—radical democratic populism and social democratic populism—played particularly important roles in leftist-political development in the country.[25] For radical democratic populism:

> ... its intellectual roots were primarily rural western American and entailed a 'co-operativist', anti-capitalist perspective on questions of economic and political power. A principled rejection of party politics and an insistence on functionally co-ordinated delegate democracy leading into a group government were the most distinctive aspects of this populism.[26]

It found clearest expression in western Canada. Here, the necessary preparty organizational structures that developed during the first party system were of particular importance. United Farmers, Non Partisan League, and grain grower cooperatives were organizations that helped popularize radical democratic populism. As Laycock concluded, the expression of radical democratic populism 'would be inconceivable outside indigenous agrarian political and economic organizations.... The most complete ... development of the radical democratic themes took place within the United Farmers of Alberta, with Henry Wise Wood and William Irvine as the principal "theoreticians".' Irvine linked this populism with social democratic populism in the CCF; Wood worked through the Progressives and the UFA.[27]

At the centre of this populism was a rather non-British notion of representation. As described by Laycock, it had closer associations with guild socialism and the 'radical' idea that representation should be closely tied to 'the people', continuous, and that representatives should act more as 'delegates' of local interests[28]; party discipline and centralized party structures were seen as obstacles to this type of political representation.[29] This populism was perhaps most closely associated with crypto-Liberalism, a strain of populism more moderate and reformist in nature—seeking to bring the Liberal Party 'back to its true economic policy home', though it also had more traditional leftist populist links in its 'delegate' view of representation.[30] William Irvine was one of the advocates for more overt political expression. A fellow Albertan associated with Wood (and a subsequent parliamentary colleague of J.S. Woodsworth), Irvine and others popularized the ideas of the Non Partisan League, first promoted in pre-First World War North Dakota. The party/non-party tension inherent in these populisms created problems for both the United Farmers and Progressives as party-political organizations. It was the main reason why the Progressives, having finished second in the 1921 election and seeing itself more as a social movement than a political party, declined to take up the role of official Opposition.

As a result, some, like Irvine, gravitated to another form of populist protest. Social democratic populism started from the assumption of unequal power relations; its variations ranged from those who thought simple equality of opportunity was the minimum goal to proponents of 'worker control'. As defined by Laycock, 'its most obvious features were rejection of the two major parties as instruments of eastern business, (and instead) support for state ownership of major industries, advocacy of a farmer-labour alliance against organized business and support for the full extension of democratic rights and practices within the parliamentary system. It was gradualist (with no) rigid orthodoxy.' It argued, as a minimum, for 'a redistribution of economic goods and societal resources . . . among classes and communities to make equality of opportunity reality'. For social democratic populists 'systematic class power in major societal institutions prevents the realization of meaningful equality'. It 'developed through the early efforts of the Non Partisan League in Alberta and Saskatchewan, the small urban labour parties across the prairies . . ., socialists working within grain producers co-operatives, and activists in the United Farmers. . . .'[31]

Because of Irvine and other supporters, the United Farmers of Alberta (UFA) was 'the "omnibus" radical party in rural Alberta. . . . From 1921 to 1935, UFA MPs and their supporters in the UFA provided a contact point for socialist and labour organizations in the prairies.'[32] This included collaboration with J.S. Woodsworth, the key figure in the founding of the CCF.

The Social Gospel was the other significant root of leftist politics in Canada from the first party system. Its exponents included clerical activists such as J.S. Woodsworth. Richard Allen has defined the Social Gospel as 'an attempt to apply Christianity to the collective ills of industrializing society'.[33] Its first expression in Canada was in the 1880s. For Avakumovic:

> ... the staunchest advocates of the Social Gospel included a group of ministers who were to play in left-wing circles a role out of all proportion to their numbers. Their awareness of social problems, their inability to get along with fellow-Christians who failed to share their concern and enthusiasm, their belief that they could play a more useful role outside what they considered to be the confining world of churches, made them susceptible to socialist overtures.[34]

For some, such as one of its main proponents, J.S. Woodsworth, moving beyond formal church association into social work and political activism did not mean an end to social preaching or social activism. With its dual urban and agrarian focus, by the First World War the Social Gospel became, as noted by Allen, 'a primary informing principle of social reform'.[35]

Both the First World War and the social unrest that followed it provided a fertile base for the Social Gospel. Its expression in the 1919 Winnipeg General Strike, and the subsequent electoral success of the Progressives in 1921, encouraged activists like Woodsworth and Irvine to move beyond formal church associations to political/party activity. The Social Gospel also brought Woodsworth and others to court, charged with various infractions, including seditious libel. In the 1920s even the creation of the United Church with its more socially conscious Christianity did not stop the focus of much of this Social Gospel-inspired protest from shifting to political party expression. Despite that shift, many involved in the formation of leftist party politics in Canada—from the Maritimes to BC—continued to be drawn from socially active Christian ministries, including subsequent Saskatchewan CCF and federal NDP leader Tommy Douglas.[36]

The Second Party System

As argued by Laycock (and later in Chapter 5), the overlapping populisms that dominated western political protest during the first party system produced several party iterations during the second party era. The first of these, the Progressives, and their United Farmer provincial variants—the latter forming governments in Ontario (in 1919), Alberta (in 1921), and Manitoba (in 1922)—contained elements of leftist ideology and action. The United Farmers also involved other more rightist forms of protest. These flowed back to the Liberal Party in many instances, or further right to the new Social Credit movement/party in the early 1930s. By then, the Progressives were politically dead, though their legacy was more long-lasting.

In the same 1921 Canadian general election that produced the election of sixty-five Progressives, J.S. Woodsworth was elected as MP for Winnipeg Centre (as a representative of the Independent Labour Party [ILP] of Manitoba);

William Irvine (as a representative of Farmer-Labour running for the Dominion Labour Party) was also elected from East Calgary.[37] The Canadian Labour Party (CLP), formed out of the Trades and Labor Congress of Canada, contested the election, but elected no one.[38] Subsequent internal party battles over communist involvement in the CLP contributed to its demise before the end of the decade, though it fought the 1925 and 1926 general elections and several provincial ones, occasionally electing MLAs.[39]

The more moderate stance represented by Woodsworth, Irvine, and others in the ILP, and the additional election of Abe A. Heaps (a Winnipeg trade union leader for Winnipeg North) to Parliament in 1925, contributed greatly to the subsequent coalescence of left/agrarian and cooperativists/socialists within the disintegrating Progressive parliamentary group.[40] The Progressives were still able to elect twenty-four MPs and twenty-two representatives in 1925–6, with the largest numbers (nine and eleven) from Alberta. The Progressives suffered from early and ongoing organizational difficulties, however: 'poorly led, courted by both Liberals and Conservatives, unable to agree among themselves on many issues, unwilling to form a close-knit parliamentary group that would extract major concessions in return for the Progressives' support, the Progressives steadily lost ground as economic conditions improved' by the mid-1920s.[41] The structural deficiencies of the Progressives were evident as early as 1922, as Young has contended:

> ... the election of sixty-five Progressives might appear to be a great start for a party but the results were actually a disappointment. Only one Progressive was elected east of the Ottawa River; the majority were from the Prairies.... They constituted a western block dedicated to the interests of the wheat farmer.... The Progressives did not become official opposition because of their principles.... By the end of 1922, cracks in the Progressive ranks were widening. [New Party leader Robert] ... Forke's ... actions were toward establishing a national Progressive *party*. The move was opposed by the Alberta members and failed.... Forke's failure in this regard—really the failure of the Progressives—marked the beginning of the end. There was nothing for them to do.[42]

Woodsworth, leading the tiny two-member labour group, was more effective, splitting the Progressives further in 1924 when his motion on the budget, mirroring a previous one by the Progressives the previous year, forced Forke and most Progressives to support the Liberals; fourteen disagreed and voted with Woodsworth, six later splitting to become the Ginger Group, joined by three more soon after.[43] Subsequently, in 1925 seventeen Progressives broke ranks and voted with the Liberals on the budget. In the 1926 election, though twenty-two Progressives were elected, only nine were pure Progressives, versus Liberal-Progressives and other like iterations.[44]

Woodsworth was also more effective, for example, in convincing Mackenzie King to legislate on old age pensions as part of his price for support during the 1926 minority period.[45] In that minority Parliament, the remaining

Progressives were involved both in the defeat of the Liberals and subsequently Meighen's Conservatives. The various splits and tensions left Progressives, in the last election in which they contested (the 1930 general election), with just twelve MPs (nine from Alberta) and a minuscule 3 per cent of the national vote.

The Ginger Group, based largely in the UFA contingent, formed an essential alliance with Woodsworth and his labour group. This was a key development leading to the creation of the Co-operative Commonwealth Federation. While Progressives were primarily rural, socialist/labour political activity was essentially urban. Independent 'Labour' MPs such as Woodsworth struggled to bridge the gap, working in association with the Ginger/Progressives. The making of a new leftist political movement was underway even before the Progressives fought their last federal election in 1930.

The economic crash of 1929 and the Depression that followed had a significant effect on Canadian parties and the Canadian party system; radical populists, whatever their stripe, and traditional parties were equally unprepared. The 1930 Canadian general election—which saw the election of 137 Conservatives, ninety-one Liberals, the last gasp of Progressivism (twelve seats) along with six 'others' (including Woodsworth and Heaps from Manitoba, an Independent and an Independent Labour from BC)—proved highly problematic for R.B. Bennett's governing Conservatives. It was to be their last victory for almost three decades until their surprising comeback in 1957.

In between, elements of the agrarian movement that spawned the Progressives gravitated back towards the two traditional parties or to two new parties of protest, the latter largely based in western Canada: the Co-operative Commonwealth Federation and Social Credit. The CCF was a leftist amalgam of the radical populism of the agrarian revolt (particularly related to the UFA and its Progressive component) and labour/socialist politics (associated with Woodsworth and the ILP). The CCF benefited from the banning of the Communist Party in the early 1930s, allowing a left-evolutionary party to replace a left-revolutionary option.[46] The other new party of protest, the right populist Social Credit, was an antecedent of the Reform Party and is discussed in some detail in Chapter 5.

The origins of this new socialist party, the CCF, can be located in the co-operation between Woodsworth, his labour group, and the Ginger Group/ Progressives. Meetings, made more urgent by the 1929 stock market crash, were held that same year in Regina. They involved trade unionists, including various representatives from the Dominion Labour Party and the Canadian Labour Party from Alberta, the Independent Labour parties of Manitoba and Saskatchewan, and the Canadian Labour Party and the Socialist Party of Canada from BC, who met 'to correlate the activities of the several labour political parties in western Canada'.[47] Though the press called this 'the beginning of a Western Canadian Labour Party', these parties/organizations did not immediately coalesce, although they did pass a number of radical resolutions. However, the lack of progress towards a consolidated socialist party did not prevent further meetings. In 1930 in Medicine Hat, what was then called the Conference of Western Labour Political Parties passed even more ideologically strident calls for political action to alleviate the extreme conditions of the early years of the Depression.

By July 1931, at the third meeting of this conference, the push was on to form a national labour party. Farmers' organizations were also invited to attend this meeting, and this Labour-Farmer alliance theme would become a feature of Woodsworth's vision of building a mass socialist alternative that would challenge the brokerage hegemony of the central Canadian-dominated Liberal and Conservative cadre parties.[48] With the final demise of the Progressives and the onset of the Depression, agrarian protest had now taken on a more socialist tinge—at least where it had not reattached itself to one of the two traditional parties. Henry Wise Wood's retirement from the UFA helped open the way for farmers to attach themselves to a new national party of the left. Ginger Group MP Robert Gardiner was Wood's successor as head of the UFA. Gardiner shared Woodsworth's vision of a new 'Co-operative Commonwealth' rather than the anti-party views of his predecessor, Wood. Gardiner's was a truly socialist vision:

> ...a community freed from the domination of irresponsible financial and economic power, in which all social means of production and distribution, including land, are socially owned and controlled, either by voluntarily organized groups of producers and consumers, or...by public corporations responsible to the peoples' elected representatives.[49]

This shift within the UFA helped energize other elements now coalescing around a new leftist party option; these included parts of the United Farmers of Ontario (UFO) and the United Farmers of Alberta, labour groups, the Saskatchewan Farmers Political Association, and the Independent Labour Party of Saskatchewan, founded by future CCF leader M.J. Coldwell. This activity, which encouraged farmer-labour collaboration in various forms, also involved young Baptist preacher Tommy Douglas, a pioneer of Canadian socialism in Saskatchewan and another future CCF and NDP leader. In Ontario and British Columbia, there were almost too many Labour or Socialist parties to foster a single focus.[50]

The main contributions from Ontario and Quebec came more at the level of ideas from academics in Montreal at McGill University and at the University of Toronto who, inspired by Woodsworth and the UK Fabian Society, formed the League for Social Reconstruction (LSR). The LSR grew to include locals in Winnipeg and Vancouver and produced the *Plan of Action*, the LSR manifesto. This was a five-paragraph, ten-point plan for leftist action in Canada. Its academic authors would later pen the most famous document in Canadian socialism, the Regina Manifesto.

In 1932 all groups interested in the formation of a Canadian 'co-opera-tive commonwealth' met at the Calgary Labour Temple. This included a wide range of people: 'construction workers, farmers, housewives, journal-ists, accountants, lawyers, miners, politicians and a movie house projec-tionist'.[51] At this founding meeting of the CCF, the *Calgary Programme* was presented and adopted by the conference. This preliminary program was brief (only two paragraphs), but called for cooperation to achieve the 'socialization of economic life [including] banking, credit and financial system', 'social ownership of utilities and natural resources', and 'encourage-ment of all cooperative enterprises'. The program advocated an evolution-ary, not revolutionary, approach, based on 'human needs instead of the making of profits'.[52]

While important, the *Calgary Programme* was intended to be superseded by another document drafted for and passed at the first formal CCF convention, the July 1933 Regina convention. This meeting brought together CCF Clubs, agrarian groups, trade union interests, labour and socialist party groupings, and LSR academics. Not all who were involved in Calgary joined the party organization and embraced the Regina Manifesto, but at Regina the CCF was formally launched as a political party.

Without a doubt, the two centrepieces of the Regina meeting were the agreement to found a new party, the CCF (with J.S. Woodsworth as its federal leader), and the passage of the Regina Manifesto. Drawing on the earlier LSR and Calgary documents, (particularly the former), the Regina Manifesto was to define much of Canadian socialism over the next few decades. It recog-nized a 'mixed economy', but, as outlined by Whitehorn, called for many of the things first suggested by the LSR:[53]

LSR Manifesto (1932) (five paragraphs, ten points)	*CCF/Regina Manifesto (1933)* (thirty-eight paragraphs, fourteen points)
1. planning	1. planning
2. socialization of finance	2. socialization of finance
3. public ownership	3. social ownership
4.	4. agriculture/co-ops
5. import/export boards	5. external trade
6. cooperative institutions	6. cooperative institutions
7. social legislation/freedom	7. labour code/social insurance
8. public health services	8. socialized health services
9. constitutional amendments	9. BNA Act (constitutional change)
10. disarmament/international cooperation	10. external relations/disarmament
11. taxation and funding	11. taxation and public finance
12.	12. freedom/civil rights
13.	13. social justice and law reform
14.	14. emergency program

The CCF was the culmination of an era of movement politics in Canada. As its name implied, the CCF was a federation that allowed many different organizations to take particular components of the Regina Manifesto as their reason to be affiliated, yet it was a formal mass party unlike the Progressives, which saw themselves as a movement. As a movement-based party with clearer ideological roots, the CCF was also unlike the two older cadre parties, which had dominated Canadian politics for sixty-six years. As such, the CCF represented a definitional challenge to Liberal and Conservative electoral hegemony. It would be two years after it was founded before there was a federal contest in which the CCF could test its political mettle. During that period, occasional labour and agrarian candidates ran and got elected provincially, but not as CCF representatives; this occurred in BC in late 1933 and in Ontario and Saskatchewan in 1934.[54] In 1935, six years into the Depression, Canadian voters, angry with the ineffective Bennett Conservative government, were able to cast votes for the first time for a nation-wide social democratic alternative. Voters were also given a decidedly non-socialist alternative to the Tories and Liberals, for Social Credit had also emerged as a significant federal party option in 1935. (See Chapter 5 for more detailed discussion of the impact of Social Credit on federal politics in Canada during this period.)

In 1935 in this first electoral contest for the two new parties, the right-wing populist alternative proved more successful, at least in winning seats. In 1935 Social Credit took seventeen, with just 4 per cent of the votes in the country; almost all victories (fifteen) were in Alberta (the other two were in Saskatchewan). The CCF, proving it had more nation-wide appeal, had more than double the vote share (9 per cent) of Social Credit nationally, but this resulted in fewer than half the seats (only seven); three of these were from BC, two from Saskatchewan, and two from Manitoba. In Ontario one UFO-Labour MP was also elected.[55] These initial CCF victories proved to be a reflection of the labour and agrarian components on which the CCF was based; they would also prove to be its durable electoral core.

In its second federal election, which was in 1940, the CCF parliamentary wing split from its first leader, J.S. Woodsworth. Woodsworth was a pacifist who in good conscience could not support the war. His fellow CCF MPs felt the need to support the war effort; Woodsworth remained party president while M.J. Coldwell was chosen to replace Woodsworth as House leader. The leadership moves produced no noticeable effect electorally, though perhaps it allowed the CCF to hold most of its vote. The party's vote dipped slightly to 8 per cent, but it actually added one MP. In British Columbia 38 per cent of the vote produced just one seat; Saskatchewan elected five CCFers with 29 per cent support; Manitoba and Nova Scotia added one seat apiece on 19 per cent and 6 per cent of the vote respectively. Party support elsewhere ranged from a high of 13 per cent in Alberta to virtually nothing, sometimes due to the lack of CCF candidates.[56]

The early Nova Scotia connection with the CCF was neither surprising nor new, though not much of this is reflected in literature on the left in Canada. In Halifax and especially in Cape Breton, where workers had early on (in 1908) replaced their conservative Provincial Workmen's Association with the much more militant United Mine Workers of America, there were strong traditions of labour protest against working conditions, low wages, and other leftist/class concerns.[57] The view that the Maritimes (and then Atlantic Canada after 1949) was a left 'dead zone' was widespread. This view was best expressed by Frank Underhill, one of the LSR drafters of the Regina Manifesto: 'As for the Maritimes, nothing, of course, ever happens down there.'[58] Somewhat later, CCF/NDP biographer Walter Young agreed, describing the apparent lack of CCF or NDP support in the region as 'the great conundrum of Canadian politics.'[59]

However, the assertion about the politics of the Maritimes was simply not accurate. Woodsworth had made several trips to the region to work with labour and socialist activists well before his efforts to create the CCF, and he and others acted on behalf of Cape Breton miners, as in 1922 when the newly formed BESCO (British Empire Steel Corporation) moved to cut wages by 37.5 per cent and sought government assistance 'to drive the Bolshevists [i.e., the United Mine Workers] out of Cape Breton'.[60] The local response by miners had been an immediate strike against the company, which received considerable attention in the Canadian Parliament. That pattern of leftist political and party activity in Cape Breton (and at times elsewhere in the Maritimes) was to continue. It reflected local efforts to define politics and party expression in more class/ideological terms, and while its parliamentary impact was small, Maritime dissent from the brokerage concept of parties was to continue.

In the 1945 federal election, mirroring Labour Party successes in Britain, the CCF had its best ever electoral showing, winning 16 per cent of the vote across the country and electing twenty-eight MPs. A higher percentage of Nova Scotians (17 per cent) and Albertans (18 per cent) supported the CCF in this election than did Ontarians (at 14 per cent). Nova Scotia's CCF MP was re-elected and subsequently returned in 1949 and 1953, though as was the case generally for the party, overall voter support in the province continued to shrink (to 10 per cent and 7 per cent respectively).[61] Nevertheless, between the 1880s and 1980s, the CCF was the most successful third party in the Atlantic region as indicated by vote share.[62]

Elsewhere in Canada, especially in the original western core of Saskatchewan, BC, and Manitoba, the CCF enjoyed a considerable degree of success: in Saskatchewan, where 44 per cent support in 1945 resulted in the election of eighteen CCF MPs (out of a total of twenty-one seats in the province); in Manitoba, where 32 per cent of the votes produced five seats; and in BC, where four MPs were elected on a 29 per cent vote share. After the 1945 breakthrough, however, the party steadily declined, partly as a by-product of the onset of the cold war. In 1949 it lost half its seats (to thirteen) and 3 per cent of its support; in 1953 it suffered a further 2 per cent decline in vote share (to 11 per cent), though because of plurality electoral vagaries, it picked up ten extra seats. In 1957 it held its 1953 vote share and added two additional seats (for a total of twenty-five), but lost more than two-thirds of its seats (dropping to eight) in the 1958 Diefenbaker landslide. During these years, the CCF strongholds remained Saskatchewan, then BC and Manitoba, followed by Ontario. Occasionally, as in 1957 and 1958, BC elected the greatest number of CCF MPs. Nova Scotia regularly provided as much voter support to the party, as did Alberta, the latter having turned after 1935 to Social Credit and then in 1958 to the Conservatives. This regional pattern of voter support reflected the different elements of the original CCF coalition. In Ontario and British Columbia, where labour unions were strongest, labour support for the party was also strongest. In Saskatchewan and parts of Manitoba, the old United Farmers/CCF elements provided a continuing base of support, even during hard political times.

The impact of the CCF was more than electoral votes and seats, however. Although it averaged just 11 per cent of the vote nationally between 1935 and 1958, it had an impact in several other ways.[63] As Wiseman has contended, the party's policy legacy remains 'embedded in the national political culture' in terms of its 'ideas and initiatives', such as 'in the development of the welfare state'. That these policies were copied by other parties, especially the governing Liberals, only added to the conclusion that the CCF (and its successor, the NDP) 'had a discernibly weighty influence on the agenda of public policy' in Canada.[64]

At its zenith in 1945, when the CCF won twenty-eight seats and 16 per cent of all the votes (just after Saskatchewan elected the first socialist government in North America in 1944), the government of Mackenzie King clearly felt the need to respond to this challenge by moving left itself. Later, the success of the Tommy Douglas-led Saskatchewan CCF government in pioneering policies and programs such as Medicare would have a profound influence on the Canadian political system.[65] The longevity and innovativeness of the Saskatchewan CCF government were important elements in terms of the CCF's overall policy impact as well.[66] As with Social Credit in Alberta (see Chapter 5), holding power in a province continuously for two decades (1944–64) was more than symbolic for a new third party like the CCF. Credibility, an arena for policy experimentation, and the chance for lessons in policy implementation and administration were just a few of the concrete benefits of provincial office for the CCF nationally.

The goals of the Co-operative Commonwealth Federation, set out in the Regina Manifesto in 1933, remained central to CCF policy for the life of the party.[67] However, a less radical statement—the Winnipeg Declaration—was adopted in 1956, partly as an attempt to stem the party's declining electoral fortunes.[68] Whether, as Whitehorn has asked, 'the CCF would have fallen further and faster without the passing of the more moderate-sounding Winnipeg Declaration is impossible to tell. . . . However, it is conceivable that coming as late as it did, the new statement made little difference.'[69] Many in the movement/party continued to prefer the wording and ideological content of the Regina document, and many saw the Winnipeg Declaration and the further electoral slide of the CCF simply as the result of 'A Protest Movement Becalmed'.[70] Alan Whitehorn's excellent review of this 'Becalmed' literature offers a more balanced corrective to such singular views of the CCF.[71]

The Third Party System

Becalmed or not, CCF support nationally never rose above 16 per cent (its high point in 1945); by 1958, at the end of the second party system, support for the party had dropped to 9.5 per cent. Both its leader, M.J. Coldwell, and deputy leader, Stanley Knowles, were among those defeated in the Diefenbaker landslide of that year. Many on the left felt there was a need to recreate the initial energy of the CCF in a 'New Party' setting. This was done—coincident with the beginning of the third party system (1962 to 1984–8)—with the creation, in 1961, of the New Democratic Party, designed to provide a more urban social democratic political appeal and a Quebec breakthrough.

If the CCF was as much a movement as a party, it clearly was one that sought to redefine Canadian politics along more ideological lines. The limited success of the CCF during the second party period perhaps said more about the capacity of the traditional brokerage parties to adjust to challenges, such as those posed by the emergence of a leftist party alternative. To overcome some of the organizational and strategic impediments of being a social movement, the NDP was more clearly designed and mandated to be a political party, with elections as the overwhelming focus of its activity. Formed out of an alliance of the CCF, the New Party Club, and the Canadian Labour Congress, the *New Party Declaration* called for a more modern, bilingual party with a closer association with organized labour and a broader electoral appeal. The NDP program was far longer than the Regina Manifesto or the Winnipeg Declaration; it contained 168 paragraphs organized around four themes:

> *Planning for Abundance*—including a commitment to 'full employment', achievable only with 'economic planning' and a 'Guaranteed Employment Act' with a job as a 'social right'; 'continuous growth' with 'a social purpose'; ending waste, opening competition, and protecting 'the family farm' as the basic unit of agriculture; democratically controlled co-ops and credit unions as 'important forms of social ownership'; programs on regional disparity, and 'help for small business'.

> *Security and Freedom*—including a 'comprehensive, far-reaching and systematic program of social security', with Medicare at its centre, extension of welfare to the elderly, a national labour code with a minimum wage, health and safety

provisions, vacation requirements and trade union and collective bargaining protections, a national housing policy, extension of 'free' education through aid to the provinces, and extended funding to national cultural institutions such as the Canadian Broadcasting Corporation and the National Film Board.

A More Complete Democracy—to improve federal-provincial relations, federalism, French-English relations; to recognize Aboriginal standing and to assist multi-cultural development while recognizing Canada as 'a nation' with 'two national cultures'; there were also provisions for Senate abolition, strengthening the roles of representatives in the House of Commons through institutional reforms, and election expenses reform.

Co-operation For Peace—including a commitment to have Canada engaged inter-nationally for freedom over totalitarianism, particularly through the United Nations and Commonwealth involvement; a 'reappraisal' of NATO; a ban on nuclear testing to lead to 'nuclear disarmament'; and a commitment to tie foreign aid to 2 per cent of GDP.[72]

The new party did have more success than the CCF. In its very first election, in 1962, led by popular former CCF Saskatchewan Premier Tommy Douglas, the NDP more than doubled the CCF parliamentary contingent to nineteen while increasing its popular vote to 14 per cent. One immediate impact of this success was the relegation of Diefenbaker's Conservatives to minority government status.[73]

When this was followed by two Liberal minority governments in quick succession (1963 and 1965), several parts of the NDP program were implemented by the Liberals as part of the ongoing price for NDP support. In 1963 the New Democratic Party essentially held its own; when the Liberals again failed to achieve a parliamentary majority in 1965, it was partly due to an increase in NDP support. With an 18 per cent vote share, the party seat total rose to twenty-one.

For a new party, having to contest three general elections in five years (1962, 1963, and 1965) stretched its organizational and financial resources to the limit. The NDP was more successful than the CCF in picking up support in Ontario and British Columbia, in part a by-product of its stronger labour ties. In Ontario, six MPs were elected in 1962 and 1963, increasing to nine in 1965 when the party received almost 22 per cent of the vote in the province. In BC (part of the NDP's stronger labour core) ten MPs were elected in 1962 and nine in 1963 and 1965 from a fairly consistent one-third share of the vote. It did suffer a decline in support when the provincial party in Saskat-chewan (minus its long-serving premier Tommy Douglas and suffering the impact of a doctors' strike over Medicare) fell to local Liberals in 1964. The federal NDP success during this initial party experience also coincided with a collapse for Social Credit in English-speaking Canada (from 12 per cent nationally to 4 per cent and just five seats).[74] (See chapters 5 and 6 for more discussion of the parallel rise of the Créditistes in Quebec.)

The federal Liberal administrations of Lester Pearson during the years 1963–8 legislated in many areas of social policy, key elements of the CCF and NDP programs. Perhaps the most important of these was the historic creation of a national Medicare program, first initiated in Saskatchewan under Premier Tommy Douglas's CCF administration. The Liberals proved once again adept at co-opting policy ideas that were popular with the Canadian population. (See chapters 2 and 3 for a more complete discussion of this phenomenon and the strategic manoeuvring of the two traditional parties during this decade in Canadian party politics.)

In the spring of 1968 the governing Liberals selected the articulate, bilingual, telegenic justice minister, Pierre Trudeau, as their new party leader. Trudeau's youthful image, intellectualism, and dynamic leadership style was accompanied by progressive policy accomplishments, such as new legislation on divorce, abortion, birth control, and homosexuality.[75] The 1968 election was characterized by a groundswell of popular support for this new leader, dubbed by the media as 'Trudeaumania'. Riding this wave, the Liberals won a solid majority. The New Democrats managed to hold their own: their vote dipped slightly, to 17 per cent, but the party managed to win the same number of seats (twenty-one) in the new Parliament. Its vote share improved in Saskatchewan by ten points to 36 per cent and held in BC (at 33 per cent) and Ontario (at 21 per cent). It appeared that the new party had won for itself a fairly reliable core electorate with regional, social, and ideological characteristics.

Trudeau's first government (1968–72) failed to meet the high expectations he had created. Here, perhaps two examples stand out: (1) despite initial popularity with Trudeau's handling of the October 1970 crisis in Quebec, the NDP was the one parliamentary party that consistently criticized the Trudeau cabinet's use of the War Measures Act; and (2) Trudeau's preference for regional desks within the prime minister's office rather than seek advice from local MPs or regional caucuses further alienated both representatives and party supporters and created the perception of an excessively centralized and bureaucratized approach to governance.[76]

While there was growing dissatisfaction within Liberal ranks and more widely with the first Trudeau government, the NDP also found itself internally divided. Its more militant, ideologically oriented activists were unhappy with the moderation and state-oriented social democratic discourse of the party; they were also critical of what they considered the more conservative influence of union leaders within the new party. This leftist tendency within the party became known as the Waffle faction. It produced a manifesto that challenged the gradualism and moderation of the party, calling instead for strong economic nationalism, sweeping democratization, and a real commitment to socialism and public ownership. Focusing on extraparliamentary activity and societal transformation, the Waffle placed itself in conflict with organized labour and the established party leadership. The timing of this

Waffle challenge was also a factor as its support seemed to grow in the run-up to the leadership contest following Tommy Douglas's resignation as leader.[77]

Initially, the Waffle had the support of a number of party notables, but when their efforts to redefine the whole direction of the NDP became apparent, both organized labour and the existing party leadership coalesced against it.[78] Labour referred to the Waffle as young 'intellectual snobs' and made it clear that they had no business interfering with the trade union movement. That labour backlash and a feeling that the strong economic nationalism of the Waffle would 'scare the hell' out of the Canadian electorate led to manoeuvres within the party to force the Waffle out of the NDP. Many Waffle supporters left rather than be formally expelled, and the attempt to redefine the NDP as a strong socialist alternative ended in failure. The new leader of the NDP, party stalwart David Lewis, reaffirmed the NDP as a moderate, labour-oriented, social democratic party. However, this would not be the end of ideological tensions within the party, nor the end of internal debates about party program and strategy.

In 1972 Trudeau's government was reduced to a minority in Parliament. David Lewis, the new NDP leader—who was, in the tradition of the party, a good, self-taught orator—had struck a chord with voters with his coining of the phrase 'corporate welfare bums'. Despite the party's previous generational and factional internal tensions around the Waffle, the campaign helped the NDP improve its parliamentary standing considerably.[79] The party was able to gather an additional ten seats, for a grand total of thirty-one. The new seats came from the West, North, and Ontario, where voter support levels for the party ranged from highs of 36 per cent and 35 per cent in Saskatchewan and BC respectively to 22 per cent in Ontario (the latter yielding eleven seats). Support levels continued to be weak in Quebec and the Atlantic provinces (where no New Democrats were elected) and where voter support ranged from lows of 5 per cent and 6 per cent (Newfoundland, Quebec, and New Brunswick) to 12 per cent (Nova Scotia).[80] Still, the overall improvement in the party's performance confirmed for many the wisdom of expelling the Waffle. A too stridently ideological party—even a leftist party—apparently was not the way to appeal to the Canadian public.

Over the 1972–4 minority government period, the Liberals acted on a number of issues long associated with the NDP. Outstanding examples of this policy 'poaching' included the establishment of the Canada Development Corporation (CDC), a review agency to screen foreign inflows of capital (the Foreign Investment Review Agency), and the creation of a publically owned oil company (Petro-Canada). In addition to the minority Liberal government's action on these initiatives, NDP support for the government was premised on passage of elections expenses legislation. The ensuing Elections Expenses Act has proven a significant and lasting reform of the Canadian electoral process. Meanwhile in Quebec, the still largely anglophone

NDP was floundering, hopelessly sidelined in the titanic struggle between the Trudeau-led federalists and the René Lévesque-led nationalists. Both developments—the ease with which Liberals incorporated some of the leading leftist/nationalist policies of the NDP and the latter's near total marginalization in Quebec—presented New Democrats with serious obstacles to any potential electoral breakthrough.

Other emerging issues of the early 1970s also affected the NDP's fortunes: the international oil crisis and the onset of other global economic ills precipitated the beginnings of a fundamental re-evaluation—and ultimate rejection—of the postwar Keynesian policy consensus. Keynesian assumptions about the operation and management of the economy had been central to NDP policy stances. The party would now be confronted with a new economic and political orthodoxy: neoconservative policy approaches and governance philosophies that were hostile towards high levels of public spending and an interventionist role for national governments.[81]

Trudeau's Liberals entered the 1974 general election, hopeful of a better showing, running on a platform opposed to the Tory proposals for wage and price controls to stem the growing problem of inflation. This made the similar stance adopted by the NDP somewhat redundant and vulnerable to strategic voting should voters shift to the Liberals in order to ensure that the Tories weren't elected. As well, the series of leftist/nationalist policies implemented by the Liberals between 1972 and 1974 had stolen most of the thunder from their erstwhile social democratic opponents. The results of the 1974 contest were therefore predictable: a rise in Liberal vote share and a parallel decline in popular vote for the NDP (to 16 per cent). Left with only sixteen seats, the party had been stripped of almost half its parliamentary contingent. For the NDP, 1974 represented the worst showing since its founding. (Indeed, the party would not again perform so poorly until the disastrous election of 1993.) While support for the party was down everywhere, it fell most in BC, one of its core areas; here the NDP vote fell sharply to 23 per cent, with the loss of nine seats.

While debates around the central tenets of the federal NDP continued throughout the early 1970s, the NDP began to experience greater success in a number of provincial arenas, particularly in western Canada. In June 1969, for example, former MP Ed Schreyer led the NDP to power in Manitoba.[82] In Saskatchewan new provincial leader Allan Blakeney managed to win back control of the province for the NDP from the Liberals in a June 1971 election.[83] Soon after in British Columbia, a one-term NDP government led by Dave Barrett brought twenty years of W.A.C. Bennett-led Social Credit rule to a close. While Barrett's term was short—just over three years (1972–5)—it represented the left's first electoral triumph over various coalitions of anti-left political forces in British Columbia.[84] These three provincial victories early in the 1970s provided a boost to NDP fortunes nationally. So did a change in NDP federal leadership with the selection of Ed Broadbent in 1975.

In 1979 the NDP regained the votes it had lost in 1974. In the federal election that year, twenty-six New Democrats were returned to Parliament on 18 per cent of the national vote. The party benefited from leftist-liberal vote switchers in English Canada who were in part disillusioned with an eleven-year-old Liberal government that seemed incapable of dealing with a stagnating economy. NDP support remained solid in its western Canada/Ontario core, but it also grew in Atlantic Canada, where the party elected one MP from Nova Scotia on 19 per cent of the vote, and a second from Newfoundland on the strength of a surprising 31 per cent vote share.[85] The minority parliamentary situation, with which Canadians had become so familiar, offered third parties like the NDP a real opportunity to exercise some policy influence. This pattern ended in December 1979 with the defeat of Joe Clark's minority Conservative government.

In the subsequent 1980 general election, the second political coming of Pierre Trudeau's Liberals was premised on a more leftist-nationalist platform that once again strayed into traditional NDP policy terrain. Despite this, the NDP was able to more than hold its own, increasing the party's parliamentary contingent to thirty-two (the party's best performance ever) on the basis of a national vote share of 20 per cent. Led by the increasingly well-regarded Ed Broadbent, the NDP played an important role in the Trudeau-led patriation of the Canadian Constitution after the 1980 Quebec referendum. Facing serious political and legal roadblocks, Trudeau had to seek out allies; federal NDP support—especially with its representation from western Canada—was considered essential by Trudeau.[86] The inclusion of Aboriginal rights in Trudeau's 'Patriation Package' was one of the conditions of that NDP support.[87]

NDP support in 1980 was again concentrated in its western core, where a third of the region elected twenty-seven of the party's thirty-two MPs. Ontario added the other five, but voter support for the party in Ontario was only slightly ahead of popular support in Nova Scotia (21 per cent), with Newfoundland and New Brunswick not far behind (17 per cent each). Only Alberta (at 10 per cent), Quebec (at 9 per cent), and PEI (at 7 per cent) seemed relatively impervious to the NDP's strengthening voter appeal.[88] The party's good showing was buoyed by the national popularity of leader Ed Broadbent and the continuing weakness of the Liberals in western Canada, due in no small measure to the Liberal government's highly controversial National Energy Program.

The Mulroney Interlude

The last government led by Pierre Trudeau between 1980–4 proved highly unpopular with the provinces and with business. A deep economic recession in the early 1980s was accompanied by record high inflation and interest rates, high unemployment, and a ballooning budget deficit. NDP fortunes did not automatically improve with these Liberal troubles, however. The NDP was trapped by the popular perception that the Liberal government's leftist-nationalist policies were close if not identical to the NDP agenda. Their failure tainted the NDP as well as the governing Liberals.

In 1984 the Liberals, now led by long-time heir-apparent John Turner, lost badly to a new Tory coalition led by Anglo Quebecer Brian Mulroney. Mulroney's Tories managed to garner about 50 per cent of all votes in the country—only the third time since the First World War that this had happened—and 75 per cent of the 282 seats in Parliament. The Liberals were reduced to forty seats and just 28 per cent support. Overall the NDP vote in the Mulroney 'sweep' of 1984 was virtually constant, down just 1 per cent—and two seats—from the party's 1980 showing. More importantly, with just a ten-seat difference and less than 10 per cent separating the NDP from the Liberals, the party could finally think of overtaking and permanently displacing one of the old-line parties. NDP vote shares varied from a high of 38 per cent in Saskatchewan, where voter support actually increased 2 per cent (though two seats were lost), and a static 35 per cent in BC (where four seats were lost); to a mid range of 21 per cent in Ontario (where an additional eight MPs were elected), 15 per cent in Nova Scotia, 14 per cent in Alberta and New Brunswick; to lows of 9 per cent in Quebec, 7 per cent in PEI, and 6 per cent in Newfoundland.[89] These shifts, it might be noted, were all downward east of Saskatchewan, and all upward from Saskatchewan west.

The 1984 election result was a combination of effective and popular party leadership—polls regularly listed NDP leader Ed Broadbent as Canada's most popular and most trusted federal party leader—and the NDP's ability to 'circle the wagons' and maintain support levels in the West and Ontario. Despite limited optimism that the NDP might displace the Turner Liberals, there were indications that larger forces of electoral change were taking place, both within older parties as they repositioned themselves and in the stirring of newer political forces, particularly as expressed in that most familiar of Canadian forms: regional discontent and protest.

In the run-up to the thirty-fourth Canadian general election of November 1988, optimism and expectations of an NDP breakthrough to second place were high. Although the party improved its parliamentary standing considerably, the two old-line parties remained firmly ensconced as government and official Opposition. The forty-three New Democrats elected to Parliament (with 20.4 per cent of the national vote) still translated into third party status in the Commons, a source of some dissatisfaction within the party. In retrospect, this was the high point for the NDP. With the polarized choices and strategic voting precipitated by the great 1988 free trade debate, NDP support further strengthened in the West, but remained static in Ontario and dropped throughout Atlantic Canada. NDP vote totals ranged from a low of 7.5 per cent in PEI and 9.3 per cent in New Brunswick to only 11 per cent in Nova Scotia and 12 per cent in Newfoundland. In Quebec the party's generally low support improved somewhat, but again no one was elected, a disappointment for party leader Ed Broadbent and many in the party. Ontario returned ten New Democrats (down from thirteen) and Manitoba two (down from four) on 20 per cent and 21 per cent of the vote respectively. In the party's western heartland, however, where the Liberals (the other party on the No side of the free trade debate) were weakest, voter support for the NDP was up: 37 per cent and nineteen seats in BC; 44 per cent and ten seats in Saskatchewan. In the Yukon the NDP candidate (future leader Audrey McLaughlin) won a majority of the votes (51.4 per cent) and the territory's one seat.

The relative success of the NDP in the 1988 contest—the best seat totals and vote share of any NDP (or CCF) result—belied emerging difficulties for the party. Despite a popular NDP leader and a Liberal Party that had been in some disarray after their 1984 shellacking by Mulroney's Tories, there were growing tensions within the party following the 1988 general election.[90] The NDP had entered the election with hopes of actually taking second place. The focus of Broadbent's 1988 campaign was on 'fairness' and 'the average family', relatively traditional NDP concerns. Campaign ads and literature directed attention to Broadbent's leadership and to the party's position on social and environmental policy. For tactical reasons, the Free Trade Agreement (FTA), the main plank of the Conservative campaign, was not placed front and centre on the advice of NDP strategists out of fear that such a strategy might benefit Liberals more than the New Democrats particularly in Ontario, where the David Peterson-led provincial Liberal government was also apposed to free trade.[91]

As an initial strategy, confronting a Liberal campaign that came close to self-destructing in the first weeks, this might have worked.[92] The televised leaders' debate affected that. Turner's emphasis on the FTA and the electorate's perceived uneasiness about Prime Minister Mulroney's trustworthiness led many to conclude that Turner had outperformed Mulroney in the leaders' debate. In the week that followed, the Conservatives fell 14 per cent in the polls, and despite doing well in that same debate, support for Broadbent and the NDP fell by a not dissimilar 10 per cent. As elections analyst Richard Johnston and colleagues have argued, the NDP had lost their advantage and were never to recover.[93] Although they had high hopes when entering the campaign, questioning from the labour movement began in the immediate 1988 electoral post-mortem; they argued that there had been a relative lack of attention to the voice of labour in developing the campaign strategy for 1988 and a view that labour's concerns had been downplayed. United Auto Workers president Bob White was one who raised such concerns. Given that Ed Broadbent had initiated CLC representation in the NDP caucus, and that organized labour had helped shape the 1988 campaign focus, some have called this more an *ex post facto* interpretation of the election than an accurate reflection of reality.[94] However interpreted, although

1988 represented the NDP's high point in results, it was appropriately described by Whitehorn as 'Dashed Hopes'.[95]

Certainly others (such as Whitehorn) have concluded that the 1988 NDP
campaign was an élite-designed game plan that de-emphasized party ideology (neither socialism nor social democracy were mentioned in the party's
twenty-four-page election manifesto)[96] and which sought to paper over divisions within the party (such as regarding Meech Lake and NATO) and which
ignored party resolutions calling for nationalization and changes to abortion legislation. All agreed that recriminations were not long in coming after
the relatively disappointing 1988 result. The first was the electoral post-
mortem that Whitehorn described as a 'labour backlash'.[97] The second was
more pronounced and more lasting: Ed Broadbent resigned not long after as
leader in response to the party's disappointment at not achieving its breakthrough second place. The increasingly negative climate also included reaction to new NDP provincial governments (especially the Rae administration
in Ontario). This resulted in considerably less labour support and assistance
as the party prepared for the federal election of 1993.

The Fourth Party System

In 1993 the New Democrats, fresh from their 1988 'success', paid the price
for alienating some of their core supporters. Regionalism also had a new
impact. The NDP vote share fell to just 6.9 per cent, a drop of almost two-
thirds; their seats in the House of Commons were slashed from forty-three to
a western rump of nine. The vote drop was dramatic; even in core support
areas voter dissatisfaction and the challenges of two new regionally based
third parties cost the NDP electorally. In Atlantic Canada, the best the NDP
under new leader Audrey McLaughlin could do was garner 6.8 per cent support in Nova Scotia. (Reform did almost twice as well with 13.3 per cent in
the province.) In the other three provinces, support was under or just over
5 per cent. In Quebec, the ascendancy of the Bloc Québécois pushed NDP
support almost off the electoral map to a miserable 1.5 per cent. Ontario was
perhaps a special case, where the provincial NDP Rae administration
(1990–5) had badly split the party. Here the NDP vote dropped to just 6 per
cent with the loss of all ten seats. Only in the West were the remnants of the
party salvaged, and even here the party was in considerable trouble. Only in
Saskatchewan and BC was the NDP able to elect more than one MP: two in BC
(where the party's vote was cut by more than half to 15.5 per cent) and five
in Saskatchewan, where the provincial NDP was once again in ascendancy.
As well, party leader Audrey McLaughlin easily won her seat in the Yukon.[98]
In the end, the newness (and relative unrecognizability across the broader
electorate) of party leader Audrey McLaughlin was one factor in the 1993
outcome. Her inability to influence the electorate, the rise of new regional

political forces like Reform and the Bloc Québécois, the 'taint' of being associated with 'suspect' approaches and policies (such as a tax-and-spend government and the Meech Lake and Charlottetown constitutional accords) and increasingly unpopular NDP governments in Ontario and BC were all factors in the NDP collapse in 1993. With party fortunes at a low ebb, the sale of national party headquarters to Ukraine was more than symbolic.

For the NDP, 1993 was the worst electoral result since the CCF fought its first election in 1935. A well-known and popular leader had resigned and been replaced in late 1989 by a relative political neophyte. Policy choices by NDP provincial governments in the context of a severe and prolonged recession proved politically unpopular. Government decisions on economic matters hurt federal party support least in Saskatchewan, its traditional stronghold, though even here Reform party strength was now noticeable. In BC leadership questions, a financial scandal, and more emphasis on the environment than jobs cost Premier Mike Harcourt his job. In Ontario decisions made in the second half of the Bob Rae government—with its emphasis on social contract debates—had a dramatic and negative impact on NDP fortunes federally in 1993 and provincially in 1995.[99]

Many labour and other core supporters, feeling betrayed by NDP governments they helped to elect, voted with their feet and wallets, reducing the NDP's capacity to mount an effective federal election campaign. Equally important was the rise of the two new parties of regional protest. The NDP had nothing to show for its considerable investment in a Quebec/French campaign in 1988 (one-third of the NDP advertising was in French).[100] And in the West, the demise of Social Credit had simply presaged the rise of Reform, which effectively challenged the NDP's claim to be the voice of western dissent. The NDP's support for the Meech Lake and Charlottetown accords made it particularly vulnerable in the West.[101] Joining the increasingly unpopular Conservative government's advertising campaign for a Yes vote on the Charlottetown Accord was, as Whitehorn has argued, 'perhaps a fatal transformation in image' for the leftist-populist party.[102]

By the mid-point of the 1993 campaign, the NDP was focused entirely on survival. The intrusion of Preston Manning and Lucien Bouchard into the leaders' debates made the leaders' individual impacts more difficult. Certainly, the debates proved no advantage for McLaughlin or the NDP. Faced with continuing poor poll showings, the party's strategy shifted in mid-campaign to one of admitting a Liberal majority was apparent so NDPers might 'come home' to the party, having helped defeat the unpopular Tories. This desperation appeal started to reverse the poor numbers, but it was too little, too late. Presiding over a western rump of nine MPs and now bereft of official party standing in the House of Commons, McLaughlin soon resigned as leader.

The 1995 NDP leadership convention selected a more seasoned political leader, Alexa McDonough, who had led the Nova Scotia New Democrats for thirteen years. Eschewing a quick run at a seat in Parliament, McDonough undertook to continue the party's re-examination and preparation for the next election. She also announced that she would run in her old provincial seat, Halifax, against a Liberal incumbent. For the 1997 campaign, a scaled-down effort was necessary for financial reasons. It was decided to maximize regional variations in the campaign and to appeal to the party's traditional core. Spending was trimmed to $6 million, advertising costs were halved, and party polling was reduced; with a relatively unknown federal leader, more emphasis was placed on local campaigns. With all the preparatory work prior to the election, stronger labour support returned. In its western strongholds, the NDP found itself facing a Reform campaign that had successfully portrayed the NDP as one of the old-line parties. For the most part, NDP losses in 1993 ended up as Liberal gains.[103] Thus, the party's 1997 strategy was to recapture this lost support: from the Liberals, whose significant shift to the right during their first mandate gave this strategy some potential, and in the West from Reform. The rightist shift also allowed the NDP to return to a more traditional party message: their role as protector of working people and supporter of social programs against corporate agendas, right-wing deficit cutters, and social program slashers. The idea was to group Reform, Conservatives, and Liberals together as like-minded exponents of neoconservative ideas and policies.

The emphasis on local campaigns was only partly dictated by smaller campaign spending. With yet another new leader who was not well known nationally, the NDP's 1997 campaign focused on an 'A' and 'B' list of constituencies, the 'A' list being forty-eight seats that were considered most winnable. This turned the campaign into what Whitehorn has described as '48 by-elections'.[104] With more locally focused advertising, the NDP were able to portray Reform as 'American-style right-wing social/health cutters' in the West where the NDP's core remained. In the East, a more traditional NDP voice spoke through the national campaign focus. That campaign focused on high unemployment numbers and Liberal government cuts to health care and education, issues that resonated with Canadian voters. The issue of national unity, which had produced little Quebec success and made the NDP vulnerable to Reform attacks in 1993, was all but ignored despite Reform's efforts to emphasize it in the latter parts of the 1997 election. The NDP campaign closed with an historical reminder to Canadians that having a social democratic voice in Parliament had 'Made a Difference'.

The NDP vote in 1997 rebounded somewhat, up from 6.9 per cent to 11 per cent. More importantly, the twenty-one MPs elected (from five provinces and one territory) represented a return to official party status in Parliament and access to research staff and other parliamentary perks. In 1997 support for the party varied from lows of 2 per cent in Quebec, 6 per cent in Alberta, and 11 per cent in Ontario (a continuing legacy of the unpopular Rae administration); to a mid-range of 15 per cent in PEI, 18 per cent in New Brunswick and BC, and 22 per cent and 23 per cent in Newfoundland and Manitoba respectively; to highs of 30 per cent in Nova Scotia and 31 per cent in Saskatchewan. Clearly, the federal election of 1997 had finally set to rest the conundrum of Atlantic Canada's electoral aversion to the left. Finally, in a region where high unemployment and regional disparities had never translated into seats for a social democratic party, more MPs (six) were elected in Nova Scotia (including popular leader Alexa McDonough) than in Saskatchewan (five), Manitoba (four), and British Columbia (three). With the two from New Brunswick, 38 per cent of the NDP caucus were Maritimers.[105]

The NDP's rebound in 1997 was partly a product of significant soul-searching and redefinition from within the party. The replacement of the Rae government in Ontario by the radically right-wing Harris Conservatives drove labour and other traditional supporters back to their social democratic allies. And Roy Romanow's NDP government in Saskatchewan regained some support after initial cuts to hospitals and social spending, which helped the federal campaign in that Prairie core. In BC Mike Harcourt was replaced by Glen Clark, who had much closer ties to organized labour in that province. When BC New Democrats were returned to power provincially in 1996 under Glen Clark, a 'friend of organized labour' who embarked on changes to the Labour Code supported by BC unions, local labour felt it had a government that was prepared to listen to—and give some policy expression to—its voice. Most importantly, each of these provincial experiences represented an instance of the party reconnecting with its core support base.

The shorter federal election campaign in 1997 (thirty-six versus forty-seven days) also helped a 'poorer' NDP contest the election on relatively even terms with the better-funded parties. In any event, the eventual outcome—a 4 per cent improvement in the NDP's popular vote, the reacquisition of official party status, and the growth of NDP support in Atlantic Canada—allowed New Democrats to breathe a sigh of relief. As Whitehorn has concluded, however, the relative improvement in party performance was offset by a disappointing show in Ontario and continuing weakness in the West, particularly in BC.[106] Indeed, only thirteen of ninety-one West/North seats went to the NDP in 1997, far below their norm during the third party system. Reform's inroads into some areas of traditional NDP support, such as parts of Saskatchewan and BC, offer pause to those who claim 1997 as the beginning of a real NDP resurgence.[107]

During the Broadbent era (1975–89) NDP fortunes were buoyed by their leader's popularity, by the party's core support in BC, Saskatchewan, and parts of Ontario and Manitoba, and by its role as a party of organized labour and leftist dissent. The Liberals' successful brokerage poaching of NDP voters and policy ideas whenever they perceived a leftist political threat attested to the continuing electoral limits on the NDP's adoption of a too radically left-wing perspective. The NDP also proved vulnerable when the electorate was polarized on key issues, such as the competition between nationalists and federalists in Quebec or on the free trade issue in parts of Canada in the election of 1988. As well, the party was vulnerable to strategic voting whenever the electorate turned to the Liberals to rid themselves of the Tories (as in 1993). Finally, with Reform on the scene, the NDP could no longer count on picking up the 'protest vote' in the West.

The 1986–93 period suggested the possibility of an actual NDP breakthrough in Canada. As noted earlier, the successes for the party in provincial contests in Saskatchewan and British Columbia, and its first ever victory in Ontario, meant that New Democrats for a time were 'governing' more than half the citizens of Canada. At the same time, in 1988 the NDP had had its best showing ever nationally, exceeding for only the second time the 20 per cent electoral threshold. Moreover, it had a party leader (Ed Broadbent) who regularly surpassed all other national party heads in 'leadership and trust' in the polls.

If this half-decade was the NDP's apogee, its very successes contained the seeds of its subsequent nadir: negative responses to policy choices in Ontario and to aspects of government policy in British Columbia, coupled with a change of national party leadership in 1989 that failed to excite party or popular support. In the wake of the 1993 fiasco, one analyst concluded that the NDP was 'intellectually bankrupt, financially broke and reeling politically'.[108] In 1997 that slide in party fortunes was reversed, though the NDP did not come close to achieving the 20 per cent support that it attained in the 1980s.

The short-term goal of returning from the electoral abyss was achieved; the possibilities and challenges of a continuing redefinition of the party's social democratic traditions remained. Here several issues—global and local—perhaps may contribute to these rebuilding and redefinition processes.

1. The Asian economic flu has forced some re-evaluation of the notion that markets are the only regulator of international currency speculation and hedge funds. It is far too early to identify strong statist responses to the global financial crises of the end of the twentieth century, but the idea that market prescriptions alone, such as those ordered by the International Monetary Fund or the World Bank, will allow countries as diverse as Russia, Malaysia, and Brazil to adjust and sustain their economies and societies is increasingly under criticism.

2. The European experience of places such as France, Britain, and Germany, where labour/socialist parties have formed new governments in the 1990s, offers encouragement and perhaps direction (though not all of this direction is ideologically undirectional as Tony Blair's New Labour suggests).

Reform's efforts to redefine Canadian politics in more ideological terms has further implications than simply trying to leave its regional, populist 'cost-cutting-cowboy' image behind.[109] In 1997 Preston Manning skipped a traditional two-week summer trail ride on horseback with family and friends

Figure 4.1 CCF/NDP Popular Vote, 1935–1997 (national)

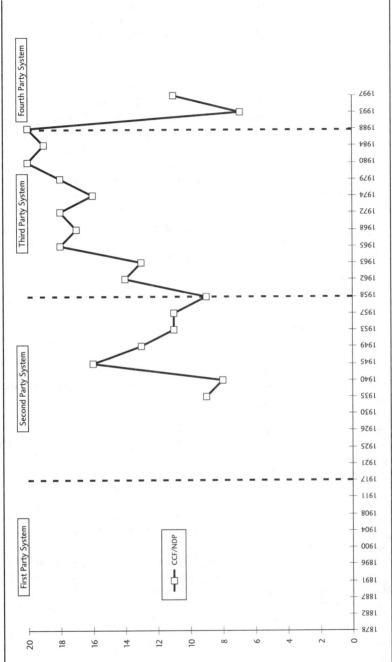

Source: Adapted from Elections Canada results.

in the Rocky Mountains to study French in Quebec.[110] Preston Manning's forsaking horse and family for a language lab in Quebec; an understanding of Quebec's Créditiste tradition; some low-level Reform success in parts of central/eastern Canada, an image make-over, and efforts to 'Unite the Right' suggest at least the potential for a party/political realignment on more polarized left-right terms. If successful (or even partially so), this may offer an opening for a party with labourist, social democratic, and new leftist ideological roots to regroup in response to the Reform challenge, with the potential for a renewed appeal to both traditional and new constituencies.

Given the initial ideological roots of Calgary and Regina (1932–3), and the angst over leftist ideological purity versus social democratic gradualism around the Winnipeg (1956) and Waffle (1969–70) manifestos, there is some irony in the fact that exposing the Canadian voter to a dose of stridently ideological conservatism may be the tonic that will fully revive the NDP as Canada's leftist alternative. While still in the process of consolidation, Canada's fourth party system appears to be producing a sharper delineation of political choices for Canadians and perhaps a fuller maturation of party and electoral politics.

Notes

The authors are grateful to the anonymous reviewers and to Alan Whitehorn, Royal Military College; David Laycock, Simon Fraser University; and Ed Broadbent, J.S. Woodsworth Chair, Simon Fraser University, for helpful comments and suggestions on this chapter.

1. See reports of the chief electoral officer, Canada, various; and Hugh G. Thorburn, ed., *Party Politics in Canada*, 6th edn (Scarborough: Prentice-Hall, 1991):522–33.
2. Ibid., 'Combined Election Results', 533.
3. See Munroe Eagles, James Bickerton, Alain-G. Gagnon, and Patrick Smith, *The Almanac of Canadian Politics* (Peterborough: Broadview, 1992), and Munroe Eagles, James Bickerton, Alain-G. Gagnon, and Patrick Smith, *The Almanac of Canadian Politics*, 2nd edn (Toronto: Oxford University Press, 1995). The former covers the 1984–8 electoral period; the latter, 1988–93.
4. Unless otherwise indicated, electoral/party data used in this paper is taken from Eagles et al., *The Almanac of Canadian Politics*, and Eagles et al., *The Almanac of Canadian Politics*, 2nd edn. Some of the ecological analysis/modelling is reported in Munroe Eagles, James Bickerton, Alain-G. Gagnon, and Patrick Smith, 'Continuity in Electoral Change: Patterns in Support for Canadian Parties, 1988 and 1993'. Association for Canadian Studies in the United States paper, Seattle, November 1995 and Munroe Eagles, James Bickerton, Alain-G. Gagnon, and Patrick Smith, 'Ecological Models of Party Support', Canadian Political Science Association paper, Montreal, June 1995.
5. See Thorburn, *Party Politics in Canada*, 6th edn, 522–33.

6. For a complete record of such early leftist party interventions in Ontario, see Roderick Lewis, *Centennial Edition of a History of the Electoral Districts, Legislatures and Ministries of the Province of Ontario, 1867–1968* (Toronto: Queen's Printer, 1968). The Hamilton/Hamilton East/Hamilton West references are on pp. 125–35.

7. Ibid., 445.

8. On this, see Walter D. Young, *Democracy and Discontent: Progressivism, Socialism and Social Credit in the Canadian West*, 2nd edn (Toronto: McGraw-Hill, 1978).

9. See C.L. Cleverdon, *The Women's Suffrage Movement in Canada* (Toronto: University of Toronto Press, 1950).

10. For a brief discussion of Owen and his ideas, see David Thomson, *Europe Since Napoleon* (London: Penguin, 1968).

11. Ivan Avakumovic, *Socialism in Canada: A Study of the CCF-NDP in Federal and Provincial Politics* (Toronto: McClelland and Stewart, 1978):18.

12. Ibid., 'Pioneering Days', 11–43.

13. Carol L. Bacchi, *Liberation Deferred? The Ideas of English Canadian Suffragists, 1877–1918* (Toronto: University of Toronto Press, 1983).

14. On this, see V. Strong-Boag, *The Parliament of Women: The National Council of Women of Canada, 1893–1929* (Ottawa: National Museums of Canada, 1976).

15. Bacchi, *Liberation Deferred?*

16. The Persons case involved five western 'suffragettes': Emily Murphy, Henrietta Muir Edwards, Louise McKinney, Irene Parlby, and Nellie McClung. It involved a challenge to the BNA Act's 1867 provision that only 'persons' could hold public office in Canada. In 1928 the Supreme Court ruled that women were not persons. The decision was overturned a year later, the JCPC noting the exclusion as a relic of more barbarous days.

17. As noted by Norman Penner, *The Canadian Left: A Critical Analysis* (Scarborough: Prentice-Hall, 1977):174–5.

18. This section on trade union/socialist development in early post-Confederation Canada is drawn from Avakumovic, *Socialism in Canada*, 11–43; Penner, *The Canadian Left*; and A.R. McCormack, 'The Emergence of the Socialist Movement in British Columbia', *B.C. Studies* 21 (Spring 1974).

19. On this period and the crossfertilization of ideas, see *The History of the TUC: 1868–1968* (London: General Council of the Trades Union Congress, 1968):56–7, 'From America and France the Syndicalist Ferment Spreads to Britain'. The US Socialist Labor Party was a doctrinaire Marxist grouping founded by Daniel de Leon. Like other syndicalists and the IWW, the TUC used the general strike as a political as well as industrial weapon.

20. The Socialist Party of Canada was based on a 1903 merging of the Canadian Socialist League and the Socialist Party of British Columbia. See, for example, Penner, *The Canadian Left*, 40–5.

21. See Roderick Lewis, *Centennial Edition of a History of the Electoral Districts, Legislatures and Ministries of the Province of Ontario, 1867–1968* (Toronto: Queen's Printer, 1968) for examples such as Hamilton East 1906, 1908, 1911, 1914, and 1919 where Labour won, and pp. 128–9 on Hamilton West where Labour won in 1919.

22. See, for example, Martin Robin, *Radical Politics and Canadian Labour, 1880–1930* (Kingston: Queen's University Press, 1968).

23. See P.J. Smith, *The Electoral Reform Question in Canada* (London: Electoral Reform Society of Great Britain and Ireland Monograph, 1979):1–6.

24. See W.L. Morton, *The Progressive Party in Canada* (Toronto: University of Toronto Press, 1950):302–5, Appendix C, for a copy of *The Farmers' Platform*.

25. On these, see David Laycock, *Populism and Democratic Thought in The Canadian Prairies, 1910 to 1945* (Toronto: University of Toronto Press, 1990). Laycock has defined these four populist forms as (1) crypto-Liberalism, (2) democratic population, (3) social democratic populism, and (4) plebiscitarian populism.

26. Ibid, 70–1. See also William Irvine's *The Farmers in Politics* (Toronto: McClelland and Stewart, 1920) and his *Cooperative Government* (Ottawa: Mutual Press, 1930). Irvine's *The Farmers in Politics* argued Henry Wise Wood's ideas on group government and economic cooperation. See Kenneth McNaught, *A Prophet in Politics: A Biography of J.S. Woodsworth* (Toronto: University of Toronto Press, 1959):144–5 on this latter point.

27. Ibid., 69.

28. These 'delegate' notions continue to find more recent expression; for example, in leftist elements of (since Tony Blair) 'old Labour'. For a study of Tony Wedgewood Benn's Bristol constituency on this, see Frances Morrell, *From the Electors of Bristol* (London: Rountree, 1977). It represents a response to Edmund Burke's Letter *To the Electors of Bristol*. G.D.H. Cole and others reflected on the British influences on this debate. See, for example, Cole's six-volume history of socialism, including *Socialist Thought—the Forerunners* (London: Macmillan, 1959).

29. Ibid., 71.

30. Ibid., 70–1.

31. Ibid., 136–8.

32. David Laycock describes this populism in detail in ibid., 136–202.

33. Richard Allen, *The Social Passion* (Toronto: University of Toronto Press, 1971).

34. Avakumovic, *Socialism in Canada*, 29–30.

35. On this period in Woodsworth's life, see Kenneth McNaught, *A Prophet in Politics: A Biography of J.S. Woodsworth* (Toronto: University of Toronto Press, 1959):30–57. See also Grace MacInnis, *J.S. Woodsworth: A Man to Remember* (Toronto: Macmillan, 1953), particularly chapters 4–7. On one 'extension' of the Social Gospel beyond traditional church expression, see McNaught on the creation of the Labour Church in Winnipeg, a 'carrying through of the social gospel to one of its logical conclusions', though authorities saw it more as 'a camouflage for the preaching of sedition and for fanning the flames of unrest', 136–7.

36. For a flavour and link of some of these Social Gospel ideas and subsequent leftist party activism by Douglas, see Dale Lovick, ed., *Tommy Douglas Speaks* (Vancouver: Douglas and McIntrye, 1979).

37. MacInnis, *J.S. Woodsworth*, 153–5.

38. See Avakumovic, *Socialism in Canada*, 36–40.

39. On this, see Penner, *The Canadian Left*, 124–70.

40. Irvine was defeated in 1925, but returned to Parliament in 1926.

41. This is the conclusion of Avakumovic, *Socialism in Canada*, 42. It was one shared by many others involved in this era, including non-socialists such as E.C. Drury (a crypto-Liberal as described by David Laycock), UFO premier of Ontario, 1919–23. Interview, P.J. Smith with E.C. Drury, Crown Hill, Ontario, October 1964.

42. Young, *Democracy and Discontent*, 32–6.
43. Ibid., 36.
44. Ibid.
45. Several sources make this point; for example, Avakumovic, *Socialism in Canada*, 41, and McNaught, *A Prophet in Politics*, 215–20.
46. On this, see Alan Whitehorn, 'The Communist Party of Canada', in *Party Politics in Canada*, 6th edn, edited by Hugh Thorburn (Scarborough: Prentice-Hall, 1991):356–8.
47. From CCF Papers, Minutes, 1929 Conference, Western Labour Political Parties, cited in Young, *Democracy and Discontent*, 51.
48. This movement/party dichotomy is addressed in Maurice Duverger's classic treatise, *Political Parties* (New York: Wiley, 1954). Duverger's typology distinguishes older élite-based cadre parties from newer mass-based parties with movement characteristics.
49. *Declaration of Ultimate Objectives*, passed by the UFA in 1932, cited in ibid., 3.
50. There were more than a dozen labour or socialist parties in Toronto alone at the start of the Depression. This count is Young's, *Democracy and Discontent*, 53–4. In British Columbia various iterations of Labour parties existed; their programs, such as the 1926 *Platform and Manifesto* of the BC ILP, were generally leftist-radical, resembling a more Marxist approach like the SPC. See Penner, *The Canadian Left*, 193–94.
51. Gordon Laird, *Slumming It at the Rodeo: The Cultural Roots of Canada's Right Wing Revolution* (Vancouver: Douglas and McIntyre, 1998):xi.
52. On the details of the Calgary Programme, see Alan Whitehorn, *Canadian Socialism: Essays on the CCF-NDP* (Toronto: Oxford University Press, 1992):35–8.
53. Ibid., 38–45.
54. See reports of the chief electoral officer, various, and for Ontario, see Roderick Lewis, *Centennial Edition of a History of the Electoral Districts, Legislatures and Ministries of the Province of Ontario, 1867–1968* (Toronto: Queen's Printer, 1968).
55. See Thorburn, *Party Politics in Canada*.
56. For a more detailed account, see Alan Whitehorn, *Canadian Socialism: Essays on the CCF/NDP* (Toronto: Oxford University Press, 1992):Appendix.
57. Discussed in Penner, *The Canadian Left*, 25, 32.
58. F.H. Underhill, *The Image of Confederation* (Toronto: CBC, 1964):63.
59. In conversation with P.J. Smith, Victoria, summer 1982.
60. This early left connection in Nova Scotia is described in several places; see, for example, McNaught's *A Prophet in Politics*, 73–180.
61. Calculated from Thorburn, *Party Politics in Canada*.
62. For a more complete account of leftist protest in Atlantic Canada, see P.J. Smith and M.W. Conley, 'Empty Harbours, Empty Dreams? The Democratic Socialist Tradition in Atlantic Canada', in *Building the Co-operative Commonwealth: Essays on the Democratic Socialist Tradition in Canada*, edited by J. William Brennan (Regina: Canadian Plains Research Centre, 1985):227–51. Here the '?' is returned to the title on Atlantic Canada; it was omitted in Brennan's *Building the Co-operative Commonwealth*.
63. Whitehorn, *Canadian Socialism*.
64. Nelson Wiseman, 'The Eclipse of the NDP', review in *Labour/Le Travail* 35 (Spring 1995):282–3, 281–95. On the policy legacy issue, see also Lynn McDonald,

The Party That Changed Canada: The New Democratic Party Then and Now (Toronto: Macmillan, 1987).

65. For a detailed examination of the early Saskatchewan experience, see, among others, S.M. Lipset's *Agrarian Socialism: The Co-operative Commonwealth Federation in Saskatchewan* (Berkeley: University of California, 1950).

66. Douglas served as provincial premier from the summer of 1944 to the autumn of 1961 when he stepped down to take up the leadership of the CCF's successor, the New Democratic Party. Woodrow Lloyd continued as CCF (then NDP) premier in Saskatchewan until 1964 when the Liberals were returned for two terms. From Loren Simerl, 'Provincial Election Results', in *Politics: Canada*, 5th edn, edited by Paul Fox (Toronto: McGraw-Hill Ryerson, 1982):655–93; and Chris Dunn, *Provinces: Canadian Political Politics* (Peterborough: Broadview, 1996):520.

67. There are numerous accounts of the development of the Co-operative Commonwealth Federation and its successor, the New Democratic Party: see, for example, Walter D. Young, *The Anatomy of a Party: The National CCF* (Toronto: University of Toronto Press, 1969); and Brennan, ed., *Building the Co-operative Commonwealth*.

68. See Whitehorn, *Canadian Socialism*, 45–50.

69. Ibid., 50.

70. See, for example, Leo Zakuta, *A Protest Movement Becalmed* (Toronto: University of Toronto, 1964); Young, *The Anatomy of a Party*; and Michael Cross, *The Decline and Fall of a Good Idea: CCF-NDP Manifestos, 1932 to 1969* (Toronto: New Hogtown, 1974).

71. See his 'Historical Writings on the CCF-NDP: The "Protest Movement Becalmed" Tradition', in Whitehorn, *Canadian Socialism*, 18–34.

72. Ibid.

73. Report of the chief electoral officer, Canada, on the 1962 general election.

74. Various sources cover this period including F.C. Engerlmann and M. Schwartz, *Political Parties and the Canadian Social Structure* (Scarborough: Prentice-Hall, 1967); John Courtney, *Voting in Canada* (Scarborough: Prentice-Hall, 1967); and Desmond Morton, *The New Democrats: 1961–1986—The Politics of Change* (Toronto: Copp Clark, 1986).

75. Trudeau's most popular 1968 leadership campaign button said simply 'It's Spring'. It was a theme of renewal that Trudeau successfully used at both the convention and in the subsequent general election. Author's conversation with Trudeau, Ottawa, April 1968.

76. P.J. Smith's interview with Senator Michael Kirby, Ottawa, April 1986.

77. See Janine Brodie, 'From Waffles to Grits: A Decade in the Life of the New Democratic Party', in H.G. Thorburn, *Party Politics in Canada*, 5th edn (Scarborough: Prentice-Hall, 1985):205–17.

78. See Terry Morley, *Secular Socialists: The CCF/NDP in Ontario, a Biography* (Montreal and Kingston: McGill-Queen's University Press, 1984), especially 211–20, for an account of both the initial popularity of the Waffle notions and the subsequent break in the party over it as a 'Manifesto'.

79. Though a long-time CCF/NDP representative and party official, Lewis was a somewhat enigmatic figure. He was closely associated with the 1956 Winnipeg Declaration, which was widely seen as a watering down of the principles of the socialist movement contained in the Regina Manifesto. His ongoing involvement

in fighting radical leftists within the trade unions and the party had created some tensions. He had also helped organize the rethinking of some of the party's ideas in the late 1960s; some of this rethinking—as expressed in the Waffle Manifesto—had produced a much more radical vision of the NDP and considerable internal wrangling. See Bob Hackett, 'The Waffle Conflict in the NDP', in *Party Politics in Canada*, 4th edn, edited by H.G. Thorburn (Scarborough: Prentice Hall, 1979); and Brodie, 'From Waffles to Grits', 205–17.

80. For a complete account of CCF/NDP electoral fortunes, see Whitehorn, *Canadian Socialism*, Appendix.

81. On the rise of the post-Keynesian neoconservative alternative, see Peter Self, *Government by the Market? The Politics of Public Choice* (Boulder: Westview, 1993).

82. From Dunn, *Provinces*, 521, and Simerl, 'Provincial Election Results', 678–81. Schreyer captured just twenty-eight seats (with 38.3 per cent of the votes) to twenty-nine for the 'combined' opposition (twenty-two for the Tories; five for the Liberals; one for the Socreds; and one for 'other'). When he ran again in 1973, Schreyer managed 42.3 per cent support across the province and thirty-one of the fifty-seven seats, with the Conservatives again second. (His government was subsequently defeated by the Tories, led by Sterling Lyon, in 1977. Lyon's one term was superseded by Howard Pawley, who led the NDP in government in Manitoba from November 1981 to May 1988.)

83. According to two officials who worked for the NDP in Saskatchewan during this period, this even included passing anonymous information that was mildly embarrassing to the Liberal government to the Conservatives when it looked as if the Tories might slip off the electoral map. The NDP vote in 1964, when it lost power, was at 40.2 per cent; in that election, the Social Credit vote provincially fell from 12.6 per cent to just 0.6 per cent. And despite losing again to the Liberals in 1967, the NDP vote actually increased to 44.3 per cent (versus 45.6 per cent for the Liberals). In the 1971 contest, Blakeney and the NDP captured 55 per cent of all votes in what was essentially a two-party race. Thereafter, according to a number of Saskatchewan party officials, Blakeney succeeded in winning the 1975 and 1978 general elections—despite lower (40.1 per cent and 48.1 per cent) support—through policy innovation, sound management, and ensuring that the now-traditional third party in the province managed to split the non-NDP vote. The latter strategy worked up to a point—the PCs moved from 2.1 per cent in 1971 to 27.6 per cent in 1975 and 38.1 per cent (and second place) in 1978—because, with the provincial Liberals in self-destruction by the late 1970s, the Tories (under Grant Devine) defeated the NDP in April 1982. They were to stay in power until their own self-destruction in the early 1990s. Roy Romanow, Blakeney's former attorney-general, brought the NDP back to power provincially in November 1991.

84. For example, Barrett was responsible for modernizing governmental structures. See T. Morley et al., *The Reins of Power: Governing British Columbia* (Vancouver: Douglas and McIntyre, 1983); Paul Tennant, 'The NDP Government in British Columbia: Unaided Politicians in an Unaided Cabinet', *Canadian Public Policy* 3, no. 3 (Autumn 1977); and Patrick Smith, 'Beyond Lotusland and Fantasyland: Public Policy and Perceptions of Governance in British Columbia', in *Canadian Politics*, edited by James Bickerton and Alain Gagnon (Peterborough: Broadview, 1994):506–26. The perception of Barrett was of a politician continuing a

tradition of BC bombast. The reality was more complex. Barrett was replaced by W.A.C. Bennett's son Bill, leading the Socreds in power between 1975 and 1986. Bennett's successors (Bill Vander Zalm and Rita Johnston) oversaw the demise of BC's post-First World War governing party, allowing the NDP to return to power in 1991 (under Mike Harcourt) and retain it—a first for the BC NDP (under Glen Clark) in 1996.

85. In 1979 the NDP elected one MP from the territories on a 29 per cent vote share, eight in BC (32 per cent of the votes), four from Saskatchewan (37 per cent support), five from Manitoba (31 per cent of the votes), and six from Ontario (21 per cent support).

86. P.J. Smith's interview with former Trudeau constitutional adviser, Senator Michael Kirby, Ottawa, April 1986.

87. See L. Cohen, P. Warwick, and P.J. Smith, *The Vision and the Game: Making the Canadian Constitution* (Calgary: Detselig, 1987) for a discussion of the role of the NDP and their 'conditions' for supporting the Trudeau package on the Constitution. Information also provided by P.J. Smith's interviews with Jean Chrétien, Vancouver, March 1986; with Svend Robinson, Vancouver, March 1986; with Michael Kirby, Ottawa, April 1986; and with Allan Blakeney, May 1986.

88. See report of the chief electoral officer, Canada, 32nd general election, 1981. The exact NDP vote share figures in the western provinces and Ontario were as follows: 36 per cent in Saskatchewan, 35 per cent in BC, 33 per cent in Manitoba, 31 per cent in the territories, and 21 per cent in Ontario.

89. See M. Eagles, et al., *The Almanac of Canadian Politics*, (Peterborough: Broadview, 1991), passim.

90. On some of the reasons for this, for example, Alan Whitehorn, 'The NDP Election Campaign: Dashed Hopes', in *The Canadian General Election of 1988*, edited by Alan Frizzell, Jon Pammett, and Anthony Westell (Ottawa: Carleton University Press, 1989):43–53.

91. On this, see Richard Johnston et al., *Letting the People Decide: Dynamics of a Canadian Federal Election* (Montreal and Kingston: McGill-Queen's University Press, 1992):20–1. According to then party leader Ed Broadbent, the party consensus was that emphasis on free trade could benefit the party in the West, but might produce very negative electoral consequences in Central Canada (P.J. Smith's discussion with Ed Broadbent, February 1999).

92. In the first weeks of the 1988 campaign, the Liberals challenged their leader and had several other public relations disasters. See ibid., 20 and particularly 23–7.

93. Ibid., 28.

94. Union leaders, such as Leo Gerrard of the United Steelworkers, confirmed this in reaction to such expressions of labour discontent by offering apologies to NDP leader Ed Broadbent days after the 1988 electoral result (P.J. Smith's conversation with Ed Broadbent, February 1999).

95. Whitehorn, 'The NDP Election Campaign', 43–53.

96. Alan Whitehorn is clearest on the features of this shift. See ibid., 46–7.

97. Ibid., 51–2.

98. See Eagles et al., *The Almanac of Canadian Politics*.

99. See Alan Whitehorn, 'The NDP's Quest For Survival' in *The Canadian General Election of 1993*, edited by A. Frizzell, J. Pammett, and A. Westell (Ottawa: Carleton University Press, 1994):43–55, on the NDP and the 1993 contest.

100. See Whitehorn, 'The NDP Election Campaign', 45–6.
101. It is a view shared by former NDP leader Ed Broadbent, as expressed in 'Why Canada Lost on the 1995 Referendum', Department of Political Science Seminar, Simon Fraser University, 27 October 1997.
102. Whitehorn, 'The NDP's Quest For Survival', 47–8.
103. See Jon Pammett, 'Tracking the Votes', in *The Canadian General Election of 1993*, edited by Alan Frizzel, Jon Pammett, and Anthony Westell (Ottawa: Carleton University Press, 1994):143–59.
104. Alan Whitehorn, 'Alexa McDonough and Atlantic Breakthrough For the New Democratic Party', in *The Canadian General Election of 1997*, edited by Alan Frizzell and Jon Pammett (Toronto: Dundurn Press, 1997):91–110.
105. Ibid. See also Jon Pammett's 'The Voters Decide' and 'The Results', in *The Canadian General Election of 1997*, edited by Alan Frizzell and Jon Pammett (Toronto: Dundurn Press, 1997):225–48 and 251–84.
106. Ibid.
107. This is argued by David Laycock in his forthcoming book on Reform. Reform's relative success in limiting the right party political terms will affect subsequent electoral success. The NDP's increasing success in Atlantic Canada—where NDP MLAs sat in all four provincial legislatures at the end of the century—represents a more positive counterpoint.
108. Wiseman, 'The Eclipse of the NDP', 281.
109. This is Gordon Laird's *Slumming It at the Rodeo* motif.
110. See Frank Dabbs, *Preston Manning: The Roots of Reform* (Vancouver: Greystone/ Douglas & McIntyre, 1997).

CHAPTER 5

THE REFORM PARTY: WESTERN POPULIST ROOTS, NEO-LIBERAL DESIGNS

While the Reform Party is clearly a product of the late third party system, some of its antecedents (particularly those of western protest) found expression much earlier in Canadian history. Some of these have links with the agrarian protests of the pre- and immediate post-First World War era; other closer links can be found in the rise of more right-wing regional dissent, particularly its party expression in Social Credit, especially in western Canada; additional (particularly ideological) elements are unique to modern expression, such as in the Reform Party itself and in political efforts to 'Unite the Right' in Canada. These ideological elements have roots both within Canada and beyond Canada's borders in broader neoconservative trends, parties, and governments.

The 1993 Canadian general election saw the emergence of two new parties with strong regional protest roots: from Quebec (as discussed in Chapter 6) the Bloc Québécois, which attained official Opposition status and, just behind in seats (with all but one of its seats from western Canada), the rightist Reform Party. The roots of Reform's success, which had been planted in the West during the 1988 election, bore electoral and parliamentary fruit in 1993. Reform placed third, with fifty-two MPs elected, two behind the official Opposition Bloc Québécois.[1]

This legislative focus is not without significance; however, it fails to provide a full explanation of what happened during the 1988, 1993, and 1997 Canadian general elections. The results of the latter election—and the events that followed—provide a slightly longer perspective to assess the position of the Reform Party and its voter base within the fourth party system. Most obviously, the achievement of official Opposition status in 1997 meant more than debates about whether Reform Party leader Preston Manning should move into the oft-scorned Stornoway (official residence of the leader of the Opposition in Ottawa), or whether re-elected Reform MPs should opt out of (or into) the parliamentary pension plan. The 1997 result actually suggested something considerably more essential for the Reform Party: namely, that

Reform was again first in the West, from where *all* sixty of its parliamentary seats emerged and where its support remained strong. In that sense, the 1997 results reflected more continuity than discontinuity in Reform Party support. Indeed, Reform's vote total over two elections remained virtually unchanged —up only 0.6 per cent nationally between 1993 and 1997.

In 1997 Reform increased its legislative seat total from fifty-two to sixty while at the same time losing its only Ontario seat and having its overall voter support remain virtually static. It was unable to make any break-through in either Ontario or Atlantic Canada. And despite a few token can-didacies in Quebec, there was no serious attempt to appeal to Quebec voters or to voters elsewhere who were sympathetic to Quebec's concerns; instead, Reform preferred to play the anti-Quebec card to solidify its support base in the West when it showed signs of softening in the midst of the 1997 cam-paign.[2] That represented a more traditional antecedent of western protest.

Other elements of the Reform Party phenomenon emerged from broader comparative ideological strains. While the latter has found clear expression in Canadian corporate culture where it has pressed for fiscal conservatism and a limited state, this component also reflects a far broader global right-wing business challenge to Keynesian interventionism, preferring what Peter Self has called *Government By the Market*.[3] Understanding both regional protest antecedents and neoconservative ideological elements is essential to making a determination about Reform's place in Canada's party system. Reform's use of former western regional protest imagery often simply reflects the party's best effort to disguise the larger rightist ideological agenda.[4] These attempts to redefine Canadian politics along ideological lines repre-sent a fairly fundamental challenge to more traditional brokerage notions of parties and their roles in Canada.

This chapter examines continuities and discontinuities for the rightist Reform Party. Its focus is on the extent and nature of continuity and change in Reform Party support—and in the Canadian party system itself.[5] It also provides a brief assessment of local dimensions of Reform Party support during the Canadian general elections of 1988, 1993, and 1997. As the only three elections contested by Reform at the end of the twentieth century, the actual electoral results, the matter of Reform's antecedents, and distinctive elements of the Reform phenomenon are all worth noting; so are more recent events, including the February 1999 'Unite the Right' convention in Ottawa led by Preston Manning and the Reform Party.

Retrospective: The First and Second Party Systems[6]

While the history of Reform as a political party in Canada is recent, it can be argued that a number of antecedents, particularly those of western protest, emerged considerably earlier. Elements of the Progressive movement, United

Farmers, and certainly the rise of the right-wing Social Credit Party nationally, as well as provincially in western Canada, can all be seen as containing harbingers of the grassroots reality and imagery of the modern Reform Party in Canada. As a relatively new party of protest, the provincial elements of this western dissent figure more prominently in understanding Reform's current position in the Canadian party system than is the case for either the Liberals or Conservatives. Often this western discontent was first and foremost a provincial expression of regional discontent, which subsequently affected federal politics, whether with the United Farmers, the Social Credit, or the Co-operative Commonwealth Federation.

There was little in the first party system (1867–1917) that suggested much about political party expression of western discontent. That is not to say there was no discontent. Even before provincial status for Saskatchewan and Alberta in 1905—and earlier in Manitoba and British Columbia—the hardship of opening the West was apparent in its regional political discourses. As described by Walter Young, 'protest movements and the political parties that sometimes grow out of them do not spring fully armed from the furrowed brow of discontent. They grow and develop slowly, particularly when they represent—as all significant movements must—a break with conventional behaviour.'[7] While different in British Columbia and the Prairies, the key factors in western discontent were predominantly geographic and economic.

In geographic terms, both isolation and physical setting presented considerable challenges in both 'regions' of western Canada (British Columbia and the Prairies) and helped shape economic and political relationships. Patterns of immigration and population settlement also played a part in shaping Canadian political parties in the West. There were three predominant sources: Manitoba was settled between 1896 and 1911 by large numbers of migrants from Ontario; Saskatchewan and British Columbia attracted large numbers of European (especially British) immigrants, who had experience with an increasingly important Labour movement and party in their British homeland; and Alberta was influenced by a significant influx of Americans from adjacent plains states, which often included former members of US farm organizations such as the Grange or more overtly political movements like the Non Partisan League and the Progressive Party.[8] The impact of these initial dynamics persist even into current assessments of western Canadian electoral politics. Wiseman, for example, has classified the provincial political culture of Manitoba as 'the Ontario of the Prairies', Saskatchewan as 'the Prairies' Britain', and Alberta as 'the Prairies' America'.[9]

The western Canadian economy, which differed significantly between BC and the Prairie region, had two central ingredients in common: (1) resource dependency and (2) outside control. On the Prairies, an economy developed that was initially almost entirely wheat-dependent, with the 1 million homesteaders who settled the Canadian plains in the pre-First World War years of this century 'almost entirely dependent upon . . . one factor—the price of wheat—[a factor] quite beyond their control'.[10] With producer costs controlled by powerful eastern-based economic interests such as the Canadian Pacific Railway and its subsidiaries, there was little interest in either of the two national parties that dominated the first party era to represent farmers' interests. Economic reciprocity with the United States, at times championed by the Liberal Party, suggested the possibility of some economic relief for Prairie farmers from high-priced eastern Canadian manufactured goods, but the tariff protection for eastern industries remained intact, even when the Liberals were in power. The result was predictable: there was a growing and deep-seated distrust of both the traditional political parties and of a governmental system dominated by eastern élite interests.[11] As summarized by Young:

> ... it was clear to the farmer that the real control of his destiny was in the hands of those who owned the land companies and the elevator companies, and those who ran the Grain Exchange. It was also clear ... that these people had more political influence. The parties were controlled by the same financial interests in the east that controlled the companies with whom the farmers had to deal. It made little difference to the farmer which party was in power ... both were the same—singularly unresponsive to his needs. The real centres of power were in the east and easterners had a vested interest in keeping the western farmer in a condition of feudal dependence.[12]

In British Columbia and in the major urban centres of western Canada, the economic base was different but the condition of resource dependency remained. Here, where there was more economic diversity (with mining, timber, and fishery sectors), the working circumstances of the labour force produced increased class consciousness, a nascent trade union movement, and a growing disassociation from the two old-line parties. Without institutional or legislative protections, workers faced low wages, industry shutdowns during periods of low commodity prices, and few advantages in the 'distribution of rewards'.[13] This was especially the case in British Columbia, where stronger trade union institutions developed. Despite this, as noted in Chapter 1, no real ideological realignment occurred in Canadian politics; instead, the two traditional parties were able to resist class definitions of politics with ethnocultural and regional alternatives. The relative failure of initial agrarian efforts to transcend ethnolinguistic/religious differences simply compounded the political failures of organized labour. Electoral politics in the first party era were tested by regional, class, and ideological strains, but traditional partisan alignments persisted.

The social and economic conditions of relative powerlessness, combined with a sense of isolation and a clear perception that existing parties and governmental institutions were unresponsive to farmers' or labour's interests, provided the basis for emerging farmers' organizations and an increasingly strong trade union response. Yet despite a shared sense of domination by eastern-based economic interests and inadequate political representation of their concerns, there was little initial interaction between farmers and workers during the first party era. This was partly a product of perceptions of economic status: farmers, for example, often employed labour and at times expressed concerns about unions and collective bargaining for wages and other benefits. Farmers also often saw themselves as owners/entrepreneurs with interests that were different from those of labour. In parts of the West, such as Alberta, this produced a 'largely *petit-bourgeois* class structure of independent agrarian producers'.[14] As a result, both farmers and labour were more intent on developing and solidifying their own institutions during this pre-First World War period.

While it preceded political party activity, this western discontent did find expression in voter turnout. In 1896, for example, voter turnout was between 68 per cent (Nova Scotia) and 73 per cent (PEI) in the Maritimes and 60 per cent and 66 per cent in Ontario and Quebec respectively; overall national turnout was 62 per cent. In contrast, in Manitoba, despite the bitterness of the Manitoba schools question, which dominated the national campaign, voter turnout was just 50 per cent; in British Columbia the figure was even lower at only 39 per cent.[15] Clearly, frustration at the lack of major party representation of western interests resulted in voters who registered discontent by not voting. Turnout did improve in Manitoba after 1904 and through to 1917, equalling or surpassing most provinces and the national average; however in British Columbia, with the exception of 1917 (an 80 per cent turnout), voter participation remained between 8 per cent and 18 per cent below the national average. When Saskatchewan and Alberta gained provincial status in 1905, voter turnout was also somewhat—and regularly—lower than the Canadian average in each of the general elections between then and 1917.[16] This muted western alienation was a strong undercurrent within the first party system even though ethnocultural brokerage within national politics remained the national norm.

In terms of electoral and party expression of this western discontent, farmers demonstrated more initial capacity at overt political action. Apart from a few independent labour candidacies, the United Farmers and then Progressives of the early second party era were the first to challenge traditional two-party Conservative/Liberal hegemony.

In the second party system (1921–57), the two-party national political template was broken beginning in Ontario (1919–23), where the United Farmers of Ontario (UFO) elected sufficient numbers[17] to form a UFO provincial government under E.C. Drury.[18] This was followed by other United Farmers provincial governments: United Farmers of Alberta (UFA) (1921–35) and United Farmers of Manitoba (UFM) (1922–8).[19] In Saskatchewan Non Partisans, Labour, Progressives, and other protest candidates won seats (sixteen of sixty-three in 1921, ten in 1925, and eleven in 1929), but except for the coalition government of 1929–34, Saskatchewan Liberals held power provincially throughout the decade.[20] These provincial expressions of western protest were fundamental to subsequent federal iterations.

In federal party terms, western/agrarian protest provided the impetus for the break-up of the traditional two-party system. Following provincial farmers' efforts, the 1921 general election returned enough Progressives to Parliament to let them capture second place with sixty-five seats (and 23 per cent of the votes).[21] This Progressive vote came from more than western Canada; in Ontario, where United Farmers were already in power provincially, the Progressives captured twenty-four federal seats and 28 per cent of the votes. But the Progressives did particularly well on the Prairies, winning twelve seats (and 44 per cent support) in Manitoba, fifteen of sixteen seats in Saskatchewan (and 61 per cent of the vote), and eleven of twelve seats in Alberta (57 per cent of the votes). In British Columbia the picture was more mixed: the Progressives won just two BC seats and 9 per cent of the vote, while union-based labour and socialist candidates captured 10 per cent of the vote.[22] The economic differences and institutional forms being developed in BC versus the rest of the West clearly had an impact in the 1921 federal contest. As discussed in Chapter 4, this BC/Prairie split was a pattern of difference that would remain throughout this second party era. Despite their parliamentary standing, the Progressives, eschewing traditional party politics, did not take on the role of official Opposition.[23]

As Laycock and others have argued, this initial agrarian protest represented early party expressions of Prairie populism and western discontent; subsequent labour/socialist and rightist dissent produced electoral breakthroughs by both the Co-operative Commonwealth Federation and Social Credit. As discussed in Chapter 4, a variety of 'populisms' formed the ideological bases of agrarian, cooperative, labour, and socialist political action related to the Co-operative Commonwealth Federation and its successor, the New Democratic Party. Others—at times the same ones—provided a base for rightist electoral responses, such as with Social Credit, and subsequent party structures, such as Reform. As such, these 'populisms' were often conflicting; they were also often overlapping.

Laycock has identified four such populist forms, each of which found electoral and party expression in western Canada both federally and provincially:[24]

1. *Crypto-Liberalism:* 'A western, rurally inclined, more socially progressive and politically experimental version of Ontario Grit Liberalism. . . . [It] marshalled and represented prairie symbols and traditions of opposition to central Canada's domination, occasionally taking clues from Clear grit reformism of mid-nineteenth-century Ontario. . . . Crypto-Liberalism generated the lowest common denominator—rurally oriented hinterland regionalism—in prairie populist discourse. . . . It was given form and substance by the National Progressive Party, and by prairie provincial Liberal parties. . . .'[25] It found expression also in the UFO, UFM, and parts of the UFA. It also 'broke least with contemporary Liberal party ideology and policy perspectives in Canada'.[26]

2. *Radical democratic populism:* 'Its intellectual roots were primarily rural western American and entailed a "co-operativist", anti-capitalist perspective on questions of economic and political power. A principled rejection of party politics and an insistence on functionally co-ordinated delegate democracy leading into a group government were the most distinctive aspects of this populism. The most complete ... development of the radical democratic themes took place within the United Farmers of Alberta, with Henry Wise Wood and William Irvine as the principal "theoreticians".'[27] Irvine linked this populism with social democratic populism in the CCF; Wood worked through the Progressives and the UFA. United Farmers, Non Partisan League, and grain-growers' cooperatives were early expressions of this populism.

3. *Social democratic populism:* 'Its most obvious features were rejection of the two major parties as instruments of eastern business, support for state ownership of major industries, advocacy of a farmer-labour alliance against organized business and support for the full extension of democratic rights and practices within the parliamentary system. It was gradualist [with no] rigid orthodoxy.' It argued, as a minimum, for 'a redistribution of economic goods and societal resources ... among classes and communities to make equality of opportunity reality'. For social democratic populists, 'systematic class power in major societal institutions prevents the realization of meaningful equality'. It 'developed through the early efforts of the Non Partisan League in Alberta and Saskatchewan, the small urban labour parties across the prairies ... socialists working within grain producers co-operatives, and activists in the United Farmers ...' Its electoral/party expression was primarily through the CCF.[28]

4. *Plebiscitarian populism:* 'The least variable and most unorthodox prairie populism was undoubtedly the "plebiscitarian" populism of the Alberta Social Credit League. [It] accepted a full extension of the technocratic logic, since its democratic vision was as unchallenging as it was unrealistic.' Given particular expression by Alberta Social Credit Premier William Aberhart (1935–43), it contained notions of 'a general will, translated into specifics and programs by "experts", as the essence of democratic government'. As expressed by Social Credit in Alberta, it was opposed to central Canadian domination and presented itself as 'radical, class-transcendent, morally-justified ... fully consistent with the basic themes of "prairie protest" crusade'.[29] Apart from Social Credit, projection of this plebiscitarian populism has continued to find expression in the modern, western-based Reform Party.[30] At question is whether Reform's right-wing, populist image is more mirage than substance.

During the second party system, several of these populist strains competed in different United Farmers organizations and, where elected, in their governments. This represented the 'dynamism' of such movement/party entities, but also ultimately contributed to their organizational and political demise. As noted, these divergent populisms stemmed in part from different patterns of settlement and immigration to the West during the first party era. Clearly, these reflected divisions were more regional than ethnocultural. In some cases, class and ideology were at play. But in the end, each failed to make a full and decisive breakthrough. Continuity ultimately prevailed over volatility, even though new political discoveries and party formations were introduced.

As discussed in more detail in Chapter 4, the Progressive phenomenon was short-lived. Their ideological eclecticism and principled rejection of the party organizational form proved their undoing. The ideological differences and overlaps were there from the beginning: crypto-Liberals essentially sought reform of the Liberal Party; small 'c' conservative elements drifted between Liberals, Conservatives, and subsequently (in the 1930s) Social Credit; and agrarian socialists and cooperativists formed one founding element of the Co-operative Commonwealth Federation, also in the 1930s.[31] In the 1925 Canadian general election, Progressive support fell to 9 per cent and twenty-four seats, twenty-two of these from the three Prairie provinces. A year later, voter support slipped again to a meagre 5 per cent and twenty-two seats, six of these from the Prairies. (A further eleven United Farmers MPs were elected from Alberta.) In its 'last' election in 1930, only 3 per cent of Canadians voted for Progressive and United Farmers candidates, returning just fifteen MPs. By then, the various populisms that had spawned the national movement began to find new political—and party—homes. The Progressives' leaders drifted into other associations and even into the leadership of other political parties, as well as into related organizations such as the wheat pools.

Apart from increasing ideological differences, not least among the reasons for the demise of the Progressive and United Farmers movement was its organizational uncertainty. The agrarian movement's longer-term political impact was negatively affected by those elements within it that eschewed organizational structure. For many, including UFO Premier E.C. Drury of Ontario, this proved to be the Achilles' heel of the movement.[32] By the 1935 federal election, alternative party forms had replaced the Progressive option: Social Credit, in its first national election, won seventeen seats; the CCF, also in its first election, won seven; Reconstruction, newly split from the Conservatives, elected only its leader (H.H. Stevens) and siphoned votes from the Tories; 'others' (including a United Farmers-Labour candidate in Ontario) won an additional seven seats. The total vote share of these new contestants in 1935 was 25 per cent, just slightly higher than that recorded by the Progressives at their peak in 1921.[33] That same year, the last strictly United Farmers government (in Alberta) fell victim to the rising tide of Social Credit in that province.[34]

If the Progressives dominated third-party formation in the early years of the second party system, it was the Co-operative Commonwealth Federation and Social Credit that provided the main non-traditional party options during the remainder of this era. Christian and Campbell have argued that apart from its populist roots in western Canada, Social Credit had one other thing in common with early leftist/socialist protest: 'both provided perspectives on what was happening [during the Depression] that absolved the individual worker of the blame for his or her plight'.[35] The CCF experience has been discussed in Chapter 4. More directly relevant to the later Reform Party phenomenon is the experience of Social Credit—both provincially and federally. As with the United Farmers, then the Progressives, the provincial Social Credit experience, particularly in Alberta, was fundamental to subsequent federal Social Credit success.[36]

Apart from its politically 'modest' origins in the 1920 writings of English mechanical engineer Major C.H. Douglas,[37] the idea of 'social credit' found a political home in parts of the United Farmers of Alberta. When UFA governments (1922–35) made little attempt to implement Douglas's ideas, they were picked up and promoted by popular lay preacher and radio host William Aberhart.[38] Aberhart had become an 'instant convert' to social credit when he read Douglas's 'A plus B theorem' in 1932. Using his well-known 'Back to the Bible Hour' radio broadcast, Aberhart popularized 'social credit' as a solution to many of the ills of the Depression of the 1930s. He formed a political party based on the idea and achieved instant success in Alberta, where Social Credit formed the government, with Aberhart as premier. In 1935, in its very first election, voters elected fifty-six Social Credit MLAs to the sixty-three-seat Alberta Legislative Assembly on 54.2 per cent of the vote.[39] This was a pattern of one-party dominance that was already well established in Alberta, one that would repeat itself in subsequent provincial and federal elections, the latter characterized by a drift to the Conservative Party and, more recently, to Reform.

In the same year (1935) that Social Credit swept to power in Alberta, national Social Credit managed to win seventeen seats and third place parliamentary standing in Ottawa. It did this with just 4 per cent of the votes nationally, less than half the 384,000 votes gathered by the new Reconstruction Party. Social Credit benefited from the vagaries of the first-past-the-post electoral system by concentrating most of its votes in western Canada, particularly Alberta.[40] This provided Social Credit with fifteen MPs from Alberta (where the party won 47 per cent of the votes) and two seats in Saskatchewan (where it tallied 18 per cent of the vote). Drawing on the appeal of Alberta Social Credit, the federal party won support across most of that province, which was still locked in the grip of the Depression.

The advantages of concentrating votes were clear, with Social Credit the 1935 beneficiary. In that same election, which was also its first, the CCF managed more than double (9 per cent) the Social Credit vote, but the new party won only seven seats because (like the Reconstruction Party) its votes were spread out across much more of the country. Alberta, with Social Credit in government after 1935, would remain the bedrock of party support throughout this second party era.

This same pattern was reflected in the results of 1940. Social Credit again finished third in seats even though it attracted only 3 per cent of the votes nationally. All ten Social Credit seats were from Alberta, a reflection of Aberhart and the emerging provincial party's hegemony in that province.[41] Social Credit's success federally clearly remained dependent upon its provincial success. For one thing, its power base in Alberta and BC provided the federal party with a base of credibility, which was reflected in much of its federal success, except later in Quebec.

When Premier Aberhart died in 1943, Ernest C. Manning, the father of current Reform Party leader Preston Manning, assumed the leadership of the Alberta Social Credit Party. Manning, a former student at Aberhart's Calgary Prophetic Bible Institute, would remain premier of Alberta for a quarter of a century, winning seven more consecutive provincial elections. In the nine electoral victories between 1935 and the party's defeat in 1971, Social Credit in Alberta won 83.4 per cent of all legislative seats—an astounding feat of political dominance.[42] Part of this success provincially was based on Social Credit's virtual abandonment of what Morley has called 'social credit fundamentalism' and its replacement with more traditional 'conservative financial and social policies'.[43]

Elsewhere provincially, Social Credit found success (somewhat later) in British Columbia. In BC, however, the party, led for twenty years (1952–72) by Kelowna hardware merchant W.A.C. Bennett, provided a home for a coalition of anti-CCF (and then NDP) business forces. Bennett represented small 'c' fiscal conservatism and adopted a province-building strategy that provided state support for projects that would open BC to development.[44] By the end of the 1960s, when Social Credit's hegemony in Alberta was coming to a close, it was also in trouble in British Columbia.[45] These provincial troubles in the only two provinces that had produced Social Credit administrations were mirrored in East-West tensions in Social Credit nationally.[46]

From the mid-1930s until the ascendancy of Réal Caouette's Créditistes in 1962–8—the fortunes and activities of Alberta Social Credit and national Social Credit were inextricably linked. Dabbs has concluded that over these several decades, Manning and his closest political adviser, Orvis Kennedy, controlled the federal wing of the party: 'the operations and finances of the national organization were controlled by Orvis Kennedy and Ernest Manning, who, at best, ran it as an Alberta branch plant and, at worst, as an afterthought. . . . As a prairie force in the House of Commons from 1938 to 1962, Social Credit never had the stature or influence of the Progressives or the CCF.'[47]

In the 1945 Canadian general election, Social Credit was 'replaced' as Parliament's 'third party' by a significant upswing in CCF support. By doubling its vote to 16 per cent, the latter more than tripled its parliamentary seats to twenty-eight. Meanwhile, the Social Credit votes remained constant—up just slightly to 4 per cent, enough to add three more MPs. All thirteen Social Credit seats were in Alberta where the party attracted 37 per cent of the votes in 1945, a far cry from the party's insignificant levels of support elsewhere.[48] The exception was Social Credit's 'version' in Quebec. As described in Chapter 6, in a 1946 by-election, the Union des Electeurs sent Social Credit's first Quebec MP to Ottawa. That MP, Réal Caouette, would return early in the third party system to play a more prominent parliamentary role as leader of the Quebec-based Ralliement des Créditistes.[49]

In the 1949 and 1953 Canadian general elections, levels of support for Social Credit remained fairly constant, with 4 per cent and 5 per cent of the vote respectively, along with ten and fifteen seats.[50] Social Credit support federally was widespread across Alberta, though strongest in more rural areas, and in urban areas where religious fundamentalism was strong. From the Calgary Prophetic Bible Institute to the national 'Back to the Bible Hour' and the Fundamental Baptist Church, Social Credit maintained close links to Christian fundamentalism.[51] This religious connection, which also characterizes the contemporary Reform Party, represents yet another clear connection between the two political parties and an element of continuity across party systems.

In the 1953 general election, apart from the eleven Alberta Socreds, four MPs were elected in British Columbia, where the party captured 26 per cent of the votes.[52] This coincided with the initial 1952 and 1953 Social Credit victories provincially. With two successive majorities for Mackenzie King's successor, Louis St Laurent, there was little Social Credit could do during this period to affect the day-to-day workings of the federal government. This partisan stability was about to change, however, with the critical realigning elections of 1957 and 1958.

The Third Party System

The prelude to the third party system was the defeat of an arrogant Liberal administration by John Diefenbaker's Conservatives in 1957. As discussed in Chapter 2, the Diefenbaker minority of 1957 was simply a hint of the landslide to follow in 1958. In the 1957 contest, Social Credit support increased nationally from 5 per cent to 7 per cent, with four more MPs elected for a total of nineteen. Social Credit support was again largely confined to western Canada: 24 per cent (six seats) in BC (where W.A.C. Bennett's Social Credit was now firmly entrenched) and 38 per cent (thirteen seats) in Alberta, along with a 10 per cent and 13 per cent vote share in Saskatchewan and Manitoba respectively. Only in Quebec in 1957 was 'other party' support as high (at 11 per cent).

Soon after, however, Social Credit was devastated by the loss of western votes to Diefenbaker's Conservatives, losing all its seats in 1958 and dropping to 2 per cent in the national vote. Even in Alberta and BC, the party was unable to hold any of its seats. As discussed in Chapter 2, Diefenbaker's stunning success was followed by disarray and internal dissension for the Tories. Despite a victory of unprecedented proportions, by 1962 national support for the Conservatives fell by 17 per cent, with a consequent loss of ninety-two seats and a return to minority government status.

Social Credit was able to take advantage of what was now increasing Conservative Party problems. With Albertan Robert Thompson chosen as party leader in 1961, and Quebec's Réal Caouette as deputy leader, Social Credit's national fortunes were revived in 1962. Party support rose from 2 per cent to 10 per cent, electing thirty MPs in the process. This eclipsed the nineteen elected for the NDP, despite the latter's higher vote total of 14 per cent. In a major reversal of historic extra-party relationship, however, twenty-six of these Social Credit MPs were elected in Quebec, where Caouette's Créditistes took 26 per cent of the vote.[53] Both Thompson and Caouette were returned. As discussed in Chapter 6, Caouette had aligned the old Union des Electeurs as a new political party—the Ralliement des Créditistes—in late 1957. Its 1962 electoral success created its own internal party tensions.[54] Support for the Créditistes in Quebec was everywhere, with the significant exception of Montreal.

In 1963 the Social Credit vote stayed at 12 per cent nationally, but six seats were lost; twenty were returned from Quebec and four from the West (two each from BC and Alberta). Rising East-West, French-English tensions within the party produced a party split in 1965. Party support that year slipped to 4 per cent and 5 seats) outside of Quebec, and 5 per cent and nine seats for the Quebec Créditistes. In the continuing circumstances of minority government, however, these small totals were still sufficient for either grouping to tip the parliamentary balance.

The political death of Social Credit outside of Quebec coincided with the May 1967 resignation of Robert Thompson, leaving the western wing of the federal party leaderless. Party fortunes were also affected by the 1968 resignation of Alberta Premier Ernest Manning. In the 1968 federal election Social Credit lost all of its seats and garnered only 1 per cent of the national vote; in Quebec fourteen Créditiste MPs were returned; in 1972 a reunited Social Credit party elected fifteen MPs, all from Quebec, enough to give the party the balance of power. Meanwhile, in its Alberta cradle, only 2 per cent of voters supported Social Credit—electing no one for the second straight election. By the early 1970s, the provincial hegemony that had aided the Social Credit party federally for so long was replaced by Conservative Party dominance in Alberta.

The slide in Alberta and elsewhere in the West was due to many factors: the nearing of the end for long-standing Social Credit regimes in both

Alberta (1971) and BC (1972); the resignation of popular Alberta Premier E.C. Manning in 1968 with no obvious successor; the phenomenon of successive one-party dominance in the province; Manning's own call—in a 1967 publication, *Political Realignment: A Challenge to Thoughtful Canadians*—for a major left/right realignment of Canada's parties, with a preference for coalescing around the Conservatives on the right nationally; the 1967 resignation of party leader Robert Thompson, criticizing the provincial organizations for too little support; tensions between Thompson and Caouette; the subsequent illness and death of Caouette (in 1976); and the re-emergence and re-election of Thompson as a Progressive Conservative.[55]

By the 1970s, Social Credit was a spent force. It managed to elect eleven MPs in 1974, keeping six in 1979. In 1980 only 1 per cent of Canadians voted for Social Credit, which meant the party had no representation in Parliament for only the second time since 1935. Still, after a few short years, others would take up the mantle of both right-wing 'western protest' and the call for political realignment.

Between the slow death of Social Credit and the birth of Reform was a second Progressive Conservative landslide. As discussed in chapters 2 and 6—the Mulroney interlude represented another 'continuity' in Canadian politics (an upward 'spike' in Conservative support), the fourth significant upswing since the end of the first party era in 1917. The initially successful coalition building by Brian Mulroney, linking 'conservatives' from all regions of Canada, including Quebec, would ultimately fail. His efforts would dramatically increase tensions and discontent among Conservative Party supporters, both in the West and elsewhere.

As the 1987 Meech Lake Constitutional Accord was being considered, dormant western voices of discontent were again being raised. And while their message—and their messenger—had a familiar ring, there were ideological and political elements particular to its new expression in the Reform Party.[56]

Reform: 'New Beginnings', 1987–1988

In May 1987, with the Brian Mulroney-led Progressive Conservative government of Canada late in its first mandate, a group of 300 politically disgruntled western Canadians met in Vancouver, British Columbia to discuss a 'new agenda' for Canada. They were motivated by a feeling of being overlooked in constitutional and economic decision making by a federal system that they felt was still dominated by Quebec and Ontario. They were determined to 'reform' that system—for example, through institutional changes such as an elected and equal Canadian Senate—and in doing so to develop a political structure more responsive to western concerns. They called themselves Reformers.[57]

If one of the antecedents of Reform was regional—that of western protest—another more important one was reflected in a more fundamental shift in Canadian politics: the shift from more communitarian, state-centred consciousness to the politics of individualism—whether in rights (as reflected in the 1982 Canadian Charter of Rights and Freedoms) or in market-defined economics and governance. The latter was reflected in the politics of public choice popularized and practised by the Thatcher government in Britain and by American President Ronald Reagan, ideological neoconservatives who were primary antecedents of the Canadian Reform Party experience. In Canada this ideological influence was apparent in some of the policy initiatives of the Mulroney Conservatives and in the studies and policy recommendations of conservative think-tanks such as the Fraser Institute.[58]

In Canada the clearest party expression of this neoconservative wave was put in place at a convention in Winnipeg, Manitoba on 30 October–1 November 1987. The Reform Party of Canada was formed with an initial membership of 3,000, a symbolic rallying cry of 'The West wants in', and Preston Manning, the son of former Alberta Socred Premier Ernest C. Manning, as its leader. Reform's initial platform was a statement of western alienation and anger—for example, over the federal government's decision to award the lucrative CF-18 fighter contract to Canadair of Montreal rather than to the lowest and technically superior bidder, Bristol Aerospace of Winnipeg. It was initially this regional protest, rather than a neoconservative ideological challenge, that motivated Reform's entry into federal politics. Of course, as a new party, claiming these roots was not without benefit for Reform.

In the 1988 Canadian general election, the Reform Party, running candidates only in the four western provinces, managed nine second-place results, all in Alberta. In doing so, they altered the federal electoral map in that province. In the ten federal elections between the 1958 Diefenbaker landslide and Brian Mulroney's own landslide in 1984, Progressive Conservatives had won 94.2 per cent of all federal seats in Alberta. That included all Alberta seats in the five elections between 1972 and 1984—with vote totals ranging from 57 per cent to 69 per cent—the latter in 1984. In 1988 this massive Conservative vote was reduced to a 51.7 per cent vote share; still, twenty-five of twenty-six MPs returned from the province were Tories.

In a province dominated by one-party hegemonies, there were two shifts of note in the 1988 contest. The new Reform Party managed to win 15.3 per cent of the provincial votes and nine second-place finishes. Moreover, in 1988 ten Alberta ridings returned MPs with less than a majority (50 per cent plus one) of the votes cast; while normal in three-plus party contests in most jurisdictions, this change suggested that for the first time in thirty years, Conservative candidates in Alberta faced a real political challenge and even the prospect of electoral defeat. It would not be long in coming.[59]

The first harbinger of a possible Reform breakthrough occurred with a by-election victory (in Beaver River, Alberta) and the unusual spectacle (for

Canada) of an election for a vacant Alberta Senate seat (which was accepted by Prime Minister Brian Mulroney, who was trying to push through his constitutional reform agenda). These provided Reform's initial parliamentary successes. To transform its base of populist discontent from a regional protest to national party status, in 1992 Preston Manning called for the nomination of Reform candidates across the country, with the exception of Quebec. In 1993 Reform managed to run in 209 of the 220 constituencies outside of Quebec.

Unlike the brokerage character of both the Liberal and Conservative parties, Reform's policies and approach to campaigning reflected a fairly distinctive set of social and cultural appeals. These provide for hypotheses concerning the socio-economic, ethnocultural, and religious foundations of its electoral support. Despite continuing efforts of party officials to moderate Reform's image, much has been made by other parties and by the media of Reform's courting of 'racist' and anti-immigrant sentiments within the electorate, evident in both its policies and candidate selections. In the West Vancouver area riding of Capilano-Howe Sound, for example, Manning was faced with a local nomination in 1993 of right-wing journalist Doug Collins, well known for his anti-immigration and anti-gay views. Manning refused to sign Collins's nomination papers. Elsewhere, Reform Party constituency organizations were infiltrated by White supremacists (e.g., York Centre and Beaches-Woodbine in the Toronto area). These early incidences added to the perception of Reform as a party of intolerance.[60]

The Fourth Party System

Early in Reform's existence as a party, Preston Manning was quoted as saying, 'I am building a kite and I need wind for it to fly.'[61] In the 1993 Canadian general election, Reform managed to reach the take-off point in the first-past-the-post plurality electoral system. With 'wind' from 18.7 per cent of the vote nationally, Reform won twenty-two of twenty-six Alberta seats and 52.3 per cent of the province's votes. Only four Edmonton seats went to the Liberals (one by just twelve votes), and only Edmonton Southeast (where longtime Tory MP David Kilgour had switched to the Liberals) had a margin of more than 1 per cent over Reform. In BC twenty-four of thirty-two ridings went to Reform on a 36.4 per cent vote share. This included most of rural British Columbia, but also a dozen seats in suburban Victoria and Vancouver. Four Saskatchewan seats taken by Reform were all agricultural or resource dependent, including the cities of Moose Jaw, Swift Current, Yorkton, and Lloydminster. The one Reform seat in Manitoba was Lisgar, the fifth most agricultural constituency in Canada. Reform also won one seat outside its western base—in Simcoe Centre, Ontario. Overall, Reform placed second in that province with 20.1 per cent of the vote. As throughout the West,

Reform's message played well in rural and suburban Ontario; siphoning votes from the Conservatives and allowing Liberals to win in twenty-five ridings where the margin of victory was less than the Reform vote.[62] A total of fifty-two Reform MPs were elected nationally, just two short of the second-place Bloc Québécois.

In this, the second election contested by Reform, there is some measurable evidence of candidate-specific or local effects. Simcoe Centre in Ontario was certainly distinct for Reform.[63] The strong Reform vote in Calgary South in 1993 was clearly affected by party leader Preston Manning's local candidacy; and Beaver River, the site of Reform's first (by-election) victory was obviously affected by high-profile Reformer Deborah Grey's incumbency; this was continued in 1997. Reform's vote was negatively affected in the Yukon (with NDP leader Audrey McLaughlin's 1993 victory) and in Vancouver Centre (with Prime Minister Kim Campbell). This was even more the case in Vancouver Centre because of high-profile Liberal and NDP candidacies.

However, there are a number of other ridings where local candidate factors do not appear central to any explanation of Reform Party showings: for example, in the northern ridings and in Saskatchewan's Battleford-Meadow Lake and Manitoba's Portage-Interlake there are high concentrations of Aboriginal peoples; Reform's poorer showings here may have been a factor of local resistance to Reform's right-wing policy stances. In Halifax the Liberal incumbent Mary Clancy's strong position on abortion—an issue that had antiabortionists dogging her local campaign—may have helped buoy the Reform vote. Conversely, in 1997 support for a local heroine, NDP leader Alexa McDonough, no doubt helped to reduce Reform support. Further research and analysis of additional elections may help identify other possible explanations of Reform's distinctive performances in particular settings.

Having been elected on a platform of differences from the traditional parties on matters of policy, party discipline, parliamentary behaviour, responsiveness to constituents, and other representational concerns, Reform found its first full term in Parliament trying. The age of sound-bite politics did not lend itself—or, on occasion, lent itself too well—to many party voices sounding forth on major and minor matters of public policy. While some new party representatives performed well, many did not, which resulted in considerable ill-temper in response to the many criticisms that Reform was forced to endure. Reformers were portrayed as unsophisticated, anti-Quebec, uncaring, bigoted, racist, homophobic, antifeminist, fundamentalist, folksy fascists. Some of the party's difficulties were simply self-inflicted, such as BC MP Bob Ringma's call (which was publically supported by Alberta Reform MP Dave Chatters) for sending Blacks and gays to the back of the store so they would not adversely affect sales.[64] When Party leader Manning suspended both of them from caucus briefly, many Reformers asked 'Why are they picking on Bob?'[65]

Many in Reform, such as party strategist Rick Anderson, came to regard the party's early troubles as 'an image problem'.[66] If the intention was to deal with this public perception problem and present a more mainstream image, Reform leader Preston Manning's 1996 commitment to a national referendum on entrenching a total ban on abortions in the Constitution did little to alter the view that the party remains Christian fundamentalist at its core.[67] The party's *Charter Task Force Report*, which called for abolition of the Canadian Charter of Rights and Freedoms' Section 15 (2) affirmative action provisions, and its attack on the policy of multiculturalism also did not help matters.[68] Much of Reform's anger at such criticisms—expressed by both caucus and the membership—was directed at 'the eastern establishment'. The media, 'they contend, at the best of times doesn't give the party a break'.[69]

Despite setbacks, some resignations (including BC's Bob Ringma), and firings (notably Calgary Southeast 'moderate' MP and internal critic of the party's far right, Jan Brown), Reform regrouped after its first parliamentary term.[70] The message for 1997 was 'A Fresh Start'. Reform needed it; however, the party's message remained substantially the same, but with more attention to its image problem. As the party faced the opening of Parliament following the 1997 election, it appeared to have at least partially adjusted: no longer would it use Question Period for lengthy issue presentations, for example; instead, it would play the parliamentary game and engage in forty-five minutes of pure political theatre. Sound-bite politics and aggressive confrontation of ministers would be the order of the day after MPs were instructed to 'think Hollywood' and become more media savvy. For a newly minted Preston Manning, the lesson learned was that 'question period is not conducive to putting forward constructive alternatives. It's essentially a place where you can hold the government accountable for its own failures.' This view was echoed by Reformer Jim Hart and his caucus colleagues: 'we have come to the reality that Question Period lends itself to more negative attacks'.[71] The abandonment of an initial party commitment to 'a new level of decorum and constructive, non-confrontational behaviour' in favour of new marching orders to be 'more dramatic, combative and nasty' was more about the politics of style than changing the substance of party positions.

In assessing the basic results of the 1988 and 1993 Canadian general elections, certain electoral patterns clearly remained, just as new ones emerged. In 1988 Reform elected no MPs and garnered a mere 2.1 per cent of the national votes, fewer than independents/other party support. However, Reform focused on a range of traditional western complaints—such as the unresponsiveness of federal institutions—and gave clearer expression to the neoconservative politics of the 'farther right'. When Conservative John Dahmer died just before being able to take up the seat he won in 1988, Reform claimed its first parliamentary victory in the subsequent December 1988 Alberta by-election. The new MP for Beaver River, Deborah Grey, proved an able representative and parliamentarian and subsequently served as

House leader and deputy leader of the Reform Party. Following that, and the passage of a Senatorial Selection Act by the provincial Conservative government of Don Getty, Brian Mulroney subsequently 'allowed' the Senate appointment of Stan Waters, the Reform candidate chosen in a special senatorial election by the Alberta electorate.[72] Mulroney, still hunting for support for his Meech Lake constitutional package, had hoped that this action might demonstrate both good will and federal responsiveness to western concerns. To date, Waters (now deceased) has remained Canada's only 'elected' senator. The failure of the Meech Lake Accord and its Charlottetown successor, and the resignation/defeat of the Mulroney/Campbell Conservatives in 1993 spelled an end to such efforts at megaconstitutional change and to Ottawa's good will towards such innovations as elected senators.[73]

In 1993 the regional Reform Party, running on a platform of 'fiscal, constitutional and parliamentary reform', took more votes nationally than either the Conservatives or the Bloc (18.7 per cent), but won two fewer seats than the Bloc Québécois.[74] 'Other' party and independent candidates saw their vote support almost triple in 1993 (from 2.6 per cent in 1988 to 6.6 per cent), most notably through the intervention of several minor party groupings. Fringe parties—such as the National Party, the Greens, and the 'yogic-flying' Natural Law Party—made some difference in a number of ridings across the country. Interestingly, and not entirely understood, the voter turnout over the two general elections fell from 75.3 per cent to 69.6 per cent, perhaps mirroring the much more dramatic electoral disengagement typical of the United States.

In anticipation of the 1997 election, Reform unveiled a six-point plan in October 1996. The party's intention was clear—to capture official Opposition status in the upcoming general election. The plan was called *A Fresh Start for Canadians*. It was a program emphasizing ideology over regional discontent with a 'new right' call for less government, real jobs, tax relief, traditional family values, tougher justice, repairs to the social safety net, and an end to national uncertainty over unity.[75]

The *Fresh Start* was intentional even if, as on families or justice, it contained 'code' for more traditional right-wing stances. Nevertheless, Reform's image problems persisted. At the start of 1997, pollster Allan Gregg conceded that 'they [Reform] need to convince people they aren't a bunch of ideological slagbrains. They still come across that way, for example, with their views on homosexuals. Canadians don't like extremists and Reform hasn't gotten beyond the perception that they're a Western-based party of extremists.'[76] It was an image that continued to hurt Reform as it devoted significant party resources to attaining a breakthrough in Ontario, which demonstrated with the provincial election of Mike Harris's radical right Conservatives in 1995 that it was open to 'public choice politics'.

Others suggested that most Canadians also simply saw Reformers as 'wingnuts' and as 'too rigid'.[77] At that point, just weeks before an election call,

Reform support was down 6 per cent from the party's 1993 general election level. Another pollster, Conrad Winn, opined that Reform had 'to decide whether it's going to be a party or a think tank'; even after the launch of its *Fresh Start Plan*, 'the public does not have a clue what Reform stands for'.[78]

Positioning Reform for an election was made more difficult by the habit of Canada's main brokerage parties to 'steal' ideas that gained popularity, regardless of which party first popularized it. Finance Minister Paul Martin of the governing Liberals did much to emphasize 'deficit reduction' as a Liberal priority, thus muddying those waters for a distinctive Reform position; Jean Charest's Tories, seeking a way back from electoral purgatory, latched onto one of Reform's key planks, one that had proven popular in Conservative Ontario: a tax cut. Almost all parties began talking tough about crime and criminals. Everyone seemed to be starting fresh at the beginning of 1997.

That did not stop Reform from focusing on other aspects of its reimaging strategy. Party leader Preston Manning began the year with what the fashion industry call 'a full make-over', which included cosmetic dental work and laser surgery to get rid of his eyeglasses, changes to his hairstyle and wardrobe, voice lessons, as well as working—along with others in the caucus—on 'TV training'.[79] As the 'personal project of Preston Manning'[80], Reform's need to project a clearer image through its leader was not misdirected.[81] Polls had suggested that Manning himself was part of the party's image problem. Despite the leader's contributions to party formation and his appeal to the party's core, Angus Reid/Southam polls leading up to the 1997 election suggested that among a broader spectrum of Canadians, the more the public knew about Manning, the less they liked him.[82]

During the winter of 1997, Reform's Okanagan-Shuswap MP Darrel Stinson challenged Liberal backbencher John Cannis to 'duke it out' 'if you've got the gonads . . . you . . . s.o.b.' after Cannis called Stinson a racist during debate in Parliament. This suggested the party's image problems were deep-seated. One strategy, according to Reform strategist Rick Anderson, was to confront the image problem—the party's 'most daunting challenge'—by presenting a 'less white, less male, less older' set of candidates for the 1997 election.[83] The party had some success in this strategy, electing five MPs from visible minorities, including Rahim Jaffer, a twenty-five-year-old business-man, in Edmonton Strathcona. Jaffer, whose family fled Uganda during the Idi Amin regime, was fluently bilingual and was added to Manning's six-member 'Unity Team'. Having a young, bilingual, visible minority MP from western Canada confront White, unilingual Justice Minister Anne McLellan on the Constitution was a Reform strategist's dream.

Apart from Jaffer's election, the results of the 1997 election gave Reform second place and official Opposition status in the House of Commons. Reform accomplished this with 46,000 fewer voters supporting the party than in 1993 (aided by a 3 per cent decline in voter turnout). Still, the party managed to marginally increase the vote share—up to 19.3 per cent from

18.7 per cent in 1993. The improved result for Reform was based on a variety of reasons that suggested both the party's strengths and its weaknesses. One concern during the 1997 contest was that Reform support in western Canada remained soft, even well into the campaign, as it had been throughout much of the previous year. In what proved a successful attempt to counter this slippage in support and to differentiate Reform from the other major parties, Manning and the party decided to play 'the Quebec card'. This strategy was to demonstrate that on unity/constitutional issues, Reform would stand up to Quebec and to a Liberal government supportive of 'distinct society' recognition for that province. In parts of western Canada, Reform knew that this idea (particularly the term 'distinct society') was a flashpoint for voters.

In a mid-campaign set of deliberately provocative advertisements, Reform placed photos of Quebec-based politicians Jean Chrétien, Jean Charest, and Lucien Bouchard with the message 'No more Quebec politicians running the country' in the now-familiar red circle with diagonal red crossbar. It played well in much of the West, particularly in rural/resource communities. However, it also provided a small positive blip for Gilles Duceppe in Quebec and allowed Chrétien, Charest, and others to rekindle Reform's 'bigoted' image. More importantly for Reform, it solidified the party's support in western Canada.

In doing so, it may also have restricted Reform to the West, which may prove to be the party's greatest weakness. In Ontario Reform lost its only seat (in Simcoe Centre), despite considerable party resources, including much of leader Preston Manning's time. Reform Party support in Ontario was actually down 1 per cent from its 1993 total. In Atlantic Canada, where discontent with the governing Liberals was palpable, Reform also hoped for more votes; instead, the Atlantic region never came close to electing any Reformers to Parliament, despite tossing out twenty of the thirty-one Liberals, including some from Chrétien's cabinet. Antigovernment sentiment served only to elect more New Democrats and Conservatives. Nova Scotia and New Brunswick produced Reform's best showings in the region. In Nova Scotia, where the party's vote share dropped from 13.3 to 9.7 per cent, Reform ran in nine of the eleven federal ridings; the party's vote only once topped 15 per cent (in West Nova, where it had 18.8 per cent support). Reform did manage more than 10 per cent of the vote in seven Nova Scotia constituencies. In New Brunswick, where 'other' parties (such as the Confederation of Regions and Christian Heritage) had some previous standing, Reform garnered 8.5 per cent support in 1993; in 1997 that total rose to 13.1 per cent. Reform ran candidates in eight of the ten federal seats in New Brunswick; in seven of the eight, party support was above 10 per cent, with four of the constituencies recording votes of over 20 per cent for Reform—the highest support was in Tobique-Mactaquac, where Reform managed a surprising 27.8 per cent in a three-way split with the Liberals (at 30.2 per cent) and the Conservatives (at 35.9 per cent).[84] Given some right-wing electoral history, New Brunswick would appear to be a potential bright spot for a more national than regional Reform Party of the future.[85]

In Quebec, largely to counter its anti-Quebec image elsewhere, Reform tried a few candidacies. However, these eleven Quebec Reform candidates were abandoned by the party's leader and strategists in mid-campaign with the 'No Quebec politicians' advertisements. Reform Party support in Quebec was just 10,766 votes, only 0.29 per cent overall; in no constituency did support for Reform rise above 2.5 per cent.

In an important sense, Reform's anti-Quebec campaign worked because the party's vote in western Canada held. Indeed, support for Reform increased across the West, especially in British Columbia and Saskatchewan, provinces where the NDP has traditionally done well. With this third electoral showing, it is arguable that Reform has become the voice of recent western protest, replacing the NDP in that role. In British Columbia, for example, Reform support in 1993 was 36.4 per cent; in the 1997 campaign it rose to 43 per cent, yielding twenty-five seats (one more than 1993). Support for Reform remained strongest in rural British Columbia and in suburban settings. In Alberta, Reform's main stronghold, more than half the voters as in 1993 supported the party. The party's 54.6 per cent vote share was a marginal increase over 1993, which produced two additional seats for a total of twenty-four out of twenty-six available seats. This performance reinforced the conclusion that in Alberta, Reform support is both urban and rural and cuts across most socio-economic divisions.

In Saskatchewan Reform managed to win eight of the fourteen seats in the province that was the heartland of the CCF/NDP; its vote, at 36.4 per cent, was up almost 10 per cent from 1993, when it had won just four seats. The Liberals were the big losers, losing four of their five Saskatchewan seats. The NDP managed to retain the five seats it had won in 1993. In Manitoba the Reform vote was almost static—up just 1.3 per cent to 23.7 per cent. However, the party took one additional seat (for a total of three); one of these was Selkirk-Interlake, captured with just 28.3 per cent of the votes. Here also the Liberals lost six of their twelve seats, while the NDP managed to take four ridings, a noticeable improvement on their one win in 1993.

It was perhaps in Ontario where Reform's anti-Quebec posture did it the most harm. Despite a massive expenditure of electoral resources in a province with a still new and relatively popular radically right-wing Conservative government, Reform's vote in the province slipped to 19 per cent and it lost its one non-western MP.

While the 1997 Canadian general election result is generally perceived as a success for Reform, at least two scenarios remain: (1) *Similarities* among Reform and the Progressives, Social Credit, and other parties emerging from western Canada as parties of protest suggest a tendency for such parties to be displaced or swallowed by other (usually older) party forms; (2) *Differences* between Reform and its regional predecessors might suggest the possibility of a breakthrough to truly national party status. Two elements in the second scenario are key if Reform is to succeed: the party's representation of new-right conservatism and the unity circumstance. Having played its 'Quebec card' in 1997 to achieve its second-place goal, Reform created certain difficulties for itself, particularly in presenting itself as a national versus regional party. However, Manning's support for the 1997 Calgary Declaration, which offered mainly symbolic concessions to Quebec, suggested that the party was hard at work on Stage Two of its plan—the goal of breaking through to form the next government of Canada.[86] The key here would appear to be to focus on developing the party's ideological (as opposed to regional or ethnocultural) appeal.[87]

Assessing the Reform Party Phenomenon

In the end, the current answer to the question of what the Reform Party's political emergence from new party to official Opposition in the course of three general elections represents in the national politics of Canada is both *continuity* and *change*. This is evident in three forms: (1) Reform's ideology, message, and method; (2) The party's leadership; and (3) Reform's support base.

One of Reform's continuities is in the continued expression of western political protest. While this is clearly and increasingly not Reform's central message, the party's effort to be perceived as the excluded western voice and its efforts to associate itself with a variety of the populist traditions from western Canada, suggest that this image continues to be important to Reform. Gordon Laird has suggested that as the reality of rural populism has faded, the mythology of the West has grown.[88] Reform's focus on representational reforms—particularly 'direct democracy' tools such as the use of referenda—is a case in point. However, as Laycock has argued, this may be the *only* case in point with regard to populist links between Reform and earlier populist movements in western Canada.[89] Laycock has noted that 'Preston Manning describes his party as the most recent Canadian expression of "democratic populism".' Ultimately, Laycock concludes that 'the logic of the Reform approach to democratic politics is largely at odds with most of the prairie populist legacy its leaders claim to be extending, save that of Social Credit's "plebiscitarian populism".'[90]

This plebiscitarian approach does provide a response to those like Sydney Sharpe and Don Braid, who have equated party leader Preston Manning's religious convictions with his politics, however. Sharpe and Braid are categorical about this. In *Storming Babylon: Preston Manning and the Rise of the Reform Party*, they conclude that 'in Preston Manning's life, evangelical Protestant religion is the first thing of all things, the source of his attitudes, beliefs, goals and dreams. . . . This religious impulse lies behind everything he stands for, from his fierce belief in capitalism to his deeply conservative views on welfare and the role of women.'[91]

Yet, while Manning is regularly prepared to defend and explain his Christianity, even in areas of policy controversy such as abortion where they are clearly on one side, Manning (as noted earlier) would prefer a national referendum to determine whether his preferred policy would be acted upon.[92] Flanagan has added the example of Manning's possible support for 'right to die' legislation, despite holding opposing religious views on the matter, following an expression of support for such legislation from his Calgary constituents.[93] According to Manning, Reform MPs 'should vote according to the majority view in their constituencies';[94] the Manning 'directive is simple here: "respect and represent majority opinion".'[95] If and when no such popular view is known, then MPs are to 'faithfully represent ... personal convictions concerning the will of God'.[96]

In assessing the Flanagan-Sharpe/Braid debate on the significance of religion as a factor in Reform policy discourse, it would appear that neither side is right; both are too categorical. Sharpe and Braid's conclusion that 'Preston Manning ... seems to see himself as a kind of Christian guerrilla working in a corrupt, secular world'[97] is in sharp contrast to Flanagan's assessment that Manning 'has never imposed [his stance on moral issues] on the Reform Party. ... having participated in policy discussions at the national office for two years, I can report that religion never played a role in considering the merits of policy positions.'[98] Manning's own response on the links between his religion and his politics—that 'I do not seek to impose my religious or political views on others'—is balanced by Sharpe and Braid's conclusion that while 'this is a fair statement of how Manning conducts his spiritual life in public, ... it does not begin to reflect the overwhelming importance of religion to his whole being'.[99] The latter is a view shared by another Manning/Reform 'biographer', Murray Dobbin. Dobbin identifies 'evangelical fundamentalism' as *one* of the early and ongoing influences on Preston Manning's politics.[100] Gordon Laird agrees. For Laird, Manning 'makes much of the persecution themes within the Bible. ... While making it somewhat clear that politics and religion should remain separate, the question of cultural survival, says Manning, quoting the Book of Psalms, is fundamental. ... By culture, Manning means ... everything ... from dualities of sin and virtue, damnation and redemption.'[101] In his own book, *The New Canada*, Manning calls for 'righteous outcomes'.

Laird cautions against reading too much into Reform's association with religious fundamentalism, however. Noting that critics have often been too quick to blame Christian fundamentalists for right-wing extremism in Canada, Laird notes that 'in fact, considerable support for social conservatism comes from Canada's political mainstream. Evangelical Christians, commonly assumed to be the foot soldiers of social conservatism, vote roughly the same way as everyone else.'[102] Despite Laird's conclusion, analysis of the 1988,

1993, and 1997 Canadian elections demonstrates a relationship between Reform votes and areas of Christian fervour such as throughout Alberta and in BC's Fraser Valley where Christian fundamentalism is strongest.

If religion is just one element of Manning's and Reform's political composition, ideology is a far more significant one. It is certainly more significant in understanding Reform's impact on the Canadian polity than the party's efforts to have itself perceived as the natural inheritor of 'Prairie populism'. On ideology, the Reform Party has become the Canadian purveyor of public choice politics, whose roots are largely not Canadian. The shift to more individualistic perspectives finds some related expression in the Canadian debates over constitutional rights in the 1970s and early 1980s. The ascendancy of individual rights over collective ones, given expression in the 1982 Canadian Charter of Rights and Freedoms, represented one expression of the increasing Americanization of Canadian politics.[103]

More significantly, the new right neoconservatism of the late 1970s and early 1980s produced what Peter Self has described as *Government by the Market*.[104] The debate about the significance of ideology in Reform's agenda setting in Canada is clear. As posed by Murray Dobbin in *Preston Manning and the Reform Party*, the argument is with 'the consistency of the right wing message'.[105] Reform's 'messages' were 'uniformly free-market policies, not the sort of eclectic mix of policies one would expect of a populist party responding to people's grievances'.[106] As Laird finds, 'the political lexicon of right-wing populism continues to suggest the limitless possibility of the West: a range of untapped prosperity and freedom, a new life at the edge of the horizon. This vision of a simple, stable and private social space, unfettered by external controls and undisturbed by strangers is inspiring to a growing number of Canadians.'[107] The reality has become instead one where such 'opportunity and security are contingent on excluding the undesirables'.[108] The result is:

> . . . a pretty long stretch from the democratic impulses of prairie populism. . . . The right-wing revolution sold itself to Canadian voters with promises of true democracy and government reform. . . . [In reality] right-wing populism appears to gain its main inspiration not from grass-roots protest but from the global frontier of high finance and Big Business—the very institutions against which old-time populists used to rail.[109]

Dobbin similarly concluded that this 'radical free-market conservatism' was at the heart of Reform and its leader, Preston Manning.[110]

Tom Flanagan has challenged this view. Terming it 'the second misconception about Manning', Flanagan contends that critical interpretations such as Dobbin's incorrectly emphasize 'every move as part of a long-term plan to 'creat[e] an ideologically consistent conservative party'.[111] Flanagan admits that there are ideological conservatives in the Reform Party, but suggests that Manning 'never refers to himself simply as a conservative', preferring to call Reform 'ideologically balanced'. The Dobbin response to this is that it is possible to place 'a person—and a political party—by who their friends are'.[112] For Dobbin, Reform's friends do not include labour unions, farm organizations, women's groups, Native leaders and organizations, nongovernmental organizations concerned about health care or poverty, or organizations defending the CBC, rural post offices, Via Rail, or the arts. This is odd for a western party that claims to have the region's populist antecedents as its roots. However, it is helpful in placing Reform in left-right ideological terms.

Central to the notion that the Reform Party and its leader are *not* radical neoconservatives are attempts by the party and Manning to claim that such 'old' left-right definitions of politics are no longer operative. It is a view often expressed by Preston Manning, as in Reform's 1990 policy *Blue Book* and in Manning's 'Hockey Analogy', which was sent to all party members in early 1990.[113] Here perhaps it is sufficient to argue that claims of 'non-ideology' are often the most ideological of all statements. Reformer's claims of non-ideological status are certainly mirrored by other 'right-wing' entities, such as the Fraser Institute think-tank; the *claim* does not negate the left-right divide inherent in their political positioning.

Flanagan's contentions that Manning demonstrated 'little interest in the revival of conservative thinking in Britain and the United States in the 1980s', that Manning never referred to Thatcher or Reagan as models, and that under his leadership 'the policies espoused by the Reform Party are far from consistently conservative' need to be balanced by an assessment of party positioning.[114] Certainly, whatever Reform's claims, it is, in Canadian terms, a 'very conservative' party.[115] Whether as a student of American right-wing thinking, or what Laird calls an exporter of 'neo-con innovation', Manning's conservative credentials have been well recognized south of the border. Former Republican House Speaker Newt Gingrich has stated that 'Margaret Thatcher and Mr. Manning are the two non-Americans we learned most from.'[116]

David Laycock has analysed much of Reform's ideology, message, and method. For Laycock, Reform's denial of ideological definition and placing is both significant and wrong. It is an ideology that transcends region in Canadian politics, and it is an ideology and party that should be taken seriously.

> While massively popular only in one region, Reform's case against the status quo in federal politics goes well beyond regionalism and a complaint about Quebec's privileged position in federal power politics. Their indictment of Canadian politics incorporates parties and the party system, organized interests in policy development processes, government bureaucracies regardless of their policy objectives, politicians as peddlers of the illusion of solutions to personal problems, and the core redistributive and market-interventionist principles of the modern welfare state.[117]

Inherent in such twentieth-century reflection of nineteenth-century classical liberalism were attacks on the central tenets of the modern welfare state.[118] According to Laycock, the new right ascendancy of the 1980s and 1990s was based *precisely* on the right's successful efforts to redefine notions of democracy, equality, freedom, and toleration and to convince voters that left-right distinctions in contemporary politics were meaningless.[119] New right parties such as Reform have equated one of the central troubles with democracy as the rise of the 'special interest', a pejorative term for the welfare state's distortion of 'true democracy' (the unaffiliated individual and the unfettered market-place). To this Barney and Laycock add 'that Reform's promotion of direct democracy is theoretically inconsistent with but strategically advantageous to their efforts to redefine democratic politics and public life in Canada'.[120]

With regard to equality, Reform and other new right formations have sought to define the argument as one between 'equality of opportunity' versus 'equality of outcome'. This 'rhetorical ploy', as Laycock describes it, allows the new right 'to appropriate the positively connoted phrase "equality of opportunity" to their own ideological purposes' while 'contrasting it with the empty yet threatening category of "equality of condition"... [confusing] many citizens as to the real implications of their agenda ... [undermining] the advances made during the welfare state's post war evolution toward a more democratic set of relations among citizens'.[121] With regard to freedom, the new right critique embodied in Reform includes an emphasis on 'negative freedom', portraying 'positive freedom' as practised by welfare states as 'a conceptual licence for ominous state infringement of such freedom from constraint'.[122]

Laycock adds an additional consideration that is often overlooked—toleration. In complex societies, toleration is a central ingredient in politics if such societies are to remain successful. Right-wing thinking on toleration tends to be based on the golden rule notion of tolerating others so you may be tolerated. As such, it views leftist-welfare liberal conceptions of the need for state action to ensure broadened toleration as intrusive and negative. Political efforts by the new right in Canada and elsewhere have been 'to undermine the conditions, the institutions and the welfare state programmes which the left claim are required to enhance toleration....'[123] Laird poses the blunt reality: 'like past assimilationists, neo-conservatives often define themselves *against* people whom they see as riddled with human imperfection and weakness. Would-be heroes preach tough love solutions and the glory of free market discipline against ... people who are dependent, vulnerable or just plain different....'[124]

In answer to ideological/non-ideological, left-right questions and assertions about Reform, Laycock's conclusion is convincing: the Reform Party gives significant expression to 'a distinctly right-wing approach to politics in Canada'.[125] As the major party purveyor of neoconservative thinking in the country, Reform has had a major impact on national agenda setting, and the ideas on which it is based will continue to affect the Canadian polity and public policy whether Reform is the conduit or not.

What are the ties that bind Reform supporters to their party and its leadership? Tom Flanagan's contention that 'to a remarkable degree, the Reform Party is the personal project of Preston Manning' is an apt starting-point.[126] Despite that clear relationship and the influence Preston Manning has had on the party, the issue of managing the membership was an early and ongoing source of difficulty for Reform. As Dobbin has contended, corporate support for Reform's free market agenda—from free trade and smaller government to deficit and debt reduction—posed little problem for the party. On Meech Lake, the goods and services tax, immigration, crime and punishment, and a range of other social policy issues, Reform attracted an array of supporters whose views gave the party an intolerant, narrow, and largely negative image. In the language of gender-defined politics in America, early Reform represented 'angry, older white men'—what Dobbin and others described as 'a sea of white heads'.[127] As Dobbin concludes, 'while Preston Manning certainly had the numbers to claim a base, it was extremely narrow, politically and demographically'.[128] Former party policy chief (and subsequent MP) Stephen Harper described such party members and supporters as a fundamental impediment to broadening Reform's base of support: 'they do more damage to us than any media outlet, any other party, and any real enemy can do'.[129]

Throughout the early 1990s, including the 1993 election campaign during which Reform had its first significant electoral breakthrough, management of both membership and supporters was clearly a major party preoccupation. Manning's response to criticisms of intolerance and extremism within the party was twofold: first, that such views were not those expressed by the party leadership; and second, that the best defence against a 'natural tendency' for a new right-wing party to attract 'people who hold extreme views of all kinds, including racial views' was to broaden its base.[130]

One outcome of the February 1999 convention regarding a United Alternative of the right (UA) was support for creation of a new political party. The fact that just 55 per cent of the approximately 1,500 delegates at the Ottawa meeting confirmed this plan suggested several things to observers, not the least of which was the probability of tough sledding for this Reform-initiated venture. Even a lesser plan, posed by Ontario Tory bagman Hal Jackman, with support from Alberta Tory treasurer Stockwell Day, of an electoral alliance for the next election where Reform and Conservatives would not oppose one another in selected constituencies offered only limited possibilities.

Several aspects of a UA remain problematic. Even the logistics of creating a new federal political party of the right were formidable: the seven-point UA steering committee plan 'Path to Victory' called for any new party to begin by November 1999; Reform Party leader Preston Manning said all the work, including leadership selection, had to be completed by the summer of 2000 in time for the thirty-seventh Canadian general election.

The most significant initial hurdle to achieve this UA party was convincing federal Tories to come on-board. At the February 1999 UA convention, the majority of delegates were from Reform, with smaller elements from provincial Tory parties in Alberta and Ontario. Few federal Tories participated—in many instances, they were officially discouraged from formal cooperation. Most of the federal Conservative membership were negative about the UA initiative, preferring Joe Clark's 'Canadian Alternative' task force/option.[131]

Two key issues stood out as impediments to a successful UA transition: leadership and ideology. On leadership, there was considerable reflection among Conservatives and other non-Reformers, within the Reform Party, and in the media. Its trend line was that if a UA option were to succeed, it would require new leadership—many saw Manning as a liability and many Reformers were sceptical about the possibility of Joe Clark leading the new right-wing party. While Reform was clearly the project of Preston Manning, Manning's failure to take a national stance during the 1997 general election —preferring instead to play an anti-Quebec card—essentially locked him and his party into a regional straightjacket.

Reform's analysis concluded that a united right alternative was the best way out of this regional perception dilemma. Reform was probably right, but in the minds of many, success required a change of leadership. Certainly no Joe Clark-Preston Manning meeting of political minds was evident following the convention.[132]

The other dilemma for a UA party was what ideological stance it would take. The tension here was between not compromising on Reform's rightist policy stances on everything from the economy to personal morality versus appealing to a broader range of voters east of the Manitoba border. The 45 per cent of UA delegates who opposed a new party were generally against compromising.[133] Right-wing sentiments were given heart by commitments from Manning that Reform 'would not sacrifice its principles' in creating a new UA.[134]

Certainly, the early support and membership for Reform was not broadly based: between 1987 and 1990, fully half of all delegates to the party's assemblies were from Alberta; like Social Credit federally a generation and more before, half of the Reform membership was also from that province; and in the 1988 general election, in which the party contested seventy-two of eighty-six seats across western Canada, two-thirds of all Reform support came from Alberta, with BC and Saskatchewan far behind and only token support in Manitoba.[135] A 1989 survey of delegates to the party's annual assembly found that 72 per cent were men; 86 per cent were over sixty; 38 per cent were retired; two-thirds had business, professional, or managerial jobs; three-quarters had some postsecondary education; and only 15 per cent had occupations that paid wages. Over three-quarters said they were former Tories, and 20 per cent former Social Credit supporters.[136]

The 1993 general election demonstrated two things: that Reform could use its neoconservative message to broaden its appeal, and that the problems of image persisted. Reform remained a party with an overwhelming percentage of its support coming from western Canada.

Reform's image as a party of extremist elements and intolerance persisted. A number of candidates and local party officials were reprimanded and, at times, asked to stand aside when they attracted excessive media attention along this spectrum. At the same time, Manning and Reform continued in their efforts to extend the base of the party beyond the West. Their primary vehicle for doing this was a renewed emphasis on their neoconservative economic agenda.

Nowhere was this more evident than in the period between the 1993 election and the 1997 general election. While more traditional western protest and appeals for representational reforms were continued, Reform, with considerable assistance from other conservative/business interests and groups—such as the Business Council on National Issues, the Fraser Institute, and the National Citizens' Coalition—managed to set the political agenda in the mid-1990s. If Canadians were asked to explain the difference between deficit and debt at the end of the 1970s, few would have known the difference. The great success of the neoconservative revolution of the 1980s and 1990s was the ability to define the language of political and policy discourse. In Canada Reform, more than any other party, is responsible for introducing this discourse. In the process, it pushed the Progressive Conservative Party into disarray and turned the Liberals into policy purveyors of new right thinking. New Democrats were simply too slow to respond to the shifts taking place in the Canadian polity of the early 1990s. Even in those settings where the NDP maintained some measure of success provincially in the face of this neoconservative onslaught (as in Saskatchewan), the politics of balanced budgets (or at least the promise of such) has come to predominate as well.

The shift in the thinking of all parties in Canada to this new right focus attests more than anything else to Reform's impact on the Canadian party system, but even more so on the broader polity itself. In the process, Reform's support has broadened somewhat from rural Saskatchewan and rural and suburban BC to Ontario, where it lost its one seat but managed to affect numerous electoral outcomes—virtually all gifts for the Liberals.

The post-1997 election focus for Reform is clearly on Ontario, though a breakthrough in Atlantic Canada (perhaps in New Brunswick) would add to its national credibility. While sitting MPs from the West have been given some responsibilities for working with Reform enthusiasts and supporters in Atlantic Canada, and party leader Preston Manning has taken several rounds of French lessons, Reform's failure to make its Ontario breakthrough despite

Figure 5.1 Social Credit/Reform Popular Vote, 1935–1997 (national)

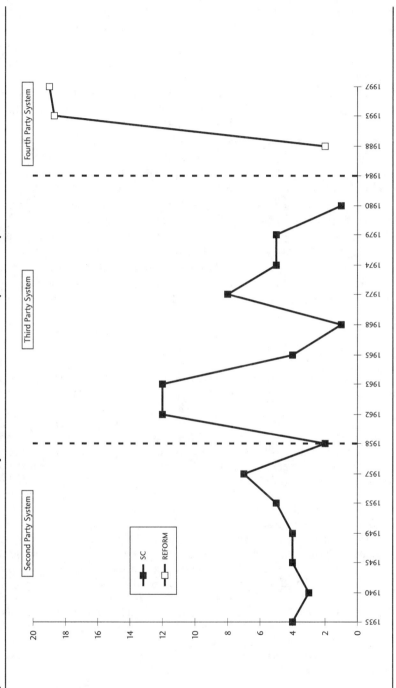

Source: Adapted from Elections Canada results.

considerable effort and expenditure has not diminished the party's enthusiasm for the task. The focus of this assault is now simple: convince Progressive Conservative voters in Ontario to switch their partisan allegiance ideally
through some reuniting of the right.[137] With the apparent continuing appeal
of the radical right agenda of fellow travellers like provincial Conservative
premiers Ralph Klein and Mike Harris, the fact that Reform represents the
'radical right' in national politics may prove its biggest asset and its true
legacy—as Reform or some United Alternative successor.[138]

The facade of a western populist protest party will now finally have to be
discarded if Reform is to meet the next (national) challenge. Signs like a
renewed interest in the regulatory relationship between states and markets
in light of global financial flu and rampant currency speculation may represent early indications of an emerging challenge to the rightist ideological
paradigm posed by Reform and other public choice proponents. If so, efforts
to 'Unite the Right' in Canada may begin to confront serious ideological
counterpressures. However, if the shift to the right that marked Canadian
politics in the 1990s is maintained in the first decade of the twenty-first century, further success for Reform or its rightist successor and an even more
fundamental ideological realignment in Canada's party system is likely.[139]

Notes

The authors are grateful to the anonymous reviewers and to David Laycock, Simon
Fraser University, for helpful comments and suggestions on this chapter.

1. The BQ's national vote was 13.5 per cent; concentrated only in Quebec, the BQ
   won fifty-four of seventy-five seats with 49.3 per cent of the votes from Quebec.
   For a detailed discussion of the 1993 Canadian general election, including an
   overview of the federal election in Quebec, see Munroe Eagles, James Bickerton,
   Alain-G. Gagnon, and Patrick Smith, *The Almanac of Canadian Politics*, 2nd edn
   (Toronto: Oxford University Press, 1995):77–9. See also A.-G. Gagnon, J. Bickerton,
   M. Eagles, and P.J. Smith, *L'Almanach politique du Québec: Portrait des circonscrip-
   tions federales* (Montreal/Québec: Editions Québec/Amerique, 1997).
2. Reform had an ongoing issue of soft support in the West leading up to the 1997
   contest. Playing the 'hard' card on Quebec in the middle of the campaign was
   clearly calculated to ensure that it would not lose votes. See, for example, Barbara
   Yaffe, 'Reform Looking For Stars to Revive Party Fortunes in BC', *Vancouver Sun*
   (12 September 1996):A3; and Angus Reid/Southam News Poll, 'The Federal Political Scene', released 31 July 1996. In the Angus Reid/Southam poll, Reform disapproval was at the highest point since the 1993 general election. Approval was
   highest in Alberta (61 per cent), split in BC, and a majority disapproval in
   Atlantic Canada. For this and other Angus Reid public opinion results, see
   http://www.angusreid.com/syndicate/reidreport.html.
3. Peter Self, *Government by the Market? The Politics of Public Choice* (Boulder: Westview, 1993).

4. A number of authors have begun to reflect on this larger ideological issue; for example, Gordon Laird in *Slumming it at the Rodeo: The Cultural Roots of Canada's Right-Wing Revolution* (Vancouver: Douglas and McIntyre, 1998); and David Laycock, *The Reform Party and Democratic Politics in Canada* (Toronto: University of Toronto Press, forthcoming).

5. Unless otherwise indicated, electoral/party data used in this article is taken from Munroe Eagles, James Bickerton, Alain-G. Gagnon, and Patrick Smith, *The Almanac of Canadian Politics* (Peterborough: Broadview, 1991), and Eagles et al., *The Almanac of Canadian Politics*, 2nd edn. The former covers the 1984–8 electoral period; the latter, 1988–93; some of the ecological analysis/modelling is also reported in M. Eagles, J. Bickerton, A.-G. Gagnon, and P. Smith, 'Continuity in Electoral Change: Patterns in Support for Canadian Parties, 1988 and 1993', Association for Canadian Studies in the United States paper, Seattle, November 1995. Analysis of the 1997 Canadian general election results are based on information from the chief electoral officer, Canada.

6. Research assistance was provided by Kennedy Stewart, doctoral candidate at the London School of Economics and research associate, Institute of Governance Studies, Simon Fraser University.

7. See Walter Young, *Democracy and Discontent: Progressivism, Socialism and Social Credit in the Canadian West*, 2nd edn (Toronto: McGraw-Hill Ryerson, 1978):1.

8. Ibid., Chapter 1, and Fred Engelmann and Mildred Schwartz, *Political Parties and the Canadian Social Structure* (Toronto: Prentice Hall, 1967):24–37. For an account of the US Progressives during the first party system in Canada, see Richard Hofstadter, ed., *The Progressive Movement: 1900–1915* (Englewood Cliffs: Prentice Hall, 1963).

9. Nelson Wiseman, 'Provincial Political Cultures' in *Provinces: Canadian Provincial Politics*, edited by Chris Dunn (Peterborough: Broadview, 1996):21–62. Wiseman assessed the significance of 'fragments' and the importance of 'immigrant ideas'. He also termed BC 'Canada's Australia'.

10. Young, *Democracy and Discontent*.

11. Apart from Young, *Democracy and Discontent*, Chapter 1, see also Engelmann and Schwartz, *Political Parties and the Canadian Social Structure*, 24–37, and David Laycock, *Populism and Democratic Thought in the Canadian Prairies, 1910 to 1945* (Toronto: University of Toronto Press, 1990), among others.

12. Young, *Democracy and Discontent*, 3–4.

13. Engelmann and Schwartz, *Political Parties and the Canadian Social Structure*, 29–31.

14. See C.B. Macpherson, *Democracy in Alberta: Social Credit and the Party System*, 2nd edn (Toronto: University of Toronto Press, 1962).

15. See, for example, Edgar McInnis, *Canada: A Political and Social History*, 3rd edn (Toronto: Holt, Rinehart and Winston, 1969):426ff and 436–77, and John Courtney, *Voting in Canada* (Scarborough: Prentice Hall, 1967):200–1.

16. See J.M. Beck, *Pendulum of Power: Canada's Federal Elections* (Scarborough: Prentice Hall, 1968); T. Qualter, *The Election Process in Canada* (Toronto: McGraw-Hill, 1970); Howard A. Scarrow, 'Patterns of Voter Turnout in Canada', *Midwest Journal of Political Science* V, no. 4 (November 1961); and *Reports of the Chief Electoral Officer* (Ottawa: Queen's Printer, various years). The BC results during this period included the 1900 general election (59 per cent), 1904 (64 per cent), 1908 (58 per cent), and 1911 (52 per cent).

17. Forty-four UFOs to twenty-eight Liberals, twenty-five Tories, and fourteen others. The latter included Labour (ten elected), Labour-UFO (one elected), Liberal-UFO (one elected), one Independent Labour, and one Soldier.

18. The best source of information on Ontario provincial results is Roderick Lewis, *Centennial Edition of a History of the Electoral Districts, Legislatures and Ministries of the Province of Ontario, 1867–1968* (Toronto: Queen's Printer, 1968). See also Loren Simerl, 'A Survey of Canadian Provincial Election Results, 1905–1981', in *Politics: Canada*, 5th edn, edited by Paul Fox (Toronto: McGraw-Hill Ryerson, 1982):674–7. On Drury, see also Charles M. Johnson, *E.C. Drury: Agrarian Idealist* (Toronto: University of Toronto Press, 1986) and Drury's own memoir, *Farmer Premier* (Toronto: McClelland and Stewart, 1966).

19. Bracken continued as premier until January 1943, though as leader of a Liberal-Progressive alliance. See, for example, Chris Dunn, ed., *Provinces: Canadian Provincial Politics* (Peterborough: Broadview, 1996):519–25; Loren Simerl, 'A Survey of Canadian Provincial Election Results, 1905–1981', 655–93; Martin Robin, ed., *Canadian Provincial Politics* (Scarborough: Prentice-Hall, 1978); and Rand Dyck, *Provincial Politics in Canada*, 2nd edn (Scarborough: Prentice-Hall, 1991).

20. Simerl, 'A Survey of Canadian Provincial Election Results, 1905–1981', 682–5.

21. See Hugh Thorburn, 'Federal Election Results', in *Party Politics in Canada*, 5th edn, edited by H.G. Thorburn (Scarborough: Prentice-Hall, 1985):338–49.

22. New Brunswick elected one Progressive MP in 1921 (with 11 per cent of the votes). There was 12 per cent Progressive support in PEI.

23. That decision in 1921 allowed Reform leader Preston Manning to make the claim seventy-six years later that he was the first *third* party/leader to achieve official Opposition standing.

24. Laycock, *Populism and Democratic Thought*, 3–22. Subsequent chapters deal with each of these in turn.

25. Ibid., 21.

26. Ibid., 23.

27. Ibid., 20–1.

28. Ibid., 20, 136.

29. Ibid., 21–2.

30. See, for example, Darin Barney and David Laycock, 'The Recline of Party: Armchair Democracy and the Reform Party of Canada', in *Changing Patterns of Governance*, edited by Edwin Black, Michael Howlett, and Patrick Smith (Vancouver: British Columbia Political Studies Association Proceedings, 1997):vol. 1, 137–58.

31. Laycock's *Populism and Democratic Thought in the Canadian Prairies, 1910 to 1945* has an extensive discussion of the 'patterns of drift' across the various populisms.

32. P.J. Smith's interview with Hon. E.C. Drury, Crown Hill, Ontario, October 1964.

33. See Howard A. Scarrow, *Canada Votes: A Handbook of Federal and Provincial Election Data* (New Orleans: Hauser, 1962).

34. A major third-party coalition continued in Manitoba until 1943.

35. William Christian and Colin Campbell, *Political Parties and Ideologies in Canada*, 3rd edn (Toronto: McGraw-Hill Ryerson, 1990):189.

36. On the significance of provincial party experience in understanding third/protest party experience federally, see, for example, Engelmann and Schwartz, *Political Parties and the Canadian Social Structure*, 34–6: 'The greatest strength of third parties has been in provincial politics. . . . it is not surprising

that parties unique to a province should spring up in response to local needs. Such was the case of the farm parties and subsequently with others such as Social Credit.'

37. Maurice Pinard, in *The Rise of a Third Party: A Study in Crisis Politics* (Scarborough: Prentice Hall, 1971):5, concluded that 'the Social Credit movement was never much of a political success in England, the country in which the doctrine was formulated in the early twenties.... [The] immediate factors seem to have been Douglas's lack of interest and talent for political action and the rudimentary means he developed when he finally decided to engage in it.'

38. Douglas's critique of capitalist society was that it was inefficient, leaving many incapable of purchasing capitalist production/goods; this required the government to distribute money or 'social credit' to rectify the imbalance between production costs and purchasing power. See, for example, John Irving, 'The Evolution of the Social Credit Movement', in *Prophecy and Protest: Social Movements in Twentieth Century Canada*, edited by S.D. Clark, Paul Grayson, and Linda Grayson (Toronto: Gage, 1975):130–52.

39. See Macpherson, *Democracy in Alberta*.

40. See Chapter 6.

41. From Thorburn's election results, see Thorburn, 'Federal Election Results'.

42. Calculated from election results in Simerl, 'A Survey of Canadian Provincial Election Results', 686.

43. Terry Morley, 'Social Credit' in *The Canadian Encyclopedia*, vol. 2 (Edmonton: Hurtig, 1985):1715.

44. On both, especially the latter, see Martin Robin's *The Rush For Spoils: The Company Province, 1871–1933* (Toronto: McClelland and Stewart, 1972) and *Pillars of Profit: The Company Province, 1934–1972* (Toronto: McClelland and Stewart, 1973).

45. The party did recover in BC after a one-term NDP victory (1972–5), with Bennett's son, Bill, governing until 1986. Bill Bennett's successor as party leader and premier, Bill Vander Zalm, managed to decimate the coalition with religious and policy fervour. By 1991, Vander Zalm's conflict of interest had left the party politically dead in all but name. The right wing in BC was now represented by a 'new' Liberal coalition. Throughout all of these almost forty years of Social Credit 'government' in British Columbia, the original 'social credit' philosophy was totally absent. The name was just a convenience for Liberals and Conservatives to team up with others to keep the 'socialist hordes' from ascending to power in Victoria.

46. There are many sources on Social Credit in BC, from Paddy Sherman's or David Mitchell's biographies of W.A.C. Bennett to more critical reviews of his successors, such as Warren Magnusson, et al., eds, *The New Reality* (Vancouver: New Star, 1984), and Warren Magnusson et al., eds, *After Bennett: A New Politics for British Columbia* (Vancouver: New Star, 1986). In Saskatchewan and Manitoba Social Credit made no clear breakthrough in provincial electoral terms; in Saskatchewan a few party members were elected; in Manitoba there was marginally better success (Social Credit 'elected' a high of five MLAs in 1936).

47. Frank Dabbs, *Preston Manning: The Roots of Reform* (Vancouver: Greystone/ Douglas and McIntyre, 1997):62–4. Kennedy had served as Social Credit MP until 1940, then as the party's national organizer. He also served on the board of the Alberta Social Credit League, the organization that Dabbs and others have

called 'the party's powerful command centre'. Apart from sharing the same strong religious convictions, Kennedy and Ernest Manning were close friends, involved in the founding of Social Credit in Alberta and nationally.

48. See Scarrow, *Canada Votes*. In BC Social Credit support in 1945 was at 2 per cent, and in Saskatchewan at 3 per cent, for example.

49. P.J. Smith's conversation with Robert Thompson, former federal Social Credit leader, at Simon Fraser University, April 1989. See also Pinard, *The Rise of a Third Party*, and Michael Stein, *The Dynamics of Right-Wing Protest: Social Credit in Quebec* (Toronto: University of Toronto Press, 1973).

50. From Thorburn, ed., 'Federal Election Results'.

51. On some of these links, see, for example, Dabbs, *Preston Manning*, 48, 65–7, 85–9; David Elliot and Iris Miller, *Bible Bill: A Biography of William Aberhart* (Edmonton: Reidmore, 1987); and Lloyd Mackey, *Like Father, Like Son: Ernest Manning and Preston Manning* (Toronto: ECW Press, 1997). For a recent critical view of these links, see also Laird, *Slumming It at the Rodeo*, 38–56 and 99–120.

52. See, for example, Thorburn, ed., 'Federal Election Results', 346–7.

53. BC and Alberta managed to elect just two MPs each, despite support levels in Alberta of 29 per cent and 14 per cent in BC.

54. P.J. Smith's conversation with Robert Thompson, former federal Social Credit leader, at Simon Fraser University, April 1989.

55. Cited in Dabbs, *Preston Manning*, 79. John Barr was editorial writer for the *Edmonton Journal* and one of the self-described 'Young Turks' who sought to revitalize Social Credit after Peter Lougheed's selection as Alberta Conservative leader. According to party insider John Barr, the demise of the provincial party was primarily attributable to the party's failure to reform: 'there is only one thing worse than to refuse to reform, and that is to promise to initiate reform and then not carry it through'. See Dabbs, *Preston Manning*, 69–70.

56. The Meech Lake Accord and the founding of the Reform Party essentially co-incided. Reform's leader Preston Manning, the son of former Alberta premier E.C. Manning, represented a continuity in the western Canadian protest.

57. For a critical account of the rise of Reform, see Murray Dobbin, *Preston Manning and the Reform Party* (Toronto: James Lorimer, 1991).

58. Some of these ideological dimensions had their roots in the neoconservatism of the public choice 'revolution', which was given initial expression in American writings by such right-wing economists as the Virginia School's James Buchanan and Gordon Tullock, and by the Chicago School's Milton Friedman and Mancur Olson. Anthony Downs's *An Economic Theory of Democracy* (New York: Harper, 1957) and William Riker's *The Theory of Coalitions* (New Haven: Yale University Press, 1962) represented other early treatises.

59. See Sydney Sharpe and Don Braid, *Storming Babylon: Preston Manning and the Rise of the Reform Party* (Toronto: Key Porter, 1992) for a less critical view. In the other three western provinces, Reform did less well, but still managed to establish a presence in 1988. In BC, for example, Reform ran in thirty of thirty-two ridings and affected outcomes in seventeen; in Saskatchewan, only one Reform candidate won more than 5 per cent of the vote, but Tory fortunes fell from nine to four MPs elected, while New Democrats went from five to ten seats; in several constituencies, Reform votes had clearly affected electoral outcomes. Reform's standing in Manitoba was similar to its standing in Saskatchewan, managing

only a third-place finish (for twelve of its fourteen candidates), but helping to reduce Conservative victories here also. See also Eagles et al., *The Almanac of Canadian Politics*, 451–84, on Reform's vote totals in Manitoba in 1988, and pp. 485–518 for similar results in Saskatchewan.

60. On this, see, for example, Dabbs, *Preston Manning*, 132–44, particularly p. 136.
61. Cited in ibid., 1.
62. See Eagles et al., *The Almanac of Canadian Politics*, 2nd edn, 237–41.
63. Cited in ibid., 1.
64. On this, see, for example, Yaffe, 'Reform Looking For Stars', A3.
65. Cited in ibid.
66. See, for example, Anderson quoted in Barbara Yaffe, 'Poll and Election Two Different Things, Reform Figures', Vancouver Sun (19 November 1996):A3.
67. See Peter O'Neil, 'Manning Wants Vote to Ban Abortion', *Vancouver Sun* (31 October 1996):A1, A8.
68. See David Laycock, 'Preston Manning's Fish Stories: At Last Weekend's Convention, Canadians Found Out What Reform Means By Equality', *Vancouver Sun* (15 June 1996):A19.
69. Barbara Yaffe, 'Spate of Reformers Bowing Out of Federal Politics Raises Doubt', Vancouver Sun (9 November 1996):A3.
70. See, for example, ibid., A3.
71. See, for example, Sheldon Alberts, 'Reform MPs Polish Act For House Opening', Vancouver Sun (17 September 1997):A5.
72. For a discussion of the politics preceding this, see Preston Manning, *The New Canada* (Toronto: Macmillan, 1992):197–214.
73. In late 1997 early 1998 more modest declarations, such as the Calgary Declaration by the nine premiers from English Canada, seemed the extent of constitutional tinkering.
74. See Manning, *The New Canada*, 215–33.
75. There were six key elements in *A Fresh Start for Canadians* plan:

   1. *A Fresh Start on the Economy:* Essentially a pledge to reduce the size of government to create 'real jobs'.
   2. *A Fresh Start For Your Pocket Book:* A pledge for tax relief, something that proved electorally popular in Mike Harris's Ontario.
   3. *A Fresh Start For Families:* A party call to make 'families', at least traditional families, a priority.
   4. *A Fresh Start For Justice:* An approach to toughen the justice system, with more emphasis on victims' rights and the punishment of criminals to 'make our streets safe again'.
   5. *A Fresh Start For Social Fairness:* A party pledge to 'repair the social safety net'.
   6. *A Fresh Start on Unity:* A promise (at least to disgruntled westerners) to 'end the uncertainty caused by the national unity crisis'; this included 'equality of provinces' versus notions like 'distinctiveness for Quebec'.

76. Allan Gregg and other analysts cited in Barbara Yaffe, '"Wing-Nut" Image Continues to Plague Reform In Ontario', Vancouver Sun (22 January 1997):A3.
77. Allan Gregg and other analysts cited in ibid.
78. Cited in ibid.

79. On Preston Manning's make-over prior to the 1997 general election 'to shake his bookish preacher's kid public persona', see Dabbs, *Preston Manning*, 117, opposite; and Laird, *Slumming It at the Rodeo*, 65: Manning himself said that 'if your teeth are crooked or your voice is strange or your clothes are out of sync, or if you stand out with your old hairdo or the wrong suit, people will not hear what you're saying. I'm interested in getting my message out.'

80. On 'The Real Manning', see Thomas Flanagan, *Waiting For the Wave: The Reform Party and Preston Manning* (Toronto: Stoddart, 1995):5–19.

81. Manning is cited in Barbara Yaffe, 'Reform Launches New Offensive in Never-Ending Image Battle', *Vancouver Sun* (7 February 1997):A3.

82. National Angus Reid/Southam news polls, for example, 'The Federal Political Scene', July 1996, 'Federal Party Leaders' Approval Ratings', cited in http://www.angusreid.com/syndicate/reidreport.html. Between January 1994 and July 1996, for example, Manning's personal approval rating dropped from 47 per cent to 32 per cent; his disapproval rating jumped 22 per cent to a majority 53 per cent, while over the same period Canadians who were 'unsure' about what they thought of Preston Manning fell from 22 per cent to 15 per cent. In contrast, then Conservative leader Jean Charest moved ahead of the Reform leader in personal political popularity, and the New Democratic Party's new leader, Alexa McDonough, provided a boost to party fortunes.

83. Cited in ibid.

84. These figures were originally calculated from '1997 Canadian Federal Election Results', UBC Faculty of Commerce and Business Administration, Policy Analysis Division, http//esm.ubc.ca/CA97/results.html, and *The Globe and Mail*. Anyone using the former UBC Faculty of Commerce figures should be prepared to do recalculations from the raw constituency results. They are all off by one constituency result. See also report of the chief electoral officer on the 1997 Canadian general election, *1997, Official Voting Results, Thirty-Sixth General Election, Synopsis* (Ottawa: Elections Canada, 1998).

85. The Reform vote in Atlantic Canada was up slightly, though in Newfoundland, where the party ran in four of the seven seats, Reform's highest support (in Humber, St Barbe, and Baie Verte) was only at 6.5 per cent. In Prince Edward Island Reform sought election in two of the four island seats; in each they placed last, their highest total at 3.3 per cent in Malpeque.

86. To ensure the latter, Reform established five party committees during summer 1997:

    1. An electoral readiness committee: To utilize the party's capacity to define much of the previous campaign focus and do better in 2000.
    2. An 'ethnic' committee: To appeal more to visible minorities (though not yet to gender gaps).
    3. A committee on 'the Single Alternative Plan': A coalition of all parties on the right, essentially a throwback to Preston Manning's father and his 1967 *Political Realignment: A Challenge to Thoughtful Canadians*. This was tied closely to future party strategy for Ontario, where a breakthrough was necessary for any subsequent hopes of forming the government. In thirty-four Ontario seats in 1997, the combined Reform/Conservative vote was higher than that for the Liberals. It provided for the appointment of an 'Ontario' party critic from among those elected in the West.

4. An 'Atlantica' committee: To bolster the party's meagre support in this region. Included here was a 'new economic vision' that would focus on North-South links with the New England states, not unlike the Pacific Northwest's Cascadia.

5. A 'unity' committee: Chaired by party leader Manning himself, with five other MPs. Despite believing that it won more votes than it lost with its controversial anti-Quebec ads during 1997, Reform's intention is to 'turn down the heat' on the unity issue.

In addition to these national party committees, Reform subsequently looked at the possibility of having provincial Reform parties; there was already one in BC because it registered before Reform registered the name. The BC precedent, pressure from Saskatchewan (where the former Devine Conservatives self-destructed over fraud charges and convictions and a 'Saskatchewan Party' sought to replace local Tories), earlier canvassing from other provinces, as well as a post-1997 election increase in Reform's national concerns have meant that provincial Reform (or Reform-like) parties are increasingly possible and might give the party a higher profile and some actual governmental experience across the country.

Flanagan has suggested three possible options: (1) riding the wave of a unity crisis, Manning will lead Reform to success; (2) as the representative of ideological conservatism, Manning and Reform will become an 'NDP of the Right' and help set the policy agenda but do not govern; and (3) Reform will fall apart because of internal dissension and some will drift to other parties, which is what happened with the Progressives. See Flanagan, *Waiting For the Wave*, 4. A fourth option might be 'None of the above' with success or failure tied to a right-wing ideological restructuring of Canada's party system.

87. Uniting the right is central to this strategy. The early indications following the February 1999 'Unite the Right' convention in Ottawa suggest some tough sledding here.

88. Laird, *Slumming It at the Rodeo*, ix–xvi.

89. On the latter, see Laycock, *Populism and Democratic Thought*, 203–66.

90. See David Laycock, *The Reform Party and Democratic Politics in Canada* (Toronto: University of Toronto Press, forthcoming): Introduction and Chapter 1.

91. Sharpe and Braid, *Storming Babylon*, 81.

92. Tom Flanagan makes this point in *Waiting For the Wave*, 8–9, in criticizing 'overstatement' on 'the religious factor'.

93. Ibid., 9.

94. Ibid., 8.

95. As expressed by Manning in 'Moral Decision Making in the Political Arena', transcript of a radio address on 'Canada's National Bible Hour' (#1008). Cited in Flanagan, *Waiting For the Wave*, 214.

96. Ibid.

97. Sharpe and Braid, *Storming Babylon*, 84.

98. Flanagan, *Waiting For the Wave*, 9.

99. Sharpe and Braid, *Storming Babylon*, 89.

100. Dobbin, *Preston Manning and the Reform Party*, 21.

101. Laird, *Slumming It at the Rodeo*, 113–14.

102. Ibid., 114.

103. On this discussion, see L. Cohen, P.J. Smith, and P. Warwick, *The Vision and the Game: Making the Canadian Constitution* (Calgary: Detselig, 1987), particularly chapters 5 and 6, 61–98.

104. Self, *Government by the Market*.

105. Dobbin, *Preston Manning and the Reform Party*.

106. Ibid., vi–vii.

107. Laird, *Slumming It at the Rodeo*, xiv–xv.

108. Ibid.

109. Ibid., xv–xvi.

110. Dobbin, *Preston Manning and the Reform Party*, 21, 206, 207–21, and passim.

111. Flanagan, *Waiting For the Wave*, 9.

112. Dobbin, *Preston Manning and the Reform Party*, 114.

113. See Preston Manning, 'Building the Reform Team: The Hockey Analogy', Reform mailout, January 1990.

114. Flanagan, *Waiting For the Wave*, 12.

115. Dobbin, *Preston Manning and the Reform Party*, 115.

116. Cited in Laird, *Slumming It at the Rodeo*, xv.

117. Laycock, *The Reform Party and Democratic Politics*, Introduction and Chapter 1.

118. For an extensive discussion of this, see Andrew Johnson, Steve McBride, and Patrick Smith, eds, *Continuities and Discontinuities: The Political Economy of Social Welfare and Labour Market Policy in Canada* (Toronto: University of Toronto Press, 1994).

119. Laycock, *The Reform Party and Democratic Politics*, Chapter 2.

120. See Darin Barney and David Laycock, 'Right-Populists and Plebiscitory Politics in Canada', *Party Politics* 5, forthcoming.

121. Laycock, *The Reform Party and Democratic Politics*, 11–12.

122. Ibid., 16.

123. Ibid., 26.

124. Laird, *Slumming It at the Rodeo*, 34–5, italics added.

125. Laycock, *The Reform Party and Democratic Politics*, 22.

126. Flanagan, *Waiting For the Wave*, 5.

127. Dobbin, *Preston Manning and the Reform Party*, 118.

128. Ibid., 119. Many of these, from constituency party officials to MPs and candidates, presented an unattractive face with negative policy pronouncements on French Canada, immigration, Aboriginal peoples, the poor, homosexuals, women, and a range of other racial groups and issues from abortion to multiculturalism and social policy.

129. Stephen Harper, cited in Dobbin, *Preston Manning and the Reform Party*, 116.

130. Manning's admission that this was a problem for Reform is cited in Dobbin, *Preston Manning and the Reform Party*, 104.

131. An initial content analysis of one national and one regional newspaper between late January and early March 1999 identified few articles that were positive about the possibility of a Reform/Conservative coalition. In the same analysis, almost three times as many articles concluded that a Tory/Reform united front was a non-starter. On Clark's 'Canadian Alternative', see Robert Fife, 'Tories Look for an Alternative to the Alternative', *National Post* (1 March 1999):A7.

132. Even an initial post-UA convention meeting between the Tory and Reform leaders proved impossible to organize. After more than a week of convoluted telephone

tag closely monitored by the media, Reform announced that it was 'getting off the merry-go-round'. On this, see, for example, Lori Culbert, 'Manning to Call Clark, Who's Prepared to Listen', *Vancouver Sun* (24 February 1999):A3; Richard Foot, 'Manning Finds Out Today Whether Clark Returns Telephone Calls, Seeks Meeting on UA', *National Post* (26 February 1999):A7; Scott Feschuk, 'Manning Calls Clark Again', *National Post* (27 February 1999):A7; Sheldon Alberts, 'Manning and Clark Get Their Wires Crossed Again', *National Post* (3 March 1999): A7; Sheldon Alberts, 'Up to Clark to Initiate Talks, Manning Says, Reform Says It Is "Getting Off the Merry-go-round"', *National Post* (6 March 1999):A7.

133. These delegates were less than amused when meeting organizers chose as the UA theme song 'Rise Up', which turned out to be an anthem of the gay and lesbian community. Glen McGregor, 'Songwriters Rise Up Against UA's Use of Gay Anthem', *National Post* (27 February 1999):A1.

134. See, for example, Peter O'Neil, 'Reform "Won't Sacrifice Its Principles": Preston Manning Says the Move to Form an Anti-Liberal Coalition with Federal Tories Doesn't Mean "Having to Give Something Up"', *Vancouver Sun* (29 January 1999):A12.

135. See Eagles et al., *The Almanac of Canadian Politics*, 451–649, for a complete discussion of results in western Canada; on support and membership, see also Peter McCormick, 'The Reform Party of Canada: New Beginning or Dead End?' in *Party Politics in Canada*, 6th edn, edited by H.G. Thorburn (Scarborough: Prentice-Hall, 1991):342–52.

136. This was the Reform Party's own survey; see Reform Party of Canada, 'Summary of Assembly Results' (Memorandum to Members), 15 December 1989.

137. See, for example, Jim Morris, 'Reform Plots New Plan For Ontario', *The Chronicle-Herald*, (30 August 1997):1.

138. See, for example Reform's recent efforts to continue the focus on debt, having managed to move the agenda so deficits are essentially banished from the political vernacular. Barbara Yaffe, 'Reform Wants to Know What You'd Do with a Few Extra Billion Dollars', *Vancouver Sun* (16 September 1997):A3.

139. On this, see, for example, Barbara Yaffe, 'Reform's Decision: Principled Purity or Compromise and Power', *Vancouver Sun* (11 March 1999):A17.

CHAPTER 6

THE BLOC QUÉBÉCOIS AND ITS NATIONALIST PREDECESSORS: THE THREAD OF CONTINUITY IN QUEBEC POLITICS

The electoral successes of the Bloc Québécois in 1993 and, with less magnitude in 1997, constitute a turning-point for Quebec nationalists. These unprecedented successes need to be understood in the context of Quebec's political history and to be presented against the backdrop of Quebec's nationalist political culture. The Bloc Québécois is not without historical roots, contrary to what many observers of the political scene would have us believe. However, it was a series of events in the 1980s and the presence of charismatic leaders that led to the rapid growth of support for a nationalist alternative at the federal level.

Many nationalist third parties have emerged over the years to defend Quebec's interests at the federal level. Among these were, in chronological order, Henri Bourassa's Nationalists, André Laurendeau's Bloc Populaire Canadien, Réal Caouette's Ralliement des Créditistes, and Marcel Léger and Denis Monière's Parti Nationaliste.

Many streams of nationalism have taken hold in Quebec during this century: from the Nationalist League, which wanted to convince all Canadians that the time had come to forge an independent Canadian identity, to the Bloc Québécois, which wants to strike a new economic and political partnership between Quebec and the rest of Canada. Reactions to such movements have varied significantly. Nationalist movements have also differed ideologically, but they tend to be on the left of the political spectrum. The exception has been the Ralliement des Créditistes, a right-of-centre populist party.

All nationalist movements emerging from Quebec have demanded that the country be organized on the principle of dualism. That is, that Canada is the result of the coming together of the two founding nations. This claim has been consistent throughout the century: first with the creation of the Nationalist League and, more recently, with the entry of the Bloc Québécois into the House of Commons. Several of these nationalist political forces were active in Ottawa only for short spans of time because of the difficulties associated with voter mobilization for a party perpetually in opposition. At best, they could only aspire to wield the balance of power in a minority Parliament (e.g., Ralliement des Créditistes) or, if they were lucky, to become the official Opposition (e.g., Bloc Québécois).

Indeed, tracing the history of the Quebec electorate's voting preferences reveals a core base of support for agendas put forth by nationalist parties. Even when supposed 'national' (pan-Canadian) parties virtually sweep Quebec (e.g., the Tories in 1984 and 1988), they do so by co-opting many of the traditional positions taken by Quebec nationalist parties. In other words, the continuity outlined earlier and its historical manifestation (as detailed later) demonstrate that Quebec voters have displayed a surprisingly consistent set of preferences. Stability rather than volatility seems to characterize voting patterns in Quebec, suggesting that such voters are not mere consumers of an ever-changing stream of goodies offered by parties acting as little more than election machines. Voter preferences linked to particular identity features of Quebec have been persistent regardless of which party caters to such issues. Voters in Quebec cannot be construed as basing their choices on individual calculations of rational self-interest. Rather than concluding that volatility characterizes the Quebec voter, the consistent presence of nationalist parties, as will be assessed later, suggests that stability is the defining feature in voter-party relationships. This contrasts with the rational choice and brokerage models of voter behaviour as outlined in Chapter 1.

In a sense, then, the advent of nationalist parties representing Quebec's interests at the federal level serves as a gauge for the extent to which the brokerage activities of the dominant parties have failed to hold this core base of support in Quebec. Again, as argued in Chapter 1, successful brokerage requires that median voters be lured while simultaneously retaining these pockets of stability—these communities of voters—within the electorate. If a core electorate's values and concerns are bypassed or voter expectations that these concerns will be adequately represented are frustrated, then a total break with the incumbent party in favour of a nationalist alternative should not be taken to signify electoral volatility. Indeed, it is the brokerage parties' inability to appreciate the stability of preferences that brings on the advent of parties whose interests lie in promoting these core values and concerns at the federal level, thereby capturing an alienated and available electorate. It is the failure of brokerage politics, in other words, that has triggered voter rebellion, heralding a watershed realignment in Canada's party system.

The First Party System: The Nationalist League

The Nationalist League is most often associated with Henri Bourassa and his pursuit of nationalist objectives for Canada as a whole.[1] The fight against British imperialism and the support of Canada's independence were key elements in the League's political program. Bourassa, who was first elected under the federal Liberal Party banner in 1896 and who later assumed the leadership of the League, had on several occasions forcefully raised these issues with Prime Minister Wilfrid Laurier, who nevertheless continued to pursue a politically pragmatic course of retaining close ties with Britain. This contributed to Bourassa's uneasiness with the Liberals.

It is important to note that Henri Bourassa tended to be distrustful of party politics; he had more confidence in other forms of political expression, such as social movements or local initiatives. He was convinced that party leaders were only interested in making short-term deals, sacrificing principles for power. He opposed the creation of a federal third party in Quebec that would compete with the traditional parties, convinced as he was that 'party', by definition, demands the complete loyalty of its members and limits the expression of independent opinions and political preferences.

The emergence in 1903 of the Nationalist League, after many years of sustained efforts by Olivar Asselin and others who finally convinced Bourassa to assume its leadership, is especially relevant here. From that moment onwards the League consistently stressed biculturalism for Canada and demanded that the country promptly sever its formal links with the British Empire.

The Nationalists advocated a progressive educational platform, inspired by European social Catholicism and American progressivism. They favoured, on the one hand, strong provincial autonomy in the Canadian context; and, on the other, they argued for as much autonomy as possible from Britain. Nevertheless, their nationalism, based on a bicultural model, was aimed more at Canada as a whole than Quebec.[2]

According to the Nationalists, building a Canadian nation required English Canadians to renounce their British connection, to escape the Dominion's authority, and to adhere unconditionally to the idea of biculturalism. Henri Bourassa felt 'that the invasion of American ideas and American capital might be only the prelude to political absorption. To meet this danger [he] advocated a bi-cultural Canada.'[3] Bourassa was leading the way towards a unique Canadian nationalism.

Historian Joseph Levitt reminds us that the Nationalists 'felt that their supreme loyalty was owed to the culture of French Canada. They felt that French Canada must keep its culture from that of English Canada but that it should not have a sovereign state of its own.'[4] This was reminiscent of Honoré Mercier's attempt during the Riel crisis of 1885 to establish a *bloc* to defend the interests of French Canadians in Ottawa and to commute his death sentence. Such efforts proved to be futile. Mercier decided to try to use the Quebec Legislative Assembly to pursue those objectives and created the Parti National in 1885. This initiative on his part proved to be successful, with Mercier elected Quebec premier in 1887.

In 1899 Henri Bourassa (at the time a Liberal MP) found himself in fundamental disagreement with Laurier on the issue of Canada's participation in the Boer War. That confrontation led to Bourassa's resignation from the House of Commons as he condemned the government's decision to send Canadian troops under the British authority. At the time, there were deep concerns and adamant opposition among most French Canadians that Canada was an integral part of an imperial federation, meaning that they could be called upon at any time to participate in any wars launched by the British Empire. Laurier nonetheless kept the confidence of most Quebecers, obtaining 56 per cent of the vote in 1900 and fifty-five out of sixty-five seats, leaving Bourassa and his League followers beaten and disheartened.

The 1903 educational program of the Nationalists focused on Canada's need to obtain its full independence, greater provincial autonomy with respect to the central government, and the establishment of progressive policies.[5] In 1904 the League began publishing a weekly newspaper, Le Nationaliste, edited by Olivar Asselin.

Six years later, Henri Bourassa started his own daily newspaper, Le Devoir, which became a major vehicle for political ideas in Quebec and French Canada in general. The principal objective of Le Devoir was to defend a Canadian nationalism based on the idea of two dominant cultures, each autonomous in its own sphere of responsibilities. Referring to his Canadian nationalism, Bourassa stated that it was 'founded on the duality of the races composed of French Canadians and English Canadians, that is to say of two elements separated by language and religion ... but united by a common attachment to a common homeland.'[6] This was the principal motivation behind Bourassa's passionate defence in the House of Commons of the rights of French Canadians living in the rest of Canada. The Manitoba schools question of 1890 acted as a reminder of things past that should never surface again.[7] Consequently, when shortly thereafter the North-West Territories schools question erupted (which involved the revocation of French language rights), Bourassa was profoundly hurt and disillusioned.

Laurier's introduction of the Naval Bill into the House of Commons in 1910 led to the inevitable clash with Bourassa and his Nationalists. In a subsequent by-election in the riding of Drummond-Arthabasca, the Liberals lost to the Nationalists. Shortly thereafter, at the general election of 1911, the Nationalist-Conservative alliance that opposed Laurier in Quebec saw no less than twenty-seven of their anti-Laurier candidates elected throughout the province, a major factor in the defeat of the Liberals that year.[8]

According to Murray Beck, the Nationalist-Conservative alliance was not difficult to realize since the two groups represented the same ideological bent. In Beck's words:

> The anti-government French-Canadian candidates—they called themselves Autonomistes—cannot be separated into Conservatives and Nationalists, but most of them had a Conservative background. While scandal and the like played some part in their campaign, they generally took their cue from Bourassa and talked almost entirely about autonomy in its anti-imperialist, anti-conscription aspects.[9]

However, Robert Borden's election as prime minister spelled bad news for the Nationalists who had mobilized to sever Laurier's imperialist ties, yet they got from the Conservatives exactly what they had fought against: imperialist-oriented policies. In addition, Bourassa's Nationalists could not, contrary to what they had hoped, exercise the balance of power in the House of Commons since Borden's Conservatives, even without the support of the Nationalists, had a majority of five seats. In the aftermath of the election, Laurier, now leader of the official Opposition, saw the gains to be made if he stressed Canada's desire to assert its independent status. In the process, the Nationalists gradually lost their appeal and the movement lost momentum. This episode clearly illustrates the difficulties that face single-issue parties: as the issues at stake evolve and the positions of the established parties shift, so do the fortunes of third parties that emerge to fill political vacuums left by unresponsive or colluding brokerage parties. The influence of the Nationalists and their appearance on the political scene acted as a reminder of the shortcomings of strict brokerage politics. Here was a party that represented a well-defined and largely taken-for-granted regional constituency. At the very least it served to demonstrate that an alternative appeal could be made to a francophone core electorate in Quebec, and as attested by the change in policy orientation by the Laurier Liberals, the success of such alternative appeals could stimulate a greater attentiveness on the part of the mainstream 'national' parties to the values and concerns of this core electorate.

Borden's Union government decision to impose conscription in 1917 was like a cold shower for francophone Quebecers. In the federal election of that year, the Unionists obtained only 25 per cent of the votes in Quebec whereas Laurier's Liberals took 73 per cent and sixty-two of the sixty-five seats. With the Conservatives delegitimized in the eyes of Quebec's francophone voters, the election of 1917 spelled the beginning of a long period of drought for the Conservatives in the province.

The Canadian political landscape changed significantly throughout Canada between 1917 and 1940. While the two major parties at the federal level remained important but highly uneven contenders in Quebec, other social movements found fertile ground. Of particular importance was the birth of the Bloc Populaire Canadien to which we now turn our attention.

The Second Party System: The Bloc Populaire Canadien

During the second party system, the Liberals received a consistently larger proportion of support in Quebec than they had prior to the First World War. The Conservatives were identified with conscription and found it difficult to rehabilitate their image with francophone voters. However, the advent of the Second World War had a negative impact on the Liberals' position in Quebec in the wake of the King government's decision to participate fully in another European war. A group of eleven Quebec Liberal MPs, led by Maxime Raymond, opposed the government's decision to hold a pan-Canadian plebiscite on the idea of releasing the government from its long-standing promise never to impose conscription. Most of these members came from ridings outside of Montreal.[10] These Liberal members were aware that, in the end, it would be the will of the anglophone majority that would prevail and that King's promise to the French Canadians not to subject them again to the hated device of conscription would be broken. At the time none of these MPs quit the Liberal Party, though the writing was already on the wall that a new Quebec party was in the offing. Once again, the basic values of Quebec's core electorate had been bypassed.

A manifesto to create the Parti Canadien was quickly produced, but failed to mobilize political forces.[11] Its leader, Liguori Lacombe, a member of the so-called Group of Eleven, attracted little support and made no electoral inroads. The urgency of the situation created a different response, as Quebecers rapidly rallied around a mass movement that became known as the League for the Defence of Canada. The opposition to King's conscriptionist bill was such among French Canadians that organized groups emerged in Ontario, Quebec, and New Brunswick.[12] Funded at the end of January 1942, the League for the Defence of Canada attracted people from all political stripes and social classes. It brought together supporters of the Union Nationale, the Group of Eleven, nationalist organizations, as well as former members of the Action Libérale Nationale. All wanted to form an alliance to stop the federal government from betraying its promise that it would not commit the population of Canada to imperial wars.

A manifesto entitled 'Manifeste au peuple du Canada' stressed what the group viewed as a betrayal by Mackenzie King, who had secured the strong support of French Canada on false promises. The League, however, had problems disseminating its program; it could not count on Radio-Canada, which denied airtime to any No partisans in the plebiscite. Nevertheless, several opinion leaders joined forces with the League, including André Laurendeau, its general secretary, and Henri Bourassa. Bourassa denounced Mackenzie King's decision and stressed the need for Canada to act independently of Great Britain. In the end, the Liberal government's Yes forces received only 27.1 per cent of the vote in Quebec, compared to 71.6 per cent for the No (1.1 per cent were wasted ballots).[13]

Conditions seemed propitious for the creation of a new political party in Quebec. Following the establishment of the League, Liberals and Conservatives in Quebec decided to work together in an unprecedented political alliance to stop conscription. Once again a federal government had overridden French Canada's clearly stated preferences, making it easier for the League to emerge in Quebec as a political force.

In May 1942 Maxime Raymond, the leader of the Group of Eleven and later head of the League, was chosen leader of the newly created Bloc Populaire Canadien. Raymond wanted to ensure that the party could be represented quickly in the House of Commons. However, only two of his colleagues in the Group of Eleven quit the Liberals to create the new party, which was officially formed on 8 September 1942. The newspaper Le Devoir and journal L'Action Nationale were particularly supportive of the initiative even if it irritated certain members of Quebec's high clergy. Not surprisingly, the new party was rapidly condemned by both the Union Nationale and the Liberals. In response to his many critics, Bloc leader Maxime Raymond evoked the party's primary goal: to defend the interests of French Canadians both in Ottawa and Quebec City.

Especially influenced by the Action Libérale Nationale's former leaders,[14] the Bloc proposed a series of progressive policies based on equality of treatment for all, and defended the principle of nationalization of several private companies.[15] The Bloc also favoured the internationalization of the economy, questioned the entry of foreign capital into the Canadian market, and condemned preferential trade arrangements as unfair practices.[16] Clearly the Bloc was ahead of its time in many sectors, advocating positions that would only be taken up again thirty years later by the NDP's progressive Waffle faction.[17]

There is no doubt that the Bloc Populaire Canadien's program was innovative, elements of which would return to the political scene in the early 1960s as the Quiet Revolution unfolded: abolition of the appointed Legislative Council (the Quebec Senate), antipatronage measures, and changes to the electoral law to prevent gerrymandering. The Bloc also proposed to sign reciprocity arrangements with any provincial government willing to guarantee their francophone population access to the same services available to anglophone Quebecers.[18]

The Bloc's constitutional philosophy was essentially built on the dualist theory of Canadian federalism articulated by Henri Bourassa, and was very critical of centralizing policies envisioned by Ottawa. The Bloc firmly opposed Canada's adoption of British symbols; it preferred 'Canada First' to 'Mother England'. The intention was to remove any colonial links; the Bloc argued that Canada should have its own independent identity.

It is possible that the surge of popular interest in the Bloc led to some initiatives to undermine the credibility of its leaders. This probably explains why important elements in the Bloc were taken to court and accused of wrongdoing.[19] As well, astute political opponents such as Maurice Duplessis, leader of the provincial Union Nationale, began co-opting the Bloc's autonomist vocabulary. Duplessis, premier between 1936 and 1939 but defeated in the provincial election that year, needed an electoral platform upon which to build his political comeback.

The Bloc Populaire Canadien competed provincially in 1944 and federally in 1945, as well as in a few by-elections. It failed to get its candidate elected in Outremont in November 1942 (this riding, which had major pockets of anglophones and allophones, had just voted Yes in the conscription plebiscite). The Bloc lost that race despite the efforts of an aged Henri Bourassa and a young Pierre Elliott Trudeau, then a student at the Université de Montréal's law faculty; both had delivered speeches in favour of the Bloc candidate.[20] Eight months later, the Bloc elected its first candidate in Stanstead, but lost the riding of Montreal-Cartier to a Communist candidate (a first for Canada).[21] Other parties accused the Bloc's candidate of helping to elect the communist candidate by stealing votes from them and several articles were written to condemn such a turn of events. Even the left-wing magazine *Canadian Forum* came out against the Bloc at the time.[22]

When the governing Liberals lost all five by-elections in 1943, King decided to try to regain former Liberal supporters that were opting for the CCF in English Canada and the Bloc Populaire Canadien in Quebec. The Liberals began to move to the left politically by adopting a package of social policies that targeted workers and low-income people. The stage was now set for the general election of 1945.

Meanwhile, the Bloc had opened a provincial front with the election of André Laurendeau as its provincial leader. The provincial election that followed in 1944 was simply a replay of the conscription plebiscite, with the Union Nationale and the Bloc candidates arguing that Quebec must have more provincial autonomy. Adélard Godbout's governing Liberals, in office since 1939, were defeated by Maurice Duplessis's Union Nationale, despite winning a higher percentage of the vote. The Bloc Populaire Canadien won a respectable 15.2 per cent of the popular vote and, according to Paul Cliche, contributed to the defeat of fifty-six candidates (forty Liberals and sixteen Unionists).[23]

The 1944 provincial election was expected to provide the Bloc Populaire Canadien with an important boost going into the federal election; instead, the mediocre showing had negative consequences. When Mackenzie King called his 1945 election, Bloquists experienced some difficulties: defections, internal rivalries between federal and provincial organizations, and the creation of yet another nationalist grouping, the Mouvement des Indépendants.[24] Camilien Houde, former mayor of Montreal and former leader of the Conservatives in Quebec (who was jailed after having opposed conscription) was named co-chair of the Bloc's campaign. The war at an end, the Bloc had difficulty recruiting candidates, fielding only thirty-six (out of sixty-five Quebec ridings). Mackenzie King was able to induce most members of the Group of Eleven (who had originally formed the backbone of the Bloc's provincial organization) back into the Liberal ranks. The Social Credit Party was another factor, entering the race in no less than forty-two ridings and skimming 4.5 per cent of the vote.

The unfavourable political winds that blew during the war were clearly changing for the Liberals in Quebec. In 1945 they obtained 50.8 per cent of the votes and fifty-eight out of the sixty-five seats. With 12.8 per cent of the votes, the Bloc elected only two of its candidates, ahead of the Conservatives who obtained a mere 8.4 per cent of the votes. Several independent candidates and third parties (such as the workers' party) received no less than one in five votes.

Ironically, King maintained his grip on power in Ottawa due to his party's strong showing in Quebec, while the Bloc—a party that was formed in response to the conscription issue—saw its support evaporate with the return of world peace. A series of events and factors negatively affected the Bloc's morale: Laurendeau's decision to quit the Bloc to become editor of *Le Devoir*; difficulties in raising funds; repeated defeats in federal and provincial by-elections; and conflict between federal and provincial leaders. The Bloc had failed to break the mould of federal politics, and it did not present candidates in the 1949 federal election.

Mackenzie King retained strong support among French Canadians throughout these years. Public opinion surveys revealed that the Liberal leader was held in high regard by francophones more so than anglophones (an ethnolinguistic difference that was paralleled in more recent times in popular perceptions of Brian Mulroney). This is said to be due to the fact that King sent Canadian troops overseas with moderation and that he was sensitive to French Canadians' concerns.[25] At the end of the war, French-Canadian voters returned to the Liberals while their distrust of the Conservatives, who had advocated more rapid and substantial troop commitments, was reinforced.

The Third Party System: Social Credit

For most of the period between 1949 and 1962, the two major parties (Conservatives and Liberals) together secured 85 per cent (1949), 90 per cent (1953), 89 per cent (1957), and 96 per cent (1958) of the votes in Quebec. Bipartisanship was shaken in 1962, however, when the two major parties obtained only 70 per cent of the popular vote. That year Social Credit won twenty-six Quebec seats on 26 per cent of the vote.

The Social Credit movement had blossomed in Alberta under the leadership of William Aberhart. In addition to its basic economic tenets, the movement demanded that provincial autonomy be fully respected, and that decentralization within Canada be encouraged. This led to several clashes with Ottawa over such powers as banking and credit.[26] This staunch defence of provincial autonomy made the party attractive to a portion of the Quebec electorate. The growth of the Social Credit movement in Quebec, however, awaited appropriate electoral conditions and the emergence of a francophone leader with political skills and magnetism comparable to that of Aberhart. That leader was Réal Caouette. Perceived as a French-Canadian nationalist, Caouette always defended bicultural and bilingual policies for the country, starting with his own party at the pan-Canadian level. Caouette's first experience in politics went back to the provincial election of 1944 when the Union des Électeurs (Créditiste) ran eleven candidates, receiving barely 1.2 per cent of the vote cast. Similar to the Bloc Populaire Canadien, the Social Credit leaders had recommended a No vote in the 1942 plebiscite on conscription. There were some doubts, however, as to where the party really stood on the issue, considering that it had joined the Social Credit Association of Canada in April 1944, and that the latter advocated Canada's participation in the war.

More generally, the Union des Électeurs was inspired by doctrines expounded in the journal *Vers Demain*. In Michael Stein's words:

> The nationalism of *Vers Demain* was carefully honed in the French-Canadian tradition, with emphasis on such distinctively French-Canadian attitudes and doctrines as anti-conscription, antagonism to English-Canadian monopolies and economic domination, cultural, linguistic, and educational autonomy for Quebec, recognition of the rights of French-Canadian minorities in other provinces, and permeation of social and economic life with Catholic, particularly papal-framed ultramontane principles.[27]

The Union des Électeurs entered its first federal election in May 1945 with forty-three candidates winning 4.5 per cent of the popular vote. Social Credit sent its first member to the House of Commons, Réal Caouette, following the September 1946 by-election in Pontiac. Caouette had promised to fight for lower taxes, to encourage the creation of wealth, to eliminate ration coupons, and to give a monthly dividend to all family members. Otherwise, the Union des Électeurs met with little success, electing only one candidate between 1940 and 1956 at either the federal or provincial level. The movement's decision in 1957 to withdraw from electoral competition led to the creation of the Ralliement des Créditistes around which Caouette, Gilles Grégoire, and some former Union des Électeurs militants decided to regroup.

The Ralliement des Créditistes competed in its first federal election in June 1962. With the exception of Greater Montreal, the party did well among most segments of Quebec society. Stein, author of *The Dynamics of Right-Wing Protest*, pointed out that, 'Of the ten traditional regions of Quebec, the Créditistes emerged as the dominant party in no less than four and also ran a strong second in four others.'[28] He also indicates that 'In the twenty-one federal constituencies of Montreal, the Créditistes placed fourth and last among the major parties in all but three ridings (Laurier, Mercier, and Saint-Jacques).'[29] The party attracted more than 50 per cent of the registered vote in no less than twelve ridings.

Economic difficulties in rural areas and Caouette's leadership skills are crucial to understanding the rapid surge in the Ralliement des Créditistes' support. In addition, Diefenbaker's success in Quebec in 1958 had not brought about favourable changes and left Quebecers unsatisfied. Many backed the Ralliement for lack of a better choice; people felt they had nothing to lose. Again, a pattern in voting behaviour emerges. The electorate's perception that Diefenbaker failed to deliver created a situation in which an alienated electorate was open to alternatives. The salient point here is that what seems to signify upheaval in the distribution of party preferences is undergirded by a certain continuity in the values and concerns of the electorate. This electorate had just seen the end of two periods of domination federally and provincially with the defeat of Louis St Laurent's Liberals in 1957 and Antonio Barrette's Union Nationale in 1960. Quebecers were suddenly willing to consider new options that Caouette's party constituted a real alternative to the old parties and he played intensely on the idea.[30]

The results of the 1963 federal election were more sobering. Caouette's political strength went down from twenty-six to twenty seats even though his Créditistes increased their popular vote from 26 per cent to 27.3 per cent. Still, the party remained a political force that could not be ignored. One should note that the presence of Social Credit on the ballot attracted some voters who normally abstained from federal politics.[31]

The Ralliement des Créditistes burst onto the scene in Ottawa at a time when Quebec nationalism was emerging as a real political force and when political discontent was growing. The party's relationship with the Liberal Party of Canada was not always clear. There are indications that the party, afraid that the western-led, antibilingual, and antibicultural Conservatives might assume power, made some deals with Pearson's Liberals to maintain them in power.[32] Pearson's establishment of the Laurendeau-Dunton Royal Commission on Bilingualism and Biculturalism was an attempt to accommodate Quebec's political claims. During that period most Quebec nationalists were refusing to enter politics at the federal level, convinced that the Quebec question could be settled only at the provincial level.

In Ottawa the Ralliement des Créditistes manifested some interest in the idea of 'associate statehood' for Quebec, a concept that was gaining popularity in Quebec. However, the division within the party rank and file was personified by the difference between their leader, Caouette, who was rather cold to the idea, and the party's deputy leader, Gilles Grégoire, who argued that the party ought to explore it further. This escalated into a significant clash within the party between nationalists like Grégoire and provincial autonomists like Caouette, who wanted a more decentralized but united country. In the end, Caouette's autonomists prevailed at the federal level, while nationalists reorganized themselves into the Ralliement National (RN) at the provincial level and distanced themselves from their former leader.

The RN firmly backed the idea of Quebec and Canada as associate states; like the Ralliement des Créditistes in Ottawa, they also condemned all leftist-oriented public policies. The party did not perform well at the June 1966 provincial election, getting only 3.2 per cent of the vote.[33] Shortly after the election, Gilles Grégoire was approached to assume the leadership of the RN. It was under Grégoire that the party decided, in 1968, to join forces with René Lévesque's recently formed Mouvement Souveraineté-Association (MSA) to form the Parti Québécois (PQ). Grégoire was elected vice-president of the PQ and René Lévesque was chosen as its first president.

Caouette was uncertain of the need for the Créditistes to have both provincial and federal wings. This was accentuated following the RN's decision to join the MSA to form the PQ. Unexpectedly, Caouette decided to push for a provincial wing, and Camille Samson was elected leader of the provincial party in March 1970. Samson broke with the nationalist musings of Grégoire's RN so that he could find a niche for his party between the Liberals and the emerging Péquistes. He opted instead for a position demanding that constitutionally guaranteed provincial jurisdictions be protected against any attempts at federal centralization. Somewhat surprisingly, the party won 11.2 per cent of the vote in 1970 and elected twelve MNAs. The nationalist PQ elected seven members to the National Assembly on 23 per cent of the vote. Several parties were then represented in the National Assembly: the newly elected Liberals, the newly defeated Union Nationale, and the newly created Parti Québécois and Ralliement des Créditistes.

Between 1970 and 1976, Quebec continued to experience a realignment of its provincial party system (see Table 6.1) and the quest for national autonomy remained essentially a matter debated in the National Assembly. Ever since the November 1976 election that first brought the PQ to power, the same two protagonists—the Liberals and the Péquistes—have been facing one another and winning power for similar periods of time.

Table 6.1: Quebec Provincial Election Results, 1970–1976

	1970		1973		1976	
	Seats	Vote	Seats	Vote	Seats	Vote
Liberal	72	45.4	102	54.5	26	33.8
Parti Québécois	7	23.1	6	30.2	71	41.4
Union Nationale	17	19.6	—	4.9	11	18.2
Ralliement des Créditistes	12	11.2	2	9.9	1	4.6
Parti National Populaire	1	0.9				

Militant Quebec nationalists stayed out of federal politics for most of the 1970s, preferring instead to invest their energies provincially. During this time there were some indications that a sovereigntist party might emerge at the federal level. PQ activist Guy Bertrand, a lawyer by profession, had frequently proposed the idea. Moreover, he had hoped to create a sovereigntist party called the Bloc Québécois in the 1972 federal election. That initiative, however, did not receive the blessing of the PQ establishment.[34]

PQ leader René Lévesque was concerned that a defeat for the nationalists at the federal level might have a demobilizing effect on the movement.[35] This does not mean that nationalists were unconcerned with federal politics; it suggests, rather, that they thought it was preferable to concentrate their efforts provincially to avoid any potential conflicts between party supporters or confrontations between a provincial and a federal wing. Instead, it was decided to invite Quebec voters to spoil their ballots at the upcoming federal election in October 1972. Approximately 165,000 did so; the same request in the federal election of 1974 resulted in more than 134,000 spoiled ballots.[36]

Following the election of the PQ in November 1976, nationalists focused their energies on providing good government for Quebecers and preparing for the promised referendum on sovereignty-association. The election in 1979 of Joe Clark's minority government, with very little support from Quebec, provided René Lévesque with a golden opportunity to launch his referendum. The same election that brought Clark to power also brought a contingent of Quebec Socreds to Ottawa. They were led by Fabien Roy, a soft nationalist who had previously voted in favour of the PQ's language legislation (Bill 101) as an Independent in the National Assembly. Roy frequently took his cues from Quebec City; having benefited from the backing of the PQ organization in many ridings, he had a political debt to repay. According to Graham Fraser:

> ... it was an open secret that in several ridings, PQ organizers were working for and even running as candidates for the Créditistes. It was part of what Lévesque's staff hoped could be 'a bridge to the right' that would enable them to reach out to the traditional conservative nationalist constituency during the referendum campaign.[37]

The political scene was to change dramatically on the night of 13 December 1979 when Joe Clark's government lost a vote of non-confidence on the budget. Having been unable to get a reply from Quebec City as to how they should vote, the Socreds abstained from voting and the Clark government fell, short of the six votes it needed.[38]

The defeat of the Conservatives—who had run in 1979 on the concept of Canada as a 'community of communities'—spelled trouble for Quebec nationalists. The fervently antinationalist Pierre Elliott Trudeau seized the opportunity; he reversed his resignation and re-entered the political fray with a renewed determination to settle matters with Quebec once and for all. Campaigning on a national energy policy favourable to consuming provinces such as Quebec, and promising Quebecers a 'renewed federalism', his Liberal Party won 44.3 per cent of vote in the February 1980 election and formed a majority government with an incredible seventy-four out of seventy-five Quebec seats. The Socreds, who had taken 16.0 per cent of the Quebec vote in the previous election, were eliminated from the House of Commons.

The Mulroney Interlude

Following the patriation of the Constitution from Britain in 1982, René Lévesque first spoke of the urgent need to establish a PQ wing in Ottawa and gave directions to form a committee to investigate such an opportunity. The PQ establishment, however, rejected the idea, though a significant contingent felt that it was essential to develop links with anti-Trudeau political forces in Ottawa in order to defeat the Liberals at the next federal election. Within the PQ, the more Conservative (Blue) nationalists generally opposed the option of a federal wing of the provincial party, preferring the option of striking a deal with the federal Conservative Party.

At first, internal polls done by the PQ pollster, Michel Lepage, indicated that the presence of the PQ at the federal level would prove successful.[39] If the PQ had entered the race federally, polls indicated there would be a significant change in the popular mood, with a large segment of support going towards the new nationalist option.[40]

With such impressive potential results, Marcel Léger, a PQ cabinet minister, did not easily give up the idea of sending a PQ wing to Ottawa. Lévesque, however, had grown cold to the idea, once again fearing a demobilizing effect on the party provincially. At this time, there were essentially two schools confronting one another within the PQ: the hard nationalists whose support went respectively to creating a federal PQ wing and the soft (Blue) nationalists who continued to advocate a deal with the federal Conservatives.[41] The name 'Parti Québécois' in fact was registered as a federal political party in the summer of 1982; this led to a major imbroglio that resulted in a decision not to run federally, but to take part in the election nonetheless. The Blue nationalists had won the day. Waiting in the wings for the departure of Lévesque as PQ leader, they were preparing for his successor and preferred to invest their energies in the federal Conservatives. No nationalist party from Quebec would enter the federal race. Still, Marcel Léger refused to quit and on 12 June 1983, the day that Brian Mulroney became leader of the Conservatives, the PQ national council announced that it was going to support the entry of the Parti Nationaliste (PN) into the federal arena. Shortly thereafter, the PN was officially launched with a mandate to defend Quebec's interests and its right to self-determination.[42]

Early polls indicated that such a party would not do well: it attracted only 5 per cent of voters' intentions. Following such poor predictions, and after intense pressure from René Lévesque's entourage, Léger resigned and left the PN leadership to Université de Montréal political scientist Denis Monière, who led the party in its first and last political campaign. The PN received only 2.5 per cent of the vote, neck and neck with the Rhinoceros Party. The PN lost its official party status in 1988 when it failed to nominate fifty candidates for that year's general election. This poor showing was a virtual certainty when many Blue nationalists decided to rally instead behind Brian Mulroney's Progressive Conservatives.[43]

With the potential election of bilingual Quebecer Brian Mulroney as prime minister of Canada in 1984, soft nationalists saw a golden opportunity to attain a 'national affirmation' within the Canadian federation. Mulroney was rapidly guaranteed the support of moderate nationalists like Lucien Bouchard, Guy Chevrette, Rodrigue Biron, and Pierre-Marc Johnson, soon to become Lévesque's successor as leader of the PQ. All favoured an affirmationist project within Canada (meaning pursuing Quebec nation building within the confines of the current federal system) rather than full sovereignty for Quebec. All had vigorously opposed the creation of a Quebec nationalist party in Ottawa on the grounds that this would have undermined Mulroney's chances of defeating the Liberals.[44] Blue nationalists placed their bets on Mulroney to accommodate Quebec's claims and tended to be suspicious of the motives the hard *indépendantistes* like Jacques Parizeau, who simply wanted to take Quebec out of the Canadian federation altogether. Provincial Liberals, also dissatisfied with the way Trudeau's federal Liberals had proceeded with the patriation of the Constitution, added their support to Mulroney's campaign. With Trudeau in retirement and the Liberals led by John Turner, Mulroney easily won the province, taking fifty-eight out of seventy-five seats.

In late 1984 Lévesque's decision to pursue the *beau risque* (the strategy of reaching an accommodation with the new Conservative government) resulted in the departure of several of the PQ's hard nationalists, including his finance minister Jacques Parizeau. These departures were a significant blow to René Lévesque's leadership. On 21 June 1985 Lévesque announced his resignation. Pierre-Marc Johnson, a Blue nationalist, was chosen as his replacement. In the subsequent provincial election, Johnson was defeated by Robert Bourassa's renewed Liberals on 2 December 1985.

Shortly thereafter, the seeds of the Meech Lake Accord were planted.[45] At Mont Gabriel in May 1986, Quebec identified five conditions to be recognized in order to bring the province back into the federal family. In August and again in November 1986, all Canadian premiers agreed to back those conditions to settle the Quebec question. The mood was upbeat and provincial premiers seemed willing to take on the challenge. The rest of the story is well known: the signing of Meech Lake proposals and the subsequent unravelling of the Accord that led to the Meech Lake débâcle in late June of 1990.[46]

The period from May 1986 to June 1992 is crucial to understanding the emergence of the Bloc Québécois in Ottawa. In many ways the election of 1988, in Quebec at least, was based first on the idea that Meech Lake was a *fait accompli* and, second, on the prospect of a free trade arrangement with the United States. These two initiatives, but especially the Meech commitment, contributed to the election of sixty-three Conservatives, a gain of five over 1984. This result was the Conservatives' best performance ever in Quebec.

It is relevant to note here that traditional support for the federal Liberals in Quebec dissipated following the repatriation of the Constitution in 1982 and that the party has not recovered.[47] The main beneficiary of this fall in popularity in 1984 and 1988 was Mulroney's Progressive Conservative Party. However, following the defeat of Meech Lake in 1990, the Conservatives were forced by anglophone opinion to tone down (if not water down) their earlier stated intention to accommodate Quebec within the federation 'with honour and enthusiasm' and instead embarked on a strategy of attempting to simultaneously placate all Canadian interests. This led to a strong sense of alienation among Quebecers who turned to the newly established Bloc Québécois and gave them almost half their votes (49.3 per cent) and fifty-four seats in 1993. The sense of urgency was not as pronounced in 1997 and voter support for the Bloc slipped to 37.4 per cent and forty-four seats.

In 1984 and again in 1988 Brian Mulroney was able to take advantage of francophone Quebecers' disaffection towards the Liberal Party by enticing both autonomists and nationalists to trust him when he promised to reintegrate the province into the federal fold. The Progressive Conservatives ran on the claim that Pierre Trudeau had denied Quebec's aspirations and betrayed his own promise, made prior to the 1980 referendum, that he would make the necessary changes to accommodate Quebec's demands in the Canadian federation.

Failing to deliver on his own solemn promise to Quebecers, which was capped by the failure of the Meech Lake Accord, Mulroney lost the support of several Quebec MPs, including his personal friend and prominent cabinet minister Lucien Bouchard. Bouchard quit the party and shortly thereafter regrouped nationalist forces around the newly created Bloc Québécois. In an attempt to regain the initiative and salvage their position in Quebec and elsewhere, Mulroney's Conservatives pursued a new constitutional settlement—the Charlottetown Accord, which was rejected in several parts of the country, including Quebec, where 56.7 per cent of the electorate voted against the deal.[48] The level of rejection in some francophone constituencies reached highs of 77 per cent (the deeply nationalist areas of Jonquière and Lac Saint-Jean), while support for the Accord in anglophone ridings was as high as 88 per cent (Mont Royal). Clearly, Quebec's language communities were once again badly divided on the key political question of ethnonational relations.

By pushing for the recognition of Quebec as a 'distinct society', the Conservative Party alienated an important group of its supporters in the West, while the October 1992 referendum on the Charlottetown Accord convinced francophone Quebecers that they were taken for granted in the federation. Third parties at this juncture were presented with a real opportunity to attract voters frustrated by this outcome. The Bloc Québécois came to be viewed by many francophone Quebecers as the only option left, short of boycotting the election itself.[49]

The difficulties experienced during the Meech Lake negotiations and its final derailment on 23 June 1990 spelled serious trouble for the Conservatives. Soft and moderate (Blue) nationalists, who had joined the Conservatives during the *beau risque* period, were compelled to reconsider their attachment to the party. The PQ was now of the view that a nationalist voice in Ottawa should be considered as part of a strategy to regain power in Quebec City and to prepare for the next referendum. Other Quebec Conservative MPs, feeling the pressure in their ridings, were more inclined to quit the party and sit as independents. The Liberal Party's 1990 decision to replace John Turner with Jean Chrétien, who had clearly stated his opposition to Meech Lake, prompted the defections of Quebec MPs Jean Lapierre and Gilles Rocheleau. A new political voice was taking shape in Ottawa, a voice that would fill the vacuum at the federal level created by the repeated frustration of the traditional demands of Quebec's core constituency. With support for the federal Conservatives plummeting, and the Chrétien Liberals unwilling to address such demands, the Bloc Québécois simply took over as vehicle for the continuing, stable preferences of Quebec voters.

On 25 July 1990, the Bloc Québécois was officially created. Lucien Bouchard, the former Conservative cabinet minister who resigned over changes made to the Meech Lake Accord, was chosen as the BQ's first leader. The Bloc's origins, then, lay in the federal Conservative Party's Quebec caucus, many of whom no longer felt comfortable within the party after the defeat of the Meech Lake Accord (considered the bottom line by all Quebec's provincial parties).

The party entered its first electoral campaign in a late summer by-election and elected its first member of Parliament, Gilles Duceppe, with an impressive 66.9 per cent of the vote.[50] It is interesting to note that in that election all candidates but one ran under a nationalist banner. The only declared federalist candidate obtained a mere 7 per cent of the vote.

Quebec had rapidly become a fertile terrain for the nationalist cause. Shocked by the failure of Meech Lake, Quebec Premier Robert Bourassa launched a major initiative to garner Quebecers' opinions and also to channel their sense of alienation towards positive ends: the building of a societal consensus of an unprecedented nature. Bourassa was said to be sympathetic to the emergence of a Quebec bloc in Ottawa, and is even said to have given his support to Lucien Bouchard's initiative.[51] Indeed, shortly after the collapse of Meech Lake, Bourassa appointed Bouchard to the Bélanger-Campeau Commission, which was established as part of a two-pronged strategy: (1) to allow time for the Liberal Party to reorganize itself and (2) to determine the future of Quebec with or without Canada.[52] Bouchard's participation on the commission afforded him further public exposure as he crisscrossed the province to take the pulse of the population. Support for the idea of sovereignty was running at an all-time high.[53]

The Fourth Party System

The most distinctive feature of the 1993 election was the Bloc Québécois's strong performance in Quebec. The party's strong showing, coupled with the fracturing of the vote elsewhere in Canada, combined to give the Bloc official Opposition status.

At stake in this election was who could best represent Quebec's interests in Ottawa: the Conservatives under the leadership of Kim Campbell; the Liberals led by Jean Chrétien; or the Bloc under Lucien Bouchard. As the campaign progressed, it became increasingly obvious that the Conservatives were going to lose badly, that the Liberals would emerge victorious, and that the Bloc might acquire the status of official Opposition.

The 1993 federal election in Quebec was in line with traditional political behaviour in at least one sense: the tendency to vote *en bloc* for the same party. Herein lies another indicator of the propensity of the Quebec electorate to act as a 'community of voters'. However, this time around Quebecers were supporting a party that was condemned to be on the Opposition side since the Bloc Québécois was not running candidates outside the province. Still, there was a sense that the Bloc could play an important role in the House of Commons if it could secure the place of the official Opposition or if it could exercise the balance of power as did the Social Credit at an earlier time. Moreover, Bouchard's strong performance in the election campaign confirmed his growing stature and popularity.

The Bloc Québécois program was essentially constructed to represent better the interests of Quebec in Ottawa, combined with a generally left-leaning approach to social policy. Several Bloc candidates came from or were closely affiliated with one of the four main labour unions in Quebec: the Quebec Teachers' Union, the Quebec Federation of Labour, the Union of Farm Producers, and the Confederation of National Trade Unions. In addition, several Bloc candidates had a prior association with the Parti Québécois.[54]

Most of the sixty-two seats that the Conservatives lost in Quebec in 1993 were snapped up by Bloc Québécois candidates. This further evinces the proposition that although parties may change, the same values and concerns govern communities of voters through various elections. Bouchard's decision to campaign only in Quebec ensured strong media coverage in each and every region of the province and allowed him to help many less well-known candidates to get elected. In fact, Bouchard went outside of Quebec only once during the entire campaign, when he travelled to Toronto to meet the press and to make a public appearance before the Empire Club.

Bloc Québécois support came primarily from people who had shifted their allegiance to the Conservative Party in 1984 and 1988. After having performed exceptionally well in these elections, popular support for the Tories in Quebec dropped thirty-nine points in 1993. The Bloc also attracted supporters from the New Democratic Party (which lost most of the 14 per cent vote share it had won in 1988).[55] If we further explore the Bloc's clientele, we see that it is made up of various segments. The important nationalist cohort who supported the Conservatives in 1984 and 1988, who were without political representation at the federal level following the departure of Bouchard and others from the PC coalition, voted for the Bloc in 1993, though somewhat less so in 1997. Polls indicate that in 1993 support for the Bloc came first and foremost from strong identifiers with the nationalist cause. According to the researchers who undertook the 1993 National Election Survey, 92 per cent of those who were favourable to sovereignty voted for the Bloc in 1993, increasing to 98 per cent for those who were very favourable.[56] Second, there is an important cohort of non-nationalist Quebecers who felt betrayed by the federal Liberals and subsequently by the Conservatives following the defeat of Meech Lake in 1990 and Charlottetown in 1992 (see Table 6.2). A similar feeling of deception was also felt among francophones who were formerly Liberal supporters, 33 per cent of whom opted for the Bloc in 1993.[57]

Table 6.2: Opinion on Sovereignty and Vote Intention, 1993

Vote		Opinion on Sovereignty (%)			
	Very Favourable	Favourable	Unfavourable	Very Unfavourable	No Opinion
Bloc	98	89	44	18	73
Liberal	1	3	25	58	11
Conservative	0	5	26	19	16
Others	1	3	4	5	0
N	112	194	115	123	26

Note: N = number of people interviewed.

Source: André Blais, Neil Nevitte, Elisabeth Gidengil, Henry Brady, Richard Johnson, 'L'élection fédérale de 1993: le comportement électoral des Québécois', Revue québécoise de science politique no. 27 (Fall 1995):28.

The table reveals that in 1993 the Conservative Party's base of support among nationalists had dried up. It also clearly indicates that the Bloc gathered its support overwhelmingly from sovereigntist forces. It should also be noted that, contrary to what is usually assumed, an important contingent of Bloc supporters are not Parti Québécois card carriers. At the time of the 1993 general election, fully 59 per cent of Bloc members were not on the PQ's list; 66,000 out of 105,000 were members of the Bloc only. What was most impressive about the Bloc's performance in 1993, then, was its capacity to appeal as well to non-sovereigntist elements: fully a quarter of its supporters were of this description.

Dissatisfaction with Conservative Party policies (e.g., the GST, the Meech Lake and Charlottetown accords, various scandals, etc.) and a continuing mistrust of the Chrétien-led Liberal Party (1982 patriation of the Constitution, Trudeau-Chrétien opposition to Meech Lake, centrist policies, etc.) contributed to the Bloc's success. These factors, coupled with the presence of a charismatic leader (Lucien Bouchard), made it possible for the Bloc to win both the nationalist vote and pick up an additional 10 per cent from non-sovereigntists in 1993. Polls also indicate that among non-sovereigntist voters, on a scale of 0 to 100 measuring leader appreciation, Bouchard, Chrétien, and Campbell obtained scores of 57 per cent, 57 per cent, and 47 per cent respectively on the day of the election. It is noteworthy that Bouchard was able to obtain the same result as Chrétien even *among opponents of sovereignty*.[58]

A final observation, the Bloc attracted a large number of voters who normally abstained from taking part in federal politics.[59] In addition, the Bloc tended to attract a high percentage of young people who had recently acquired the right to vote federally. It should be remembered that the Parti Québécois had asked Quebecers to express their alienation from federal politics by spoiling their ballots in 1972 and again in 1974: a risky strategy in the event that people would not follow the suggestion. Both in 1993 and 1997, Quebecers again expressed more than other Canadians their discontent by spoiling 3.3 per cent and 3.5 per cent of their ballots respectively compared to a low 1.41 per cent and 1.42 per cent in 1997 for Canada as a whole.

Contrary to the 1984 and 1988 federal elections when they tended to assist the Mulroney Conservatives, the governing provincial Liberals in Quebec abstained from the political fray in 1993. As expected, Parti Québécois activists took part in the campaign on the side of Bloc candidates. Profound differences of opinion on the wisdom of Quebec nationalists seeking representation in Ottawa were put aside.[60] Several unions also got involved; for instance, the Public Service Alliance of Canada targeted several ridings to unseat Conservatives, an objective often accomplished by backing Bloc candidates. Other major unions officially supported the Bloc Québécois.

Political conditions changed between 1993 and 1997; in the interim the Bloc had formed the official Opposition and the Parti Québécois had taken power in Quebec in September 1994. Lucien Bouchard was no longer leader of the Bloc, having assumed the role of leader of the Parti Québécois and premier of Quebec in February 1996. The election of his first successor, Michel Gauthier, by a small group of party cadres immediately after his departure, led to many internecine conflicts due, in part, to the fact that the legitimacy of the new leader did not rest on a broad mandate from party members. Gauthier was made to feel that he did not have the support of his organization, which eventually forced him to call a real leadership convention in March 1997. In the middle of these troubled times for the Bloc, another fight was looming and came to a climax during the leadership convention: a conflict between the leftist social democrats in the party led by Gilles Duceppe and Francine Lalonde (both of whom came from the labour movement), and the rightist neoliberals inspired by Rodrigue Biron, Yves Duhaime, Daniel Turp, and Pierrette Venne. In the end, the main protagonists were Duceppe and Duhaime. Duceppe won on the second ballot with 52.8 per cent of the vote, while Duhaime received 33.9 per cent and Biron 13.3 per cent. All defeated candidates save one, Duhaime, decided to rally immediately behind the new leader.

Left-of-centre nationalists led by Duceppe and right-of-centre nationalists led by Duhaime were positioning themselves for the day after the federal election; meanwhile, moderate Blue nationalists and nationalists *purs et durs* were at each other's throats trying to take control of the party. The stakes were high, considering that Parizeau was no longer in charge in Quebec City and that Bouchard, a Blue nationalist, now had a firm grip on the Parti Québécois. In this context, Duhaime's defeat was difficult to accept for Parizeau's hard nationalists, who now felt expelled from Quebec City. The playing out of these internal conflicts contributed to the popular impression that Duceppe was a weak political leader and unable to rally all elements of the Bloc coalition around him as Bouchard had done.

Contrary to the 1993 campaign, most labour unions did not rally behind the Bloc in 1997. This time support was muted. In fact, the leader of the Quebec Federation of Labour, Clément Godbout, publicly mused whether a separatist party was still necessary at the federal level. This led to a profound malaise within the nationalist ranks. The Quebec Federation of Labour did not want to be perceived as giving a blank cheque to nationalists both in Quebec City and Ottawa. Following Lucien Bouchard's arrival at the helm in Quebec, and his decision to significantly cut social programs, it was much more difficult to convince the public that nationalists were favourable to the establishment of a more equitable society. To make matters worse, BQ leader Duceppe's election performance was below expectations. Day after day, he was caught contradicting his former boss and new Quebec premier. Duceppe did not appear to be in charge of his party or the party's agenda. Campaign events were poorly conceived and organized; at one point, the campaign bus got lost en route to an event, which led to the firing of the bus driver. It was an event that captured and highlighted the overall problems the Bloc was experiencing under Duceppe's leadership.[61]

A Léger-Léger poll completed between 20 and 23 February 1997 indicated that as Quebec's preferred leader, Duceppe was running well behind Charest (43 per cent) and tied with Chrétien (18 per cent); nevertheless, his party remained the clear favourite to defend Quebec's interests in Ottawa (39 per cent), with 23 per cent going to the Liberals on this score and 19 per cent to the Conservatives. Among francophones only the portrait was slightly different, with Charest leading with 43 per cent, Duceppe at 22 per cent, and Chrétien at 13 per cent. The Bloc far outdistanced its rivals in francophone public opinion on which party was best positioned to defend Quebec's interests in Ottawa (45 per cent versus 17 per cent and 17 per cent).[62] Duceppe's personal approval rating remained low, however, throughout the campaign while Conservative leader Jean Charest ran an impressive campaign, promising (as did Mulroney in 1984 and again in 1988) to find a way to reconcile Quebec with the rest of Canada.

These problems were highlighted in the election of 2 June 1997. Federalist and sovereigntist voters' attitudes towards the parties and their leaders had evolved significantly between the elections. Favourable opinion towards the Bloc had diminished significantly, though the decrease of support appears to have been due more to the new leader's lack of appeal than to the party itself. Federalist francophone Quebecers were definitely less impressed by Duceppe than they had been with the charismatic Bouchard.

One notes an important downward shift in sovereigntists' support for the Bloc in 1997 versus 1993 (a loss of thirteen points). This was compounded by an even higher drop (a loss of seventeen points) among federalists who had been tempted to vote for the Bloc in 1993. The Liberals, however, failed to make any gains among sovereigntists. They did win back some federalist identifiers, thanks to the polarization. Jean Charest's Conservatives, on the other hand, took advantage of the Bloc's troubles by attracting the support of an important cohort of Bloc identifiers with smaller gains among federalists. On election day, this shift in public opinion resulted in a drop in vote share for the Bloc, a slight gain for the Liberals, and a more significant gain for the Conservatives.

The results obtained by the Bloc are deceiving, however, considering that the nationalists attracted nearly 50 per cent of the vote in the 1995 Quebec referendum on sovereignty partnership.[63] In any event, the Bloc kept forty-four of the fifty-four seats it won in 1993 and remained the principal voice for Quebec in Ottawa. The party was once again able to convince Quebecers that it was the political organization best suited to defend Quebec's interests in Ottawa, even though it failed to appeal to some Blue nationalists. Jean Charest made inroads into this latter group of voters, particularly those who felt that Canada should be given yet another try.

From 1968 until 1981 there was a strong sentiment among non-sovereigntists in Quebec that the Liberal Party of Canada was their best available option in Ottawa. There was a feeling that Pierre Elliott Trudeau had made important contributions, putting French on an equal footing with English in the federal civil service and, among other things, advancing individual rights through the entrenchment of the Canadian Charter of Rights and Freedoms. However, these initiatives were intended to 'deterritorialize' the language issue and, to be frank, to constrain the role of Quebec's National Assembly (for example, in the areas of language legislation, culture, education, and manpower training) while giving Ottawa overarching political authority over the country.

The last four elections testify to a significant break with traditional patterns of voter support in favour of the Liberals. First, francophone Quebecers clearly distanced themselves from the Liberals. This is noteworthy considering that between 1900 and 1984 the Liberals lost their Quebec stronghold only once: in 1958 with the landslide re-election of Conservative John Diefenbaker. In 1984 Brian Mulroney's Conservatives easily carried the province, a feat he repeated in 1988. In 1993 and again in 1997 the Bloc won a clear majority of the province's seats.

Quebec francophones turned their back on the Liberals for a number of reasons: the 1982 patriation of the Constitution, which weakened the Quebec National Assembly without its consent; the imposition of an amending formula that deprived Quebec of its historic veto; and the entrenchment of the Charter of Rights and Freedoms that threatened, among other things, Quebec's language legislation and undermined Quebec's own Charter of Human Rights and Freedoms. As a consequence, the level of support for the Liberals among Quebec francophones gradually dropped from one-third in 1984 to one-fourth in 1988 and down to one-fifth in 1993. The drop was even sharper in the Greater Montreal region where the Liberals claimed only 15 per cent to 20 per cent of the francophone vote. Indeed, Liberals have been largely confined to non-francophone ridings since 1984. Jean Chrétien's lack of popularity among francophone Quebecers was confirmed during the 1993 and 1997 campaigns. In contrast, the Liberals attracted overwhelming support from both anglophone and allophone (other minority-language speakers) Quebecers. The 1997 election brought only marginal gains as the Liberals improved their popular vote by 2.3 per cent and won seven additional seats.

In Canada, as in western Europe, there appears to have been a growing distrust of politicians and political institutions.[64] This frustration with traditional political representation—the established political parties, bureaucrats, and legislatures—has caused people to become more interested in looking after the protection of their rights through legal instruments such as the Charter of Rights and Freedoms.

While structural factors (economic reversals and perceived unresponsiveness of the major parties) provided a fertile terrain for the Bloc to grow, it also benefited from a happy combination of skilled leadership and good fortune. The Conservatives' poor campaign in 1993, along with Kim Campbell's failure to convince nationalist francophones in Quebec that she stood for anything new or that she could represent their interests any more effectively than had Brian Mulroney, played a large role in the Bloc's 1993 success. In 1997 it was Jean Chrétien's threat not to respect Quebecers' right of self-determination that mobilized nationalists behind the Bloc and attenuated the impact of the Bloc's poor campaign.

Common sense suggests that the Bloc is more than a protest party; it constitutes a serious challenge to the existing federal party system. While the

Bloc has drawn support from Quebec voters dissatisfied with their economic position, its more fundamental appeal is to those francophone Quebecers who lean towards sovereignty or favour some radically reconstituted federal arrangement.[65] In this connection, the results of October 1993 and June 1997 federal elections merely confirm the results of the Charlottetown referendum in 1992 and the Quebec referendum of 1995.[66] The Bloc, like its mirror opposite, the Reform Party, appeals to a fairly cohesive, disaffected social group that is regionally concentrated. As a result, whether or not the Bloc Québécois poses the ultimate challenge to the prevailing brokerage parties, it is nonetheless unlikely that it will simply vanish in the foreseeable future.

To reiterate, as long as there is a community of core concerns and values among Quebec's francophone electors, this fact will be reflected at the federal level. The success of a third party is predicated on the extent to which the traditional brokerage parties are willing or able to cater to that core electorate. As long as the Quebec electorate can be conceptualized as forming a community of voters exhibiting a clear set of voter preferences rather than an amalgamation of individual voters acting on rational self-interest, then the idea of continuity seems more effective than the notion of volatility in explaining Quebec's role in Canadian elections. Though no longer 'Her Majesty's Loyal Opposition', the Bloc continues to represent the majority of francophone Quebecers in Canada's federal Parliament, pledged to defend Quebec's interests in Ottawa until sovereignty for that province is attained.

Notes

1. For a thorough account of the Nationalist League and the role played by Bourassa, see Hélène Pelletier-Baillargeon, *Olivar Asselin et son temps: le militant* (Montreal: Fides, 1996):225–346.
2. There are divergent opinions on this interpretation, see Pelletier-Baillargeon, 255, who underlines the point that, according to many League supporters, defending autonomist ideas at the federal level might prove illusory. The priority ought to be at the provincial level considering that it is the only order of government that matters for French Canadians.
3. Joseph Levitt, *Henri Bourassa and the Golden Calf: The Social Program of the Nationalists of Quebec, 1900–1914*, 2nd edn (Ottawa: Les Éditions de l'Université d'Ottawa, 1972):3.
4. Ibid., 145.
5. The fight for social justice has also been central to the League's initiatives. See Pelletier-Baillargeon, 319; Olivar Asselin, 'Les étudiants au "Nationaliste"', *Le Nationaliste* (30 September 1906):1.
6. Quote given in Levitt, *Henri Bourassa*, note 32, 26.
7. The settlement reached between the province of Manitoba and the federal government did not satisfy Bourassa. See Pelletier-Baillargeon, *Olivar Asselin*, 305.
8. It should also be noted that Henri Bourassa's support came from both Conservatives and Liberals who shared his binational vision. With hindsight, the coalition

of political forces that opposed Laurier in Quebec resembles the one that led Brian Mulroney to victory in 1984.

9. Murray Beck, *Pendulum of Power: Canada's Federal Election* (Scarborough: Prentice-Hall, 1968):132.

10. These eleven ridings were Gaspé, Rimouski, Témiscouata, Kamouraska, Québec-Montmorency, Beauce, Quebec West and South, Lévis, Portneuf, Laval-Deux-Montagnes, and Beauharnois-La Prairie.

11. Liguori Lacombe, 'Un manifeste du parti canadien', *Le Devoir* (31 January 1942):3.

12. According to historian Michel Sarra-Bournet, the opposition to the bill was aimed at the eventual participation in an imperial war, but that was not to apply if the Canadian territory was under a foreign threat.

13. See Paul-André Comeau, *Le Bloc populaire, 1942–1948* (Montreal: Québec/Amérique, 1982):87.

14. The Action Libérale Nationale emerged out of the Depression as many liberal party activists felt ill at ease with Louis-Alexandre Taschereau's provincial liberals. Mobilized around a left-wing political agenda and led by Paul Gouin, the son of Lomer Gouin and predecessor of Taschereau from 1905 to 1920, the party developed an ambitious social program that appealed to many Quebecers.

15. The Bloc was also a tributary of the École Sociale Populaire's teachings that had popularized innovative ways to tackle economic and social difficulties facing the Western world during the Depression. For an account of intellectual contributions during this period, see Stephen Brooks and Alain-G. Gagnon, *Social Scientists and Politics in Canada: Between Vanguard and Clerisy* (Montreal: McGill-Queen's University Press, 1989).

16. Comeau, *Le Bloc populaire*, 210.

17. Ibid., 210.

18. Paul-André Comeau develops this point particularly well in ibid., 200–1.

19. Ibid., 100. For instance, Pierre Gauthier is brought forward to face a court martial, and a political organizer of Jean Drapeau, who is a potential candidate, is thrown in jail.

20. Ibid., 303.

21. Fred Rose won Montreal-Cartier with 30 per cent of the vote ahead of Paul Massé (Bloc populaire) who received 29 per cent, as well as of David Lewis (CCF) and Lazarus Philips (Liberal) who got 19 per cent and 22 per cent of the vote respectively.

22. 'The Cartier By-Election', *Canadian Forum* 23 (September 1943):126–7.

23. Paul Cliche, 'Les élections provinciales dans le Québec de 1927 à 1956', MA thesis, Political Science, Université Laval, 1960, 46–8, cited in Comeau, *Le Bloc populaire*, 317.

24. Led by two Quebec Conservative MPs, Frédéric Dorion and Sasseville Roy, the Mouvement tried to mobilize supporters of the provincial Union Nationale for action at the federal level. Eventually the Mouvement joined forces with the Bloc candidates in an attempt to form a common front against the Liberals.

25. As of November 1945, 200,000 men had been sent to Europe. See Comeau, 328.

26. James Mallory, *Social Credit and the Federal Power in Canada* (Toronto: University of Toronto Press, 1954).

27. Michael B. Stein, *The Dynamics of Right-Wing Protest: A Political Analysis of Social Credit in Quebec* (Toronto: University of Toronto Press, 1973):52.

28. Ibid., 86.
29. Ibid.
30. Vincent Lemieux, 'Les dimensions sociologiques du vote créditiste au Québec', *Recherches sociographiques* 6, no. 2 (1965):181–95.
31. Ibid., 191–2.
32. Stein, *The Dynamics of Right-Wing Protest*, 92, 99: Six Créditistes had offered to support Pearson's minority government in writing if the government was threatened by a vote of non-confidence. Five of those MPs were defeated at the general election of 1965 at which the Ralliement des Créditistes still attracted 19 per cent of the vote in Quebec.
33. Winning even less than its arch nationalist rival, Pierre Bourgault's left-wing Rassemblement pour l'Indépendance Nationale (RIN), which took 5.6 per cent of the vote. It was at that point that Pierre Bourgault invited RIN members to join the PQ on an individual basis to form a common nationalist front, illustrating that the long-standing divisions that had hampered the nationalists were starting to heal.
34. Jean Crête and Guy Lachapelle, 'The Bloc Québécois', in *Party Politics in Canada*, 7th edn, edited by Hugh Thorburn (Scarborough: Prentice-Hall, 1996):419.
35. René Lévesque, 'Le Parti Québécois et le scrutin fédéral', *Journal de Québec* (1 February 1972):4.
36. Chief electoral officer of Canada.
37. Graham Fraser, *René Lévesque and the Parti Québécois in Power* (Toronto: Macmillan of Canada, 1984):182.
38. See Fraser, *René Lévesque*, 203–5, for his recounting of the event.
39. See Marcel Léger, *Le Parti québécois: ce n'était que le début* (Montreal: Québec/ Amérique, 1986):195. Here is a revealing sequence of internal polls:

Percentage of Voters' Intention

	Liberal	Conservative	NDP	Others	Abstained	Undecided
Oct. 81	31	22	9	2	9	28
Nov. 81	29	25	10	5	12	19
Dec. 81	40	24	8	3	10	15
Jan. 82	35	21	9	2	11	23
Mar. 82	28	26	8	3	9	27
June 82	30	25	15	3	7	28

40. The percentage of voters' intention for such an event is as follows:

	Liberal	Conservative	NDP	PQ	Abstained	Undecided
Oct. 81	22	8	3	35	2	30
Nov. 81	22	7	3	41	4	22
Dec. 81	30	7	3	37	3	21
Jan. 82	25	8	3	37	5	23
Mar. 82	21	10	3	34	4	27
June 82	24	12	3	37	3	20

41. Hard nationalists counted on the support of Marcel Léger, Bernard Landry, Jacques-Yvan Morin, and Jean Garon, while soft nationalists were supported by Marc-André Bédard, Rodrigue Biron, Guy Chevrette, Yves Duhaime, and Pierre-

Marc Johnson. Two of these would enter the race for the leadership of the Bloc in March 1997.

42. Pierre O'Neill, 'Le PN veut s'imposer comme seule voix du Québec à Ottawa', *Le Devoir* (15 September 1983):1, 8.

43. A provincial incarnation of the PN, the Parti Indépendantiste, again led by Denis Monière, presented candidates in the December 1985 election. The PI did abysmally; it finished fifth and received only 0.45 per cent of the popular vote.

44. See Léger, *Le Parti québécois*.

45. 'Meech Lake' refers to an agreement between the central government (Ottawa), the nine anglophone provinces, and Quebec (the only province where franco-phones constitute a majority) that was intended to bring the latter back into the federal family. In 1982 the federal government of Pierre Trudeau, along with the nine anglophone provinces, decided to patriate the British North America Act from London, to entrench a Charter of Rights and Freedoms that was to super-sede Quebec's Charter of Human Rights and Freedoms, and to add an amending formula that did not consider Quebec's rights as a founding member of the Canadian federation. In sum, Quebec's powers were diminished without its con-sent; this represented a breach of trust between Quebec and the rest of Canada.

46. Alain-G. Gagnon, 'Quebec: Variations on a Theme', in *Canadian Politics*, 2nd edn, edited by James P. Bickerton and Alain-G. Gagnon (Peterborough: Broadview, 1994):462–3.

47. Liberal fortunes in Quebec went from 53.6 per cent (fifty-six out of seventy four seats) in 1968 to 49.1 per cent (fifty-six out of seventy-four) in 1972, back up to 54.1 per cent (sixty out of seventy-four) in 1974, 61.6 per cent (sixty-seven out of seventy-five) in 1979, and 68.2 per cent (seventy-four out of seventy-five) in 1980. In 1984 Liberal support plunged to 35.4 per cent (seventeen seats) and con-tinued its fall to 30.2 per cent (twelve seats) in 1988. It inched up to 33.0 per cent (nineteen seats) in 1993, and 36.1 per cent (twenty-six seats) in 1997, slightly higher than they were in 1984 following Mulroney's sweep of the province.

48. It was said that Ottawa was willing to vacate secondary fields of *exclusive provin-cial jurisdictions* that had been invaded over the years by the federal government, but not before having signed reversible deals with provinces, *de jure* recognizing federal supremacy. In addition, Ottawa would continue to be responsible for country-wide economic and social programs (leaving provinces totally depen-dent on Ottawa's approach to economic development) and would make changes to federal institutions that would have officialized the equality of provinces principle. For a more detailed discussion of the Charlottetown proposals from a Quebec perspective, see *Référendum, 26 octobre 1992: les objections de 20 spécia-listes aux offres fédérales* (Montreal: Éditions Saint-Martin, 1992).

49. Richard Nadeau, Daniel Guérin, and Pierre Martin, 'L'effrondrement du parti Progressiste-Conservateur à l'élection fédérale de 1993', *Revue québécoise de science politique* no. 27 (Spring 1995):127.

50. The Bloc decided to enter the race following results of an internal poll taken by the provincial Liberals and provided by Robert Bourassa's office. The results indicated that the Bloc could win the riding of Laurier-Sainte-Marie with 60 per cent of the vote. See Jean-François Lisée, *Le tricheur: Robert Bourassa et les Québé-cois 1990–1991* (Montreal: Boréal, 1994):82.

51. Ibid., 78–88.

52. Alain-G. Gagnon and Daniel Latouche, *Allaire, Bélanger, Campeau et les autres* (Montreal: Québec/Amérique, 1991):431–521; and Lisée, *Le tricheur*, 81.

53. See Lisée, *Le tricheur*, 124. See also polls taken at the time, which indicated that support in favour of sovereignty was reaching highs of 61 per cent in September 1990 (Léger and Léger), 64 per cent in November 1990 (CROP), and 70 per cent in December 1990 (Léger and Léger). These results are reproduced in Robert Bourassa, *Gouverner le Québec* (Montreal: Éditions Fides, 1993):note 17, 233.

54. Namely, former PQ minister Francine Lalonde (Mercier) and former MNAs Michel Gauthier (Roberval) and Laurent Lavigne (Beauharnois-Salaberry). Some Bloc candidates had been defeated running under the PQ banner in recent provincial elections: Amin Achem (1989), Maurice Bernier (1985), Maurice Dumas (1981), and Francine Lalonde (1985, 1989). There were also some former PQ political attachés who decided to stand as Bloc Québécois candidates: Stéphane Bergeron and Réal Ménard are two notable cases.

55. For a similar interpretation, see William Christian and Colin Campbell *Political Parties and Ideologies in Canada*, 3rd edn (Toronto: McGraw-Hill, 1990):188. In a number of ridings, NDP candidates finished fourth or fifth, often behind fringe party candidates such as Natural Law and Rhinoceros. Disaffection with the NDP in Quebec was partly due to the shift to the right that the party was perceived to have taken following the 1988 federal election. After the formation of the Bloc, most nationalists distanced themselves from the NDP to join forces with the Bloc. But the most detrimental development for NDP candidates was the fact that the political debate in Quebec was dominated by the Constitution.

56. André Blais, Neil Nevitte, Elisabeth Gidengil, Henry Brady, and Richard Johnson, 'L'élection fédérale de 1993: le comportement électoral des Québécois', *Revue québécoise de science politique* no. 27 (Fall 1995):26–8.

57. Manon Cornellier, *The Bloc* (Toronto: James Lorimer and Company, Publishers, 1995):43.

58. Blais et al., 'L'élection fédérale de 1993', 41. Furthermore, a poll taken between 24 and 28 September 1993 revealed that Bloc supporters felt that they could back the party without necessarily supporting independence.

59. Richard Johnson, Elisabeth Gidengil, Neil Nevitte, and Henry Brady, 'The 1993 Canadian Election: Realignment, Dealignment or Something Else?', a paper presented to the Annual Meeting of the Canadian Political Science Association, Brock University, St Catharines, Ontario, 2–4 June 1996.

60. Cornellier, *The Bloc*, vii–xi.

61. This item made the news repeatedly during the campaign. It is interesting to note that, at the end of the campaign, Jean Chrétien ran into the same problem with his bus driver, who got lost several times in the prime minister's riding. The Bloc could not use this incident; it was time to vote.

62. Richard Nadeau, 'Le dilemme des Québécois: choisir le chef ou le parti', *La Presse* (30 May 1997):B-3.

63. For a detailed analysis of the referendum, see Alain-G. Gagnon and Guy Lachapelle, 'The Quebec Referendum of October 30, 1995: Two Competing Societal Projects Searching for Legitimacy', *Publius* 26, no. 3, (Summer 1996):177–91.

64. This section borrows from Alain-G. Gagnon and A. Brian Tanguay, 'Minor Parties in the Canadian Political System', in *Canadian Parties in Transition*, edited by A. Brian Tanguay and Alain-G. Gagnon (Toronto: Nelson Canada, 1996):127–8.

65. Alain Noël, 'Distinct in the House of Commons: The Bloc Québécois as Official Opposition', in *Canada: The State of the Federation, 1994*, edited by Douglas Brown and Janet Hiebert (Kingston: Queen's University Institute of Intergovernmental Relations, 1994):24.

66. Alain Gagnon and Alain Desruisseaux, 'Le succès du Bloc Québécois dépasse le vote de protestation circonstanciel', *La Presse* (10 November 1993):B3.

CHAPTER 7

CONTINUITY AND CHANGE IN A NEW ERA OF PARTY POLITICS

The elections of 1993 and 1997 marked the emergence of a new era of party politics in Canada. With the Progressive Conservatives reduced to the status of a minor party and the apparent stability of two new political parties (each of which has served as the official Opposition in Parliament), political alignments, voter loyalties, and competitive dynamics have been dramatically altered. In effect, party and electoral politics again have gone through a systemic change. However, as with past system transformations, the profound changes associated with the emergence of this fourth party system in Canada have been accompanied by a significant thread of continuity.

Change

The changes that have taken place are readily identifiable. Most important has been the change in the distribution of votes and seats among parties in the system. Two of the three parties associated with the third party system suffered calamitous declines in both their vote and seat totals in 1993. The NDP went from their highest totals in party history to their lowest; after their historic achievement of forming two successive majority governments, the Progressive Conservatives were reduced to minor party status in terms of their proportion of the vote and were almost completely eliminated in terms of seats. Both parties lost their official status in the House of Commons. While there was a modest revival of their electoral fortunes in 1997, neither recovered to anything close to their former status, finishing well behind the other three parties in Parliament. Most of the votes and seats that went 'missing' from the Conservative support base in 1993 ended up with the two new parties: the Reform Party in the West and Ontario, and the Bloc Québécois in Quebec. This electoral base was not recovered in 1997. Similarly, the New Democrats' stubbornly faithful social democratic constituency was whittled down to its nub in 1993 and only partially recovered in 1997. In particular, the party failed to repatriate both its hard-won, urban-labourist support in Ontario and its historic leftist vote in British Columbia; the party survives, but only as a somewhat emaciated remnant of its former self.

The flip side of the coin to these significant changes in the levels of popular support upon which individual parties in the system can rely are concomitant shifts in the partisan loyalties of Canadian voters. Voters in western Canada (especially Alberta and BC) and francophone voters in Quebec have forsaken (in the main) the established, moderate, mainstream parties. New ties of partisanship now bind these voters to recently created parties (Reform and the Bloc) that are more regional and ideological in their appeal. These shifts have increased the balkanization of the Canadian electorate and party system. The divisions between parties and among voters have been magnified and multiplied; the regional bases of party support and activity are more sharply delineated; and the pattern of voter loyalties and preferences is more spatially differentiated.

Another dimension of change has been in party leadership. This was yet another consequence of the disastrous electoral result for these established parties in 1993 and, conversely, the immediate and substantial success of the new parties in the system. Following the election, both Kim Campbell (PC) and Audrey McLaughlin (NDP) announced to their parties their resignation as leader. Their successors, Jean Charest and Alexa McDonough, appeared secure in their immediate futures by leading their respective parties to modest comebacks. The Tories, however, had yet another (unanticipated) leadership change thrust upon them following the 1997 election when Charest switched electoral arenas and party allegiances. The other new leadership figures after 1993 were Lucien Bouchard (Bloc) and Preston Manning (Reform). Each brought a new leadership style and ideological appeal to Canadian party politics. Bouchard's subsequent replacement as leader prior to 1997 by Gilles Duceppe, again as the result of a leader changing electoral arenas and party labels, brought the total of new federal party leaders to six in five years. Clearly, then, the cumulative change in national party leaderships has been extensive.

Nor have these changes in voters and parties been merely a matter of a simple increase in the number of interchangeable party organizations and personalities; they were not just more of the same. The policy and program agenda of individual parties—their ideological orientation—also changed, as well as the ideological scope and character of the party system as a whole.[1] In the new era of party politics, the general ideological cast of party appeals has been revamped, either because of the presence within the system of new parties bearing a different message for voters, or because the older, established parties themselves made alterations to their traditional appeal to voters. This change in the policy and ideological content of Canadian party politics began in earnest with the 1993 election campaign. It was both consolidated and increased by that astounding election result, which affirmed the strategies and discourse of the new protest parties while acting as a catalyst for the traditional parties to re-evaluate their own 'messages' and the policy-related reasons for the massive shift that had occurred in voter allegiances.

What actually changed in terms of party appeals on the key dimensions of conflict in Canadian electoral politics? On the socio-economic dimension, the most dramatic change in partisan political discourse was that introduced by the Reform Party. On matters of social, economic, and fiscal policy, Reform presented Canadians with a strongly antistatist approach shaped by its ideological conservatism and its populism. The party proposed a dramatic downsizing of the size and role of government; it asserted the primacy of the free market (and the need to sharply reduce taxes on individuals and businesses); and it championed private sector solutions to the country's social and economic problems. Its first order of business would be to carry out deep cuts in government spending in order to eliminate the federal deficit and pay down the federal debt. Although individual Progressive Conservative MPs had sometimes articulated similar views, the Tory party itself (and certainly its leadership) had never embraced the antistatist philosophy that underpinned the views, nor the policy priorities it mandated.

On the ethnocultural and regional dimensions of Canadian politics, Reform opposed official bilingualism and adopted an uncompromising position on Quebec's demands for some form of special status based on its claim to be a 'distinct society'. On the contrary, Reform expressed an absolutist commitment to the idea of provincial equality and to the redesign of federal institutions to fully reflect this, in particular the creation of a 'triple E' Senate similar to that of the United States. It also advocated a much more decentralized federation that would reduce the federal government's role in areas such as social policy or minority language rights. This would instead be left to the provinces. In general, Reform advocated complete autonomy for the provinces in their constitutional spheres of jurisdiction and reduced responsibility and oversight capabilities for the federal government. On multiculturalism and Aboriginal rights, the 'other' realities in Canada's ethnocultural mosaic, Reform insisted on the absolute primacy of individual rights and individual equality as the basis of a common Canadian citizenship while resisting the notion of special rights or differential treatment of individuals based on ethnic, racial, or cultural attributes (such as affirmative action programs). This clearly differentiated Reform's message from other political parties in Canada, all of whom supported (in one form or another) official bilingualism, the idea of Quebec's distinct society, special Aboriginal rights (Aboriginals as 'citizens plus'), and the need for (and legitimacy of) equity legislation and affirmative action programs for visible and other minorities.

The other new party in 1993, the Bloc Québécois, did not introduce any new elements into the socio-economic dimension of Canada's partisan discourse. Its social-democratic leanings were reminiscent of positions taken by the NDP or (when free to do so) 'welfare liberals' within the Liberal Party.

However, the Bloc did dramatically alter the ideological complexion of the ethnocultural dimension of federal party politics. For the first time, the 'hard nationalism' of the Quebec separatist movement was represented within the federal party system and incorporated into the daily posturings and strategic manoeuvrings of parties within Parliament and the national media. No longer was the deep divide within the Quebec polity between nationalists and federalists masked by the dominance of one of the traditional federal parties in Quebec. The struggle had been brought decisively into the federal arena, and the dynamics of party debate on the 'Quebec question' were fundamentally changed as a result.

The traditional parties, of course, were not left unmoved or unaffected by the successful debut of Reform and the Bloc. In response, both the Liberals and the Progressive Conservatives made adjustments in their ideological and policy positioning. Clearly, the Liberals have benefited most from the presence of Reform on the federal scene. It has allowed the 'government party' to adopt a much more conservative political discourse and policy orientation than would have been possible prior to 1993. This shift to the right in the name of deficit elimination, debt reduction, and 'prudent' financial management has been highly satisfying for the business liberal element of the party while simultaneously rebuilding ties between the Liberals and the business community. Yet Liberals were still able to present themselves as the moderate party-of-the-centre, with Reform portrayed as the party-of-the-right and the NDP and Bloc as left-wing Canadian nationalists and Quebec nationalists respectively. This *relative* positioning of Liberals within the new party system, however, obscures the fact that the party moved significantly to the right in the 1990s in both its rhetoric and its policies.

The Progressive Conservatives were faced with more difficult and unsavoury strategic choices after 1993. Displaced from the right by Reform and the centre-right by the Liberals, ideological and policy positioning has been a problematic affair for the Tories. They have alternately staked out policy ground on the right in an attempt to 'reclaim' conservative voters lost to Reform, or moved to a left-of-centre position where voters have been demonstrably unhappy with Liberal cuts to social spending. This period of ideological flux can be understood as a tactical response to a highly unfavourable and still unclear political environment. The Tory party's voter base may have largely disappeared, but its centrist, brokerage instincts survived intact.

Among the traditional parties, only the NDP in the 1990s remained fairly consistent and unwavering in its ideological and policy orientation. While the party did make a leadership change in response to the disastrous 1993 election result, it did not engage in a prolonged period of introspection or re-evaluation regarding the continued validity of its program and its social democratic ideology.[2] One significant change associated with the NDP, however, concerns its regional bases of support. Perhaps the most surprising aspect of the 1997 federal election result was the strong support received by the party in Atlantic Canada, particularly Nova Scotia and New Brunswick, where the NDP took eight of twenty-one seats. In a region where the party had never won more than one seat, this was a breakthrough of major proportions. A number of factors accounted for this breakthrough (see Chapter 4), which suggests the potential (for the first time) for competitiveness throughout English-speaking Canada. This change in the regional base of NDP support (should it be sustained) also harbours important implications for the other parties.

The surge of voter support in Atlantic Canada for the NDP ironically was accomplished without any change in the party's message or policy orientation; indeed, consistency and continuity on this score was perhaps the main reason for the party's newfound support. Such ideological steadfastness is characteristic of New Democrats, who have always placed a high value on remaining true to their social democratic principles regardless of the short-term electoral consequences. This means NDP leaders are more constrained than their counterparts in other parties when it comes to departing from approved party policy. Archer and Whitehorn have shown that NDP activists are more internally consistent in their ideological views and demonstrate fewer divisions on policy matters than other party activists. Party leaders, as a result, have less latitude to change policy direction or to ignore party ideology in favour of pragmatism or electoral opportunism as Liberal and Conservative leaders have often done.[3] For better or worse, the NDP is likely to remain firmly ensconced as the party-of-the-left in Canada, though party activists may periodically seek to redefine the true meaning of this role.

Continuity

Perhaps the most striking element of continuity in the new era of party politics has been the relative stability of the ideological structure of Canadian politics. As well, the same key themes and dimensions of political conflict that have always shaped Canadian electoral politics have persevered. And these conflicts continue to be underpinned by the same regional and ethno-cultural bases of voter support. This is most strikingly evident with regard to the national unity question and Quebec's place within the federation. All parties have been forced to continue their competitive positioning and manoeuvring around this issue; moreover, the partisan and electoral cleavages incited by the issue were clearly a major determinant of party support levels in both 1993 and 1997. In general, Quebec nationalism and western populism (often involving some anti-Quebec sentiment) continue to be important ideological forces in the shaping of voter attitudes, priorities, and preferences in those regions. Reform and the Bloc are the latest partisan manifestations of these motive ideologies. The constancy of the New Democratic Party's social democratic appeal has already been noted, and with the notable exception of Atlantic Canada, its modest comeback in 1997 occurred in traditional pockets of NDP support in western Canada. A similar observation can be made about support for the Progressive Conservative Party if one considers the regional contours of its support. The Tory comeback (again, modest) in 1997 occurred primarily in areas of Atlantic Canada that have been traditionally supportive of the party. The same could be said of the party's performance in Ontario, with the important proviso that (in contrast to Atlantic Canada) their traditional vote had to be shared with Reform. Of course, the most striking symbol of continuity in the Tory party is the return of Joe Clark as national leader in November 1998.

It is also worth noting that Liberal Party behaviour in the new era of party politics has been consistent with Canadian party history, whereby Liberals have tended to campaign from a centre-left position but govern from the centre-right. Chrétien's Liberals remained sensitive to the need to maintain their *relative* standing as a party-of-the-centre, while showing little concern for adherence to ideological principles. Indeed, there has been little sign of reluctance to embrace policies in government that previously had been anathema to the party faithful. In the 1990s the Liberal Party élite rebuilt its traditional links to the business community, while at the same time restating the party's traditional concern for the underprivileged and disadvantaged. In program terms, this resulted in a combination of continuity with the past (equalization payments), broad and deep cuts in social programs such as health and welfare (as represented by the introduction of the Canada Health and Social Transfer), and some new program initiatives in the areas of child poverty and student scholarships. In sum, the Liberals returned in the 1990s to play the role of pragmatic, centrist, brokerage party focused on courting the median voter, criticized by its detractors for its hypocrisy and opportunism, and celebrated by its supporters for its hard-headed realism and managerial competence. *Plus ça change, plus c'est la même chose.*

There is also continuity in the pattern of fragmentation of the fourth party system, which, considered as a whole, bears a resemblance to the pre-Diefenbaker era of party politics in Canada when there was only one national party (the Liberals) competing with several regionally based minor parties. The effect of this party alignment is the same in both eras: one-party dominance with the Liberals ensconced as the 'government party'. Of course, the overall competitive dynamics within the new party system differ significantly from previous eras, clearly distinguishing the current party system from its forerunners. The second party system featured four parties; the third party system (for the most part) three parties; the fourth party system five parties. The third party system was bifurcated, with a different pattern of party competition in eastern versus western Canada; the fourth party system is fully regionalized, with distinctive patterns of party competition in each region (Atlantic, Quebec, Ontario, the West). The second and third party systems featured a Liberal-dominated Quebec; the fourth party system a Liberal-dominated

Ontario; the second (and somewhat less so the third) party system featured a division of conservative supporters between the Tories and the Socreds; and the fourth party system between the Tories and Reform. Of course, a dramatic new element in the competitive dynamics of the current party system is the presence of the Bloc Québécois. As long as francophone Quebec's sympathies remain tied to this nationalist party, leaving the other four parties to struggle over the votes of English-speaking Canada, a new and incalculable unpredictability is introduced into Canadian electoral politics.

Finally, an element of institutional continuity in the new era of party politics is the role that Canada's electoral system continues to play. As Alan Cairns argued in 1968, the 'first-past-the-post' electoral system rewards parties with regionally concentrated support while penalizing those with weak but diffuse national support. This effect can be seen once again in the results of the 1993 and 1997 elections when regional parties (the Bloc and Reform) did very well, while another party with broad but weak national support (the Tories) did very poorly. This bias in the electoral system provides parties with an incentive to focus their efforts and their appeals on regional electorates and to play on regional fears, concerns, and demands. It creates a party system that overlays and reinforces regional divisions with partisan divisions. At the same time, the electoral system tends to produce majorities for the strongest party (even if that party receives much less than majority support from the electorate, as in 1993 and 1997), thereby permitting the continuation of a system based on strict party discipline and one-party government. This in turn encourages rabid and relentless adversarialism. In such a system that is almost devoid of incentives to consensus-building and cooperation across party lines, voter discontent and political legitimacy problems should be expected.[4]

The Ties That Bind Parties and Voters

This book has argued that political parties in Canada have established enduring bonds with core groups of voters within the electorate. These 'ties' between parties and voters have been constituted on the basis of shared ideological orientation as well as party 'iconologies' (powerfully charged symbols, vague concepts, and core policies that tap into shared values and myths).[5] These are in turn related to key policies and programs, voter loyalty to particular party leaders (either the leader or other members of a party's collective leadership), and to historic patterns of 'communal partisanship' that generate and perpetuate a community preference for particular parties or particular kinds of parties. These communities of voters may be constituency-based, regional, or ethnocultural. Their existence reflects the spatial predominance of religious, linguistic, class, ethnic, rural, or other sociodemographic and economic characteristics that can and do shape community values and partisanship over time.

Political parties are acutely aware of these ties to their 'traditional' electorates and are conscious of the need to continually reinforce and refresh
them, especially during election periods. The most used and most effective
technique for doing so is to remind these voters of their traditional partisan
loyalties, and to refresh the communal political memory with regard to those
key societal cleavages and political conflicts that are most immediately associated with the core values and policy orientations that in the past cemented
the voter-party relationship.[6] As noted in the work of Lipset and Rokkan on
European party systems,[7] and subjected to historical analysis in Canada by
scholars such as Brodie and Jenson,[8] once firmly established, the pattern of
voter-party relations within a party system is highly resistant to major changes,
with a strong bias towards *continuity* in the level and character of party
support and (associated with this) in the substance and foci of partisan
political discourse.

At the same time, parties must be cognizant of the need in a diverse and
divided polity to reach out beyond a core electorate that is insufficient to
carry the party to power. Each party must craft an appeal to voters outside
its traditional support base; to be successful, this appeal must present the
party's leadership, values, and program as broadly affirmative (if not all-
encompassing) of the interests of society taken as a whole.[9] In this sense,
all parties aspiring to become hegemonic or governing parties must to some
extent become 'catch-all' parties. Additionally, particular groups within the
polity may be targeted and promised specific benefits should the party be
elected. Again, all parties can be expected to engage in such brokering
behaviour, though the extent to which they do so (and the groups they
target) may vary considerably.

The difficulty for parties lay in determining how far they may stray from
the concerns and preferences of voters who comprise their core base of support in their attempt to make a broader electoral appeal. As argued by Rose
and Mackie, a party's failure to respond to electoral pressures by modifying
or adapting its traditional message and appeal (in the search for a wider—
or changing—audience) can lead to a steady loss of vote share and eventual
disappearance; on the other hand, too great a change can lead to a party
split, as groups of activists, traditionalists, and core supporters refuse to go
along with such electorally necessary change.[10]

This suggests that parties face a number of dangers to their organizational
health and political survival in the competitive struggle to attract, build, and
hold voter support. One of these is the danger of striving to be all things to
all people. To pursue this strategy recklessly is to court electoral disaster.
Developing an exclusive focus on the need to broker for the support of the
weakly committed median voter and/or diverse special interests can lead
parties to ignore or even abandon their traditional supporters. In such circumstances, a party places at risk its core vote without any guarantee that
this vote once lost is recoverable. As noted by political strategists Axworthy

and Goldfarb, 'Knowing the interests and concerns of one's stable coalition is the beginning of political wisdom . . . taking one's core support for granted is an error of major proportions.'[11] The Liberals and the Conservatives— Canada's centrist brokerage parties—have been perhaps most susceptible to this danger; each has on occasion flirted with such an outcome as they react to changing political climates, sometimes shifting policies and leaders, and recasting their voter appeals while they chase the floating vote. At the same time, it is clear that these parties generally have recognized the limits of brokering, how far their ties with their core electorate can be stretched, and the importance of renewing these ties between and especially during election periods. Even so, on rare occasions in Canadian party history, party vote shares have crashed through their traditional 'floors' and such incidences have usually heralded the death of one party system and the emergence of another, featuring a different set of parties and a different pattern of party support and competition. Of course, each such occasion has its own confluence of factors that explain the event, while also determining the contours and character of the emergent party system.

On the other hand, parties may fall prey to another danger that lay at the opposite end of the spectrum: that of remaining rigidly true to only one thing. If a party becomes exclusively identified with one narrow constituency or wedded to one unchanging set of policies or ideas, it may suffer inexorable decline as its electoral prospects stagnate while change occurs all around it —in its core constituency, in society more generally, or in the character and appeal of competitor parties. The fate of the CCF in national politics, or Social Credit, serve as examples. In the current context, to ensure its survival and future electoral prospects, the Bloc Québécois must seek to avoid being perceived in Quebec as a 'one trick pony': a narrow nationalist party unconcerned about any issue save the Constitution and Quebec sovereignty.

There are other threats or dangers to the ties that bind parties and voters. The reward for electoral success is to become a party in government, which provides a range of potential rewards and benefits to party activists and supporters, as well as certain advantages to the party in power over their erstwhile rivals in Opposition. Husbanded and used wisely, the powers and resources available to the party in government can contribute to future electoral successes by helping to maintain party solidarity and a core support base, on top of which can be rebuilt a winning electoral coalition. But there is no permanent safe harbour for parties repeatedly forced to weather the stormy seas of an election, and in the long run winning power can sometimes be more of a curse than a blessing. With power comes unavoidable responsibility and accountability to the whole electorate for the actions (or non-actions) of the government, as well as for the general welfare of society during a party's term of office. This leaves a party in government open to criticism and punishment for its own inevitable errors, as well as forces and events over which it may have little control. Even core supporters may become disillusioned and alienated during a period in which their party wields power (and therefore must take decisions and act). As exemplified by the electoral fate of R.B. Bennett's Conservative government during the Depression, the Mulroney-Campbell Conservatives in 1993, or the Rae NDP government in Ontario in 1995, voter retribution for the unpopular actions and perceived shortcomings of a party in government can be devastating and long-lasting.

Parties relegated to endless Opposition status face different challenges. Not being saddled with the responsibilities of government leaves Opposition parties free to criticize and unconstrained in their need and desire to play to the audience, and in particular to *their* audience. Under these circumstances, refreshing ties to their core electorate can be an ongoing and relatively painless task. Difficulties may arise for the party, however, should the promise of gaining power be continually frustrated. This can lead to disenchantment, discord, and even desertion as party activists and core supporters argue over strategy, tactics, policy and personnel, and re-evaluate their own partisan commitment. As argued by Perlin about the Progressive Conservative Party during its long periods in Opposition in the second and third party systems, internal factionalism can plague a party too long in Opposition, and this preoccupation with internal battles (and especially leadership) only worsens the chances of eventual electoral success.[12] Moreover, a creeping desperation may seep into the decisions of key party leaders and strategists, leading them to radically alter traditional policies and to craft new electoral appeals designed to break out of their entrenched but stagnant competitive position within the party system. In certain favourable conjunctures, such departures from tradition can be successful and highly rewarding—witness both the immediate and long-term impact on Conservative support of the Diefenbaker revolution or (in hindsight) the short-term change in electoral fortunes that accompanied Mulroney's leadership. As made abundantly clear in the latter case, however, the problems of moving a party and its supporters through such a transformation can be considerable, and the costs of failure extremely high.

Finally, there are the dangers for the voter-party relationship that attend a change of party leadership. Leaders are both inheritors of a party legacy and creators of their own. As such they are charged with the complex task of maintaining an enduring core of supporters while forging a new and expanded voter coalition. To accomplish this task, they must tap key party icons, play on pre-existing loyalties, and judiciously use tangible rewards in order to carry the party; they must also initiate changes in the party's sociological and electoral base in ways beneficial to the long-term interests of the party. Great party leaders are those who succeed in this difficult task. 'Macdonald created a coalition of Quebec and Ontario; Laurier's coalition was built of Quebec and the West. Pierre Trudeau changed the sociological profile of his party to include many more ethnic Canadians.'[13]

For better or worse, modern electoral politics focus sharply—sometimes almost exclusively—on party leaders, but leaders have always been central to the fortunes of Canadian political parties. Commenting on Canadian politics in 1907, Andre Siegfried noted, 'it is of the first importance to the success of a party that it should be led by someone ... whose mere name is a programme in itself.'[14] The process of changing party leaders, therefore, carries high stakes for parties, with implications for their partisan identity, policy orientation, and voter appeal. Over time, the norms of leader selection and removal have evolved in a rather halting and haphazard fashion, and continue to be marked by considerable uncertainty. Still, some of the traditional concerns about the process have remained the same. The potential divisiveness of leadership contests is one of these. Often struggles over leadership will be destabilizing for a party. According to one study of party leadership contests, the most important consideration for party stability is not which process is adopted for choosing a leader, but the competitive situation in which a party finds itself at the time of choosing a leader, especially whether a party is in government or opposition. With regard to the latter, endemic instability is largely an Opposition Party phenomenon. Yet not all Opposition parties are equally affected; generally, the closer a party moves to being a serious contender for power, the more conflictual leadership politics become. 'The character of these battles and their scrutiny by the media can threaten the legitimacy of a leader's claim to respect and authority.'[15]

Thus, the competitive situation of a party undergoing a leadership change and the character of the leadership struggle itself are factors affecting the overall impact of leadership change on the party and its electoral prospects. This should not be taken to imply, however, that the method of selection is irrelevant. Parties in recent times have become conscious of the need to convince voters that they are progressive, open, and democratic organizations. In an example of Duverger's 'contagion effect' at work, all parties have moved inexorably (and in competition with one another) towards broader and more direct membership participation in leadership selection.[16] However, there are clearly trade-offs for the parties in doing so. Latouche has argued that moving away from delegate conventions deprives the party of important media attention and a venue for building and reinforcing party networks and solidarity.[17] Similarly, Woolstencroft argues that important intraparty processes of interest aggregation and brokerage politics (building consensus and support among activists) will be weakened in favour of image building and candidate-centred electioneering. Thus, the strong tendency already extant to focus on the leader's image and personality will likely be further exaggerated. It may well be that this change in selection process will dilute the importance of party history and iconology to leadership aspirants, as well as the need for these leaders to acknowledge and pay homage to the values and concerns of a party's activists, core electorate, and enduring coalition. If so, then most assuredly the stability of voter-party ties will be affected.

Leadership, of course, can affect the stability of these ties in other ways, as well. All political parties provide their leaders with some measure of autonomy on policy and strategy matters to allow them room to manoeuvre in the arenas of parliamentary and electoral politics. A host of personal and institutional factors determine the degree of leader autonomy from both the caucus and the extraparliamentary party, and this will vary over time and between parties. The benefits of maximizing leadership autonomy lay in the enhanced capacity this gives leaders (and their coterie of advisers) to take advantage of political opportunities that arise as the result of Opposition mistakes, shifts in public opinion, or unforeseen events. A leader may be able to exploit such opportunities in order to solidify, build, or extend the party's base of support (and/or to erode that of opposing parties). In this sense, leader autonomy is the *sine qua non* of brokerage politics.

At the same time, too much leader autonomy on policy and strategy matters can present dangers for a political party. Reckless use of such autonomy, without due regard for a party's iconology or long-standing elements of its program and for the policy predilections as well as the class, regional, and sociodemographic characteristics of the party's core electorate, invites the serious and rapid erosion of the party's core support base. Party leaders in government, it seems, are most likely to incite such partisan backlash, since party leaders in Opposition are both more constrained by their own caucus and party membership, and at the same time less likely to be drawn away from a partisan perspective by the broader considerations and discipline imposed by wielding power. The potential for unfettered leader autonomy is also greater when party élites are shielded (institutionally and/or by party culture) from the systematic input of party members (or even the parliamentary caucus).[18] It will also vary with a leader's personality and leadership style.[19] Leader autonomy will also be affected by the electoral cycle, increasing in the aftermath of a majority victory or when leaders have decided they will not lead their party into another election.[20] When such leader autonomy has been used or abused in ways that have alienated large numbers of party supporters, movements of reform have inevitably sprung up from within the party and/or the caucus, the objectives of which have been to renew the ties between the party and its supporters as well as reshape the relationships between party, caucus, and leadership.[21] Finding the right balance in these relationships is a key factor for the long-term health of the party, but it is never fully settled and the tensions inherent in these relationships never fully resolved.

It is no doubt true that the majority of Canadians no longer feel strong emotive or patron-client ties to a specific political party in the fashion of their political ancestors. Nonetheless, communities of voters across the country are still likely to conform to an established pattern of preferences and tendencies when they cast their ballots either for a particular party or for a particular kind of party. These communities of voters exist in every region and they constitute the enduring coalitions or core support base from which parties broker for the additional support of more weakly committed or volatile voters. Dramatic changes in party support levels have occurred, but these have been exceptional. More often, party vote shares have remained relatively stable, with only minor shifts between elections. It is generally the electoral system that then translates these minor shifts into more significant results at the level of seats. At other times, changes in party vote share reflect the movement of voters within an ideological family of parties (historically, NDP-Liberal or Conservative-Social Credit-Reform). Voter volatility clearly is a factor in modern elections, but voter continuity in its various forms is also strikingly apparent and, in the long run, more important. It is the ballast in the hull of every political party without which parties may easily lose their stability and their bearings, as well as their chances of electoral success and long-term political survival. Interpreting party politics in Canada, then, means more than accurately reading the entrails of the latest permutations in voting behaviour. It means understanding the ties that bind core electorates to their parties of choice and the manner in which such ties are renewed or broken in the competitive context of electoral politics.

Notes

1. On the idea of 'ideological space' in party systems and the ideological dynamics of party competition, see Giovanni Sartori, *Parties and Party Systems: A Framework For Analysis* (New York and Cambridge: Cambridge University Press, 1976).

2. This decision not to re-evaluate some of the party's ideological 'sacred cows' has come under fire from a number of high-profile New Democrats, including intellectuals like John Richards and James Laxer, and former provincial premiers Allan Blakeney and Bob Rae. For example, see James Laxer, *In Search of a New Left: Canadian Politics After the Neo-Conservative Assault* (Toronto: Viking, 1996), and Bob Rae, *The Three Questions: Prosperity and the Public Good* (Toronto: Penguin, 1998).

3. Keith Archer and Alan Whitehorn, *Political Activists: The NDP in Convention* (Toronto: Oxford University Press, 1997):27, 34, 37.

4. Alan Cairns, 'The Electoral System and the Party System in Canada, 1921–1965', *Canadian Journal of Political Science* 1, no. 1 (March 1968):55–80.

5. Leslie Pal, 'The Cauldron of Leadership: Prime Ministers and Their Parties', in *Canadian Political Party Systems*, edited by R.K. Carty (Peterborough: Broadview Press, 1992):89.

6. For the first comprehensive statement of this argument, see E.E. Schattschneider, *The Semisovereign People: A Realist's View of Democracy in America* (Hinsdale: Dryden Press, 1960).

7. Seymour Martin Lipset and Stein Rokkan, 'Cleavage Structures, Party Systems and Voter Alignments', in *Party Systems and Voter Alignments: Cross-national Perspectives*, edited by S.M. Lipset and S. Rokkan (New York: Free Press, 1967). Lipset and Rokkan spoke of 'the freezing of party alignments' and emphasized the importance of past history for present electoral choice.

8. Janine Brodie and Jane Jenson, *Crisis, Challenge and Change: Party and Class in Canada* (Toronto: Methuen, 1980).
9. For a discussion of this feature of party appeals, see Gilles Bourque, 'Class, Nation and the Parti Quebecois', *Studies in Political Economy* 2 (Autumn 1979):129–58.
10. R. Rose and T.T. Mackie, 'Do Parties Persist or Disappear? The Big Tradeoff Facing Organizations', in *When Parties Fail*, edited by K. Lawson and P. Merkyl (Princeton: Princeton University Press, 1987).
11. M. Goldfarb and T. Axworthy, *Marching to a Different Drummer: An Essay on Liberals and Conservatives in Convention* (Toronto: Stoddart, 1988):5.
12. George Perlin, *The Tory Syndrome* (Montreal: McGill-Queen's University Press, 1980).
13. Pal, 'Cauldron of Leadership', 416.
14. Andre Siegfried, *The Race Question in Canada* (Toronto: McClelland and Stewart, 1970):136.
15. R.K. Carty, L. Erickson, and D.E. Blake, 'Parties and Leaders: The Experiences of the Provinces', in *Leaders and Parties in Canadian Politics: Experiences of the Provinces*, edited by R.K. Carty, L. Erickson, and D.E. Blake (Toronto: Harcourt, Brace, Jovanovich, 1992):10.
16. Duverger was the first party theorist to take note of the tendency for organizational innovations by one party that produce some competitive advantage to be quickly taken up by other parties in the party system. See Maurice Duverger, *Political Parties: Their Organization and Activity in the Modern State* (London: Methuen, 1964).
17. Daniel Latouche, 'Universal Democracy and Effective Leadership: Lessons from the Parti Québécois Experience' in *Leaders and Parties in Canadian Politics: Experiences of the Provinces*, edited by R.K. Carty, L. Erickson, and D.E. Blake (Toronto: Harcourt, Brace, Jovanovich, 1992):174–202.
18. For a discussion of how the ascent to power leads to the insulation of brokerage party élites from their own party supporters, activists, and backbench MPs, see Christina McCall-Newman, 'Power in Trudeau's Liberal Party', in *Party Politics in Canada*, 5th edn, edited by Hugh Thorburn (Scarborough: Prentice-Hall, 1985); Peter Woolstencroft, 'The Progressive Conservative Party, 1984–1993: Government, Party, Members', in *Party Politics in Canada*, 7th edn, edited by Hugh Thorburn (Scarborough: Prentice-Hall, 1996):280–305.
19. For example, both Trudeau (arrogance and disinterest) and Mulroney (hubris and affectation) had certain leadership traits that ultimately are thought to have had negative organizational and/or electoral consequences for their respective parties.
20. For a discussion of how this affected the content and style of Pierre Trudeau's last mandate, see Stephen Clarkson and Christina McCall, *Trudeau and Our Times, Volume 2: The Historic Delusion* (Toronto: McClelland and Stewart, 1994).
21. For a discussion of these historic tensions and tendencies within the Liberal Party, see Stephen Clarkson, 'Democracy Within the Liberal Party: The Experiment with Citizen Participation under Pierre Trudeau', in *Party Politics in Canada*, 4th edn, edited by Hugh Thorburn (Scarborough: Prentice-Hall, 1979); Joseph Wearing, *The L Shaped Party: The Liberal Party of Canada* (Toronto: McGraw-Hill Ryerson, 1981).

APPENDICES A, B, AND C: CANADIAN FEDERAL ELECTION RESULTS BY PARTY SYSTEM, 1867–1997 AND BY PROVINCE AND PARTY, 1925–1997

Compiled by Tony Coulson

Appendix A includes overview tables of the election results for the period 1967–97. These tables are organized according to the four party systems: 1867–1917, 1921–58, 1962–80, and 1984-present. In Appendix B, detailed election results by party and province are presented for the elections between 1925 and 1997. Voter turnout figures are also presented for each election in Appendix A, and by province in Appendix B.

Data Sources

The overview data for the elections between 1867 and 1921 are pieced together primarily from three sources: J. Murray Beck's *Pendulum of Power*, Howard Scarrow's *Canada Votes*, and *A History of the Vote in Canada*, published for the chief electoral officer of Canada by Public Works and Government Services Canada. It should be noted that the votes by party in the earliest elections are, in Beck's words, 'little more than informed guesses' (Beck 1968:preface). Indeed, Scarrow chose to exclude the first three federal elections from his work since 'the formation of national political parties had not been completed' (Scarrow 1962:3).

It is also noteworthy that the vote totals presented for the elections in the period 1867 through 1921 are the total votes cast, including rejected ballots. The total votes cast for the elections up to and including 1921, and the turnout information for all elections considered here are drawn from *A History of the Vote in Canada*. The tables included in *A History of the Vote in Canada*, which were compiled by Alain Pelletier and I (see page xi), are based on the *Report of the Clerk of the Crown in Chancery* (1867–1917); *Reports of the Chief Electoral Officer* (1921–93), and unpublished summary data prepared by Elections Canada.

The tables for the period 1925 through 1962 are based on unpublished summary data maintained by the Office of the Chief Electoral Officer of Canada (for votes by party and province) and on *The Canadian Parliamentary Guide* (party affiliation of elected members). The vote totals presented for these and all subsequent elections are the total valid votes, excluding rejected ballots.

The *Report of the Chief Electoral Officer* for the elections of 1963 and 1965 contained a summary description of the votes obtained by political party and province, but did not include summary information on the number of candidates elected. Consequently, voting data for the elections of 1963 and 1965 are drawn from the official *Report of the Chief Electoral Officer*, while the data on the number of candidates elected by party and province are drawn from *The Canadian Parliamentary Guide*.

The tables for the period 1968 through 1997 are based entirely on the *Reports of the Chief Electoral Officer*, which include summaries by party and province of the members elected and the number of votes.

Any calculation or transcription errors are solely my own.

Tony Coulson is an evaluation officer in the Program Evaluation Directorate of the Policy Group at Transport Canada. From 1994 through 1998, he was a research project officer at Elections Canada.

References

Beck, Murray J. (1968). *Pendulum of Power Canada's Federal Elections* (Scarborough: Prentice-Hall).

Canada, Chief Electoral Officer. 1963. *Report of the Chief Electoral Officer*. Ottawa: The Queen's Printer.

——. 1965. *Report of the Chief Electoral Officer*. Ottawa: The Queen's Printer.

——. 1968. *Report of the Chief Electoral Officer*, parts I, III, and IV. Ottawa: The Queen's Printer.

——. 1972. *Report of the Chief Electoral Officer*, parts I, III, and IV. Ottawa: Information Canada.

——. 1974. *Report of the Chief Electoral Officer*, parts I, III, and IV. Ottawa: Information Canada.

——. 1979. *Report of the Chief Electoral Officer*, parts I, III, and IV. Ottawa: Minister of Supply and Services Canada.

——. 1980. *Report of the Chief Electoral Officer*, parts I, III, and IV. Ottawa: Minister of Supply and Services Canada.

——. 1984. *Report of the Chief Electoral Officer*, parts I, III, and IV. Ottawa: Minister of Supply and Services Canada.

———. 1988. *Report of the Chief Electoral Officer: Appendices (Revised)*. Ottawa: Minister of Supply and Services Canada.

———. 1993. *Official Voting Results: Synopsis*. Ottawa: Chief Electoral Officer of Canada.

Info Globe. (1993). 'Summary of General Election Results', pp. 471–5. In *The Canadian Parliamentary Guide*. Toronto: Info Globe.

Scarrow, Howard A. (1962), *Canada Votes: A Handbook of Federal and Provincial Election Data*. New Orleans: Hauser.

APPENDIX A:

ELECTION RESULTS BY PARTY SYSTEM

FEDERAL GENERAL ELECTIONS, 1867–1997

Table A.1: First Party System, 1867–1917

Party	1867[1]	1872	1874	1878	1882	1887	1891
Liberal	49.0% 72	49.1% 96	53.8% 138	45.1% 65	46.6% 73	48.9% 87	46.4% 91
Conservative	50.1% 108	49.9% 104	45.4% 67	53.2% 140	53.4% 138	50.7% 128	52.0% 122
Other	0.9% —	0.9% —	0.8% 1[2]	1.7% 1[3]	0.1% —	0.4% —	1.6% 2[4]
Total votes	268,387	318,329	324,006	534,029	508,496	724,517	778,495
Total seats	181	200	206	206	211	215	215
Turnout (%)	73.1%	70.3%	69.6%	69.1%	70.3%	70.1%	64.4%

Party	1896	1900	1904	1908	1911	1917[7]
Liberal	45.1% 118	52.0% 132	52.5% 139	50.6% 135	47.8% 87	40.1% 82
Conservative	46.3% 88	47.4% 81	46.9% 75	47.0% 85	51.2% 134	57.0% 153
Other	8.6% 7[5]	0.6% —	0.7% —	2.4% 1[6]	1% —	2.9% —
Total votes	912,992	958,497	1,036,878	1,180,820	1,314,953	1,892,741
Total seats	213	213	214	221	221	235
Turnout (%)	62.9%	77.4%	71.6%	70.3%	70.2%	75.0%

Table A.2: Second Party System, 1921–1958

Party	1921	1925	1926	1930	1935	1940
Liberal	40.7% 116	40.4% 99	43.6% 116	43.9% 88	44.4% 171	54.9% 181[14]
Conservative	30.3% 50	46.6% 116	46.2% 91	49.0% 137	29.8% 39	30.6% 40
Progressive	23.1% 65	8.8% 24	6.2% 22	2.3% 5	— 2[11]	— —
Labour/CCF	2.2% 2	1.6% 2	1.5% 3	1.2% 3[10]	8.9% 7	8.5% 8
United Farmers	0.1% —	— —	1.9% 11	2.2 10	— 1[12]	— —
Social Credit	— —	— —	— —	— —	4.1% 17	2.7% 10
Reconstruction	— —	— —	— —	— —	8.7% 1	— —
Others	3.6% 2[8]	2.6 4	0.6 2	1.4 2	4.1 7[13]	3.3% 6[15]
Total valid votes	3,139,306[9]	3,144,337	3,256,508	3,898,995	4,406,854	4,620,260
Total seats	235	245	245	245	245	245
Turnout (%)	67.7	66.4	67.7	73.5	74.2	69.9

(Continued)

Table A.2: Second Party System, 1921–1958 (*Continued*)

Party	1945	1949	1953	1957	1958
Liberal	41.4% 127	50.1% 193	50.0% 172	42.3% 106	33.8% 48
Progressive Conservative	27.7% 68	29.7% 41	31.0% 51	39.0% 112	53.7% 208
CCF/NDP	15.7% 28	13.4% 13	11.3% 23	10.8% 25	9.5% 8
Social Credit	4.1% 13	3.9%[17] 10	5.4% 15	6.6% 19	2.6% —
Bloc Populaire	3.3% 2	— —	— —	— —	— —
Others	7.8% 7[16]	2.9% 5	2.3% 4[18]	1.3% 3[19]	0.4% 1[20]
Total votes	5,246,130	5,848,971	5,641,272	6,605,980	7,287,297
Total seats	245	262	265	265	265
Turnout (%)	75.3	73.8	67.5	74.1	79.4

Table A.3: Third Party System, 1962–1980

Party	1962	1963	1965	1968	1972	1974	1979	1980
Liberal	37.4% 99	41.7% 128	40.2% 131	45.5% 155	38.5% 109	43.2% 141	40.1% 114	44.3% 147
Progressive Conservative	37.3% 116	32.8% 95	32.4% 97	31.4% 72	34.9% 107	35.4% 95	35.9% 136	32.5% 103
New Democratic Party	13.4% 19	13.1% 17	17.9% 21	17.0% 22	17.7% 31	15.4% 16	17.9% 26	19.8% 32
Ralliement des Créditistes	— —	— —	4.6% 9	4.4% 14	— —	— —	— —	— —
Social Credit	11.7% 30	11.9% 24	3.7% 5	0.8% 0	7.6% 15	5.0% 11	4.6% 6	1.7% 0
Others	0.2% 1[21]	0.4% 1	1.2% 2	0.9% 1	1.2% 2	0.9% 1	1.5% 0	1.7% 0
Total valid votes	7,690,134	7,894,076	7,713,316	8,125,996	9,667,489	9,505,908	11,455,702	10,947,914
Total seats	265	265	265	264	264	264	282	282
Turnout (%)	79.0	79.2	74.8	75.7	76.7	71.0	75.7	69.3

Table A.4: Fourth Party System, 1984–1997

Party	1984	1988	1993	1997[23]
Liberal	28.0% 40	31.9% 83	41.3% 177	38.5% 155
Progressive Conservative	50.0% 211	43.0% 169	16.0% 2	18.8% 20
New Democratic Party	18.8% 30	20.4% 43	6.9% 9	11.0% 21
Social Credit	0.1% 0	** 0	— —	— —
Bloc Québécois	— —	— —	13.5% 54	10.7% 44
Reform	— —	2.1 —	18.7% 52	19.4% 60
Others	3.0% 1	2.6% 0	3.6% 1	1.6% 1
Total valid votes	12,548,721	13,175,599	13,667,671	12,985,964
Total seats	282	295	295	301
Turnout (%)	75.3	75.3	69.6[22]	67

Notes to Tables in Appendix A

General

- The first federal election for the Cooperative Commonwealth Federation (CCF) was in 1935.
- The name Progressive Conservative Party was first utilized in the election of 1945.
- The first federal election for the New Democratic Party (NDP) was in 1962.
- Columns may not total 100 per cent due to rounding.
- ** Indicates less than 0.1 per cent.

First Party System, 1867–1917

1. Members elected do not equal the total seats due to no return from one district (Kamouraska) due to rioting (see Beck 1968:12).
2. An Independent.
3. An Independent.
4. Two Independents.
5. Includes four McCarthyites, two Patrons, and one Independent.
6. An Independent.
7. The 1917 Union government was comprised of Conservatives and 'Unionist Liberals' (see Scarrow 1962:28).

Second Party System, 1921–1958

8. Includes one Independent Liberal and one Independent.
9. The vote total for the election of 1921 (and all prior elections) is the total vote, including rejected ballots. For 1925 and subsequent elections, the total valid votes are presented excluding rejected ballots.
10. Includes one Independent Labour and two Labour.
11. The votes obtained that correspond to these seats (two Liberal Progressives) are included under Liberal.
12. The votes obtained that correspond to this seat (one United Farmer of Ontario-Labour) are included under Other.
13. Includes five Independent Liberals, one Independent Conservative, and one Independent.
14. 181 Liberal includes three Liberal Progressives.
15. Includes three Independent Liberal, one United Reform, one Unity, and one Independent.
16. Includes one Labour Progressive, one Independent Progressive, and five Independents.
17. Includes 1.5 per cent of votes received by the Union des Electeurs, the French Canadian affiliate of Social Credit. See *The Canadian Encyclopedia*

(Edmonton: Hurtig Publishers, 1988):532; Thomas T. Mackie and Richard Rose, *International Almanac of Electoral History*, 2nd edn (New York: Facts on File, 1982):76; or Maurice Pinard, *The Rise of a Third Party* (Montreal: McGill-Queen's University Press, 1975).

18. Includes one Liberal Labour and three Independents.
19. Includes one Liberal Labour and three Independents.
20. Liberal Labour.

Third Party System, 1962–1980

21. Liberal Labour.

Fourth Party System, 1984–1997

22. Due to the inclusion of duplicate names and the names of deceased persons on the 1993 final list of electors, the official turnout reported for that election was artificially low (see: 'Note to the Reader', in the *Official Voting Results, Thirty-Fifth General Election, 1993*, published by the Chief Electoral Officer of Canada). On the basis of the growth of the electoral lists over time, Blais et al. have estimated the voter turnout rate in 1993 at approximately 73 per cent (see A. Blais, A. Bilodeau, and C. Kam, 'Déplacement des votes entre les élections de 1993 et 1997'. Montreal: Typescript).
23. As of 18 January 1999, the composition of the House of Commons was: 155 Liberal, fifty-nine Reform, forty-four Bloc Québécois, twenty-one NDP, nineteen PC, two Independent, and one Vacancy (see Party Standings under reference materials on the Parliamentary web site at www.parl.gc.ca).

Appendix B:

Election Results by Party and Province

Federal General Elections, 1925–1997

Table B.1: 1925 General Election

Province	Liberal	Conservative	Progressive	Labour	Others	Totals	Turnout (%)
Nova Scotia	41.9% 3	56.4% 11	— —	1.6% —	— —	222,010 14	70
New Brunswick	40.3% 1	59.7% 10	— —	— —	** —	151,660 11	61
Prince Edward Island	52.0% 2	48.0% 2	— —	— —	— —	49,430 4	76
Quebec	60.4% 59	33.4% 4	** —	0.2% —	5.9% 2	805,881 65	72
Ontario	32.0% 11	57.2% 68	8.3% 2	0.8% —	1.6% 1	1,213,253 82	65
Manitoba	19.5% 1	41.7% 7	27.3% 7	9.7% 2	1.7% —	168,694 17	68
Saskatchewan	40.6% 15	26.6% —	31.8% 6	— —	1.0% —	196,419 21	57
Alberta	25.6% 4	32.7% 3	31.1% 9	6.0% —	4.5% —	162,468 16	57
British Columbia	34.1% 3	49.8% 10	9.2% —	5.8% —	1.1% 1	173,272 14	75
Yukon Territory	40.6% —	59.4% 1	— —	— —	— —	1,250 1	78
Totals	1,269,401 99	1,466,324 116	276,757 24	51,045 2	80,810 4	3,144,337 245	66

Notes: Rows may not add up to 100 per cent due to rounding.
**Less than 0.1 per cent.

Table B.2: 1926 General Election

Province	Liberal	Conservative	Progressive	Labour	United Farmers	Others	Totals	Turnout (%)
Nova Scotia	43.5% 2	53.7% 12	— —	2.8% —	— —	— —	228,958 14	72
New Brunswick	46.1% 4	53.9% 7	— —	— —	— —	— —	161,545 11	68
Prince Edward Island	52.7% 3	47.3% 1	— —	— —	— —	— —	55,439 4	84
Quebec	63.2% 60	35.7% 4	— —	— —	— —	1.1% 1	803,386 65	71
Ontario	36.1% 23	55.7% 53	7.2% 6	0.5% —	— —	0.4% —	1,222,106 82	64
Manitoba	18.4% 4	42.2% —	30.7% 11	8.7% 2	— —	— —	197,007 17	77
Saskatchewan	51.3% 16	27.5% —	21.1% 5	— —	— —	— —	245,110 21	70
Alberta	24.5% 3	31.5% 1	— —	5.2% 1	38.7% 11	0.1% —	157,016 16	57
British Columbia	37.0% 1	54.2% 12	— —	6.4% —	— —	2.3% 1	184,470 14	71
Yukon Territory	44.0% —	55.9% 1	— —	— —	— —	— —	1,471 1	80
Totals	1,504,855 116	1,421,804 91	200,680 22	49,793 3	60,740 11	18,636 2	3,256,508 245	68

Note: Rows may not add up to 100 per cent due to rounding.

Table B.3: 1930 General Election

Province	Liberal	Conservative	Progressive	Labour	United Farmers	Others	Totals	Turnout (%)
Nova Scotia	47.5% 4	52.5% 10	—	—	—	—	267,702 14	83
New Brunswick	40.3% 1	59.3% 10	—	—	—	—	185,060 11	78
Prince Edward Island	50.0% 1	50.0% 3	—	—	—	—	59,390 4	89
Quebec	53.1% 40	44.7% 24	—	—	—	2.2% 1	1,020,261 65	76
Ontario	43.4% 22	54.8% 59	0.9% —	**	1[2]	0.8% —	1,359,576 82	69
Manitoba	15.9% 1	47.7% 11	25.3% 3	8.5% 2	—	2.5% —	233,401 17	72
Saskatchewan	46.5% 11	39.2% 8	5.5% 2	—	6.9% —	1.9% —	330,192 21	81
Alberta	30.0% 3	33.8% 4	—	4.4% —	30.4% 9	1.4% —	200,376 16	66
British Columbia	40.9% 5	49.3% 7	—	6.5% 1[1]	—	3.3% 1	241,633 14	73
Yukon Territory	39.7% —	60.2% 1	—	—	—	—	1,404 1	82
Totals	1,909,955 88	1,714,860 137	90,148 5	45,302 3	83,690 10	55,040 2	3,898,995 245	73

Notes:
Rows may not add up to 100 per cent due to rounding.
**Less than 0.1 per cent.
[1]Independent Labour.
[2]The votes that correspond to this seat are included under Progressive.

Table B.4: 1935 General Election

Province	Liberal	Conservative	Reconstruction	CCF	United Farmers	Social Credit	Progressive	Others	Totals	Turnout (%)
Nova Scotia	52.0% 12	32.1% —	13.9% —	— —	— —	— —	— —	1.9% —	273,767 12	76
New Brunswick	57.2% 9	31.9% 1	10.5% —	— —	— —	— —	— —	0.4% —	175,762 10	77
Prince Edward Island	58.2% 4	38.4% —	3.4% —	— —	— —	— —	— —	— —	61,448 4	80
Quebec	54.4% 55	28.2% 5	9.0% —	0.6% —	— —	— —	— —	7.7% 5	1,146,521 65	74
Ontario	42.4% 56	35.3% 25	11.4% —	8.1% —	1¹	— —	— —	2.7% —	1,594,247 82	74
Manitoba	35.8% 12	26.9% 1	5.8% —	19.4% 2	— —	2.0% —	— —	10.0% —	280,992 17	75
Saskatchewan	39.0% 16	20.6% 1	0.6% —	21.3% 2	— —	18.4% 2	2²	— —	345,570 21	77
Alberta	21.2% 1	16.9% 1	0.7% —	12.2% —	— —	46.8% 15	— —	2.2% —	238,513 17	65
British Columbia	31.8% 6	24.6% 5	6.6% 1	33.6% 3	— —	0.6% —	— —	2.8% 1	288,783 16	76
Yukon Territory	— —	— —	— —	— —	— —	— —	— —	100% 1	1,251 1	70
Totals	1,955,727 171	1,311,459 39	384,215 1	390,860 7	1	182,767 17	2	181,826 7	4,406,854 245	74

Notes: Rows may not add up to 100 per cent due to rounding.
¹The votes that correspond to this United Farmers of Ontario-Labour seat are included under Others.
²The votes that correspond to these two Liberal-Progressive seats are included under Liberal.

Table B.5: 1940 General Election

Province	Liberal	Conservative	CCF	Social Credit	Progressive	Others	Totals	Turnout (%)
Nova Scotia	53.9% 10	39.8% 1	6.3% 1	—	—	—	281,652 12	70
New Brunswick	56.2% 5	43.4% 5	0.4% —	—	—	—	172,793 10	68
Prince Edward Island	55.3% 4	44.7% —	—	—	—	—	62,692 4	78
Quebec	74.1% 61	19.8% 1	0.6% —	0.9% —	—	4.4% 3[3]	1,171,497 65	66
Ontario	51.8% 55	42.7% 25	3.8% —	** 	2[1]	1.6% 1	1,609,414 82	69
Manitoba	47.8% 14	25.9% 1	19.4% 1	1.8% —	1[2]	5.0% —	316,883 17	74
Saskatchewan	43.0% 12	14.1% 2	28.6% 5	3.3% —	—	11.0% 2[4]	371,134 21	77
Alberta	38.0% 7	13.0% —	13.0% —	34.5% 10	—	1.5% —	269,343 17	63
British Columbia	37.5% 10	30.5% 4	28.4% 1	0.1% —	—	3.5% 1	363,144 16	76
Yukon Territory	46.4% —	53.6% 1	—	—	—	—	1,708 1	82
Totals	2,536,214 178	1,416,257 40	393,230 8	123,443 10	— 3	151,116 6	4,620,260 245	70

Notes:

Rows may not add up to 100 per cent due to rounding.

** Less than 0.1 per cent.

[1] The votes that correspond to these two Liberal-Progressive seats are included under Liberal.

[2] The votes that correspond to this Liberal-Progressive seat are included under Liberal.

[3] Three Independent Liberals.

[4] Includes one Unity Reform and one Unity Saskatchewan.

Table B.6: 1945 General Election

Province	Liberal	Progressive Conservative	CCF	Social Credit	Bloc Populaire	Others	Totals	Turnout (%)
Nova Scotia	45.7% 8	36.8% 3	16.7% 1	—	—	0.8% —	310,667 12	72
New Brunswick	50.0% 7	38.2% 3	7.4% —	1.1% —	—	3.2% —	201,886 10	78
Prince Edward Island	48.4% 3	47.3% 1	4.2% —	—	—	—	63,406 4	81
Quebec	51.1% 56	9.8% 2	2.4% —	4.5% —	11.9% 2	19.3% 5[1]	1,414,169 65	73
Ontario	41.1% 34	41.7% 48	14.3% —	0.2% —	0.3% —	2.4% —	1,814,967 82	75
Manitoba	34.6% 10	24.9% 2	31.6% 5	3.2% —	—	5.7% —	322,815 17	76
Saskatchewan	32.9% 2	18.8% 1	44.4% 18	3.0% —	—	0.8% —	376,886 21	85
Alberta	21.8% 2	18.7% 2	18.4% —	36.6% 13	—	4.5% —	310,773 17	73
British Columbia	29.2% 5	30.0% 5	30.8% 4	2.3% —	—	7.7% 2[2]	428,441 16	80
Yukon Territory	— —	40.0% 1	27.5% —	—	—	32.4% —	2,120 1	63
Totals	2,170,625 127	1,455,453 68	822,661 28	214,998 13	173,427 2	408,966 7	5,246,130 245	75

Notes: Rows may not add up to 100 per cent due to rounding.
[1] Includes four Independent and one Labour Progressive.
[2] Includes one Independent and one Independent Progressive.

Table B.7: 1949 General Election

Province	Liberal	Progressive Conservative	CCF	Social Credit	Others	Totals	Turnout (%)
Newfoundland	71.9% 5	27.9% 2	0.1% —	— —	— —	104,635 7	58
Nova Scotia	52.7% 10	37.4% 2	9.9% 1	— —	— —	337,378 13	75
New Brunswick	55.2% 8	39.4% 2	4.2% —	1.0% —	0.2% —	223,657 10	79
Prince Edward Island	49.2% 3	48.4% 1	2.4% —	— —	— —	68,095 4	85
Quebec	61.8% 68	24.9% 2	1.1% —	5.1% —	7.1% 3	1,593,300 73	74
Ontario	46.0% 56	37.5% 25	15.1% 1	0.3% —	1.1% 1	2,022,174 83	75
Manitoba	47.9% 12	22.0% 1	25.9% 3	— —	4.1% —	320,911 16	72
Saskatchewan	43.4% 14	14.4% 1	40.8% 5	0.9% —	0.4% —	372,915 20	79
Alberta	34.5% 5	16.8% 2	9.3% —	38.7% 10	0.6% —	338,131 17	69
British Columbia	36.7% 11	27.9% 3	31.5% 3	0.4% —	3.4% 1	461,068 18	69
Yukon	49.0% 1	— —	17.0% —	— —	34.0% —	6,707 1	76
Totals	2,929,391 193	1,746,276 41	782,410 13	225,013[1] 10	169,881 5	5,848,971 262	74

Notes:
Rows may not add up to 100 per cent due to rounding.
[1] The Social Credit total includes 85,198 votes obtained by Union des Electeurs candidates, who ran unsuccessfully in New Brunswick (2,172 votes in one district), Ontario (2,036 votes in four electoral districts) and Quebec (80,990 votes in fifty electoral districts; see Beck 1968:272). Beck's numbers are corroborated by Elections Canada data.

Table B.8: 1953 General Election

Province	Liberal	Progressive Conservative	CCF	Social Credit	Others	Totals	Turnout (%)
Newfoundland	67.2% 7	28.1% —	0.6% —	— —	4.0% —	110,583 7	57
Nova Scotia	53.0% 10	40.1% 1	6.7% 1	— —	0.2% —	333,203 12	72
New Brunswick	54.6% 7	41.9% 3	3.0% —	0.4% —	— —	223,086 10	78
Prince Edward Island	51.1% 3	48.0% 1	0.8% —	— —	— —	66,262 4	83
Quebec	64.7% 68	29.5% 4	1.5% —	— —	4.2% 3	1,546,773 75	69
Ontario	46.9% 50	40.3% 33	11.1% 1	0.3% —	1.4% 1[1]	1,915,420 85	67
Manitoba	40.6% 8	27.0% 3	23.6% 3	6.3% —	2.4% —	272,777 14	59
Saskatchewan	37.7% 5	11.7% 1	44.1% 11	5.3% —	1.1% —	354,153 17	74
Alberta	34.9% 4	14.5% 2	6.9% —	40.8% 11	2.8% —	340,241 17	63
British Columbia	30.8% 8	14.1% 3	26.6% 7	26.2% 4	2.2% —	471,523 22	65
Yukon & Mackenzie River	53.7% 2	26.7% —	— —	13.7% —	5.8% —	7,251 2	76 & 63
Totals	2,819,813 172	1,751,215 51	636,310 23	305,973 15	127,961 4	5,641,272 265	67

Notes: Rows may not add up to 100 per cent due to rounding.
[1] Liberal Labour.

Table B.9: 1957 General Election

Province	Liberal	Progressive Conservative	CCF	Social Credit	Others	Totals	Turnout (%)
Newfoundland	61.8% 5	37.8% 2	0.3% —	— —	— —	92,109 7	52
Nova Scotia	45.1% 2	50.4% 10	4.4% —	0.1% —	— —	392,157 12	81
New Brunswick	48.0% 5	48.7% 5	0.8% —	1.0% —	1.3% —	234,158 10	81
Prince Edward Island	46.6% —	52.3% 4	1.0% —	— —	— —	66,807 4	85
Quebec	62.3% 64[1]	31.4% 9	1.8% —	0.2% —	4.2% 2	1,790,060 75	72
Ontario	37.3% 20	48.8% 61	12.1% 3	1.7% —	0.1% 1[2]	2,264,571 85	74
Manitoba	26.8% 1	35.8% 8	23.6% 5	13.1% —	0.5% —	348,110 14	74
Saskatchewan	30.3% 4	23.1% 3	36.0% 10	10.4% —	0.1% —	390,098 17	81
Alberta	27.9% 1	27.6% 3	6.3% —	37.9% 13	0.2% —	427,652 17	73
British Columbia	20.5% 2	32.6% 7	22.3% 7	24.2% 6	0.4% —	591,539 22	74
Yukon & Mackenzie River	58.6% 2	41.4% —	— —	— —	— —	8,719 2	89 & 63
Totals	2,796,039 106	2,578,045 112	707,659 25	437,049 19	87,183 3	6,605,980 265	74

Notes: Rows may not add up to 100 per cent due to rounding.
[1] Includes one Independent Liberal.
[2] Liberal Labour.

Table B.10: 1958 General Election

Province	Liberal	Progressive Conservative	CCF	Social Credit	Others	Totals	Turnout (%)
Newfoundland	54.4% 5	45.2% 2	0.1% —	— —	0.1% —	159,745 —	79
Nova Scotia	38.4% —	57.0% 12	4.5% —	— —	— —	416,359 12	84
New Brunswick	43.3% 3	54.1% 7	1.8% —	0.6% —	— —	247,484 10	85
Prince Edward Island	37.5% —	62.2% 4	0.3% —	— —	— —	68,973 4	88
Quebec	46.2% 25	49.6% 50	2.2% —	0.6% —	1.3% —	2,024,249 75	79
Ontario	32.6% 14	56.4% 67	10.5% 3	0.3% —	0.2% 1[1]	2,504,513 85	79
Manitoba	21.5% —	56.7% 14	19.6% —	1.8% —	0.4% —	382,560 14	80
Saskatchewan	19.6% —	51.4% 16	28.3% 1	0.4% —	0.1% —	397,712 17	82
Alberta	13.7% —	60.0% 17	4.3% —	21.6% —	0.3% —	449,889 17	74
British Columbia	16.1% —	49.3% 18	24.5% 4	9.5% —	0.4% —	625,542 22	76
Yukon & Mackenzie River	50.1% 1	49.8% 1	— —	— —	— —	10,271 2	90 & 74
Totals	2,459,700 48	3,910,852 208	692,398 8	188,717 —	35,630 1	7,288,297 265	79

Notes: Rows may not add up to 100 per cent due to rounding.
[1] The votes that correspond to this Liberal Labour seat may be included under Liberal.

Table B.11: 1962 General Election

Province	Liberal	Progressive Conservative	New Democratic Party	Social Credit	Others	Totals	Turnout (%)
Newfoundland	59.0% 6	35.9 1	4.9% —	0.1% —	— —	154,040 7	72
Nova Scotia	42.4% 2	47.2% 9	9.4% 1	0.9% —	— —	420,875 12	84
New Brunswick	44.6% 6	46.5% 4	5.2% —	3.6% —	— —	249,500 10	83
Prince Edward Island	43.3% —	51.2% 4	4.2% —	0.2% —	— —	72,946 4	90
Quebec	39.8% 35	29.7% 14	4.3% —	25.9% 26	0.2% —	2,089,923 75	78
Ontario	41.7% 43	39.3% 35	17.0% 6	1.8% —	0.1% 1[1]	2,687,645 85	80
Manitoba	31.1% 1	41.6% 11	19.6% 2	6.8% —	0.8% —	389,338 14	77
Saskatchewan	22.8% 1	50.4% 16	22.0% —	4.6% —	** —	423,470 17	85
Alberta	19.4% —	42.8% 15	8.4% —	29.2% 2	0.1% —	501,985 17	74
British Columbia	27.3% 4	27.3% 6	30.9% 10	14.2% 2	0.2% —	686,189 22	78
Yukon & Northwest Territories	45.7% 1	47.6% 1	6.7% —	— —	— —	14,223 2	88 & 72
Totals	2,874,076 99	2,868,295 116	1,036,853 19	896,574 30	14,336 1	7,690,134 265	79

Notes: Rows may not add up to 100 per cent due to rounding.
**Less than 0.1 per cent.
[1] The votes that correspond to this Liberal Labour seat may be included under Liberal.

Table B.12: 1963 General Election

Province	Liberal	Progressive Conservative	New Democratic Party	Social Credit	Others	Totals	Turnout (%)
Newfoundland	64.5% 7	30.0% —	4.2% —	— —	1.3% —	151,374 7	69
Nova Scotia	46.7% 5	46.8% 7	6.4% —	** —	— —	417,736 12	82
New Brunswick	47.3% 6	40.4% 4	3.6% —	8.6% —	— —	243,447 10	81
Prince Edward Island	46.4% 2	51.6% 2	1.6% —	— —	— —	69,178 4	84
Quebec	45.6% 47	19.5% 8	7.1% —	27.3% 20	0.4% —	2,118,045 75	76
Ontario	46.3% 51	35.3% 27	15.9% 6	2.0 —	0.4% 1	2,776,662 85	81
Manitoba	33.8% 2	42.3% 10	16.7% 2	7.0% —	0.2% —	399,553 14	78
Saskatchewan	24.1% —	53.7% 17	18.2% —	3.8% —	0.1% —	418,126 17	83
Alberta	22.1% 1	45.3% 14	6.5% —	25.8% 2	0.2% —	549,526 17	79
British Columbia	32.3% 7	23.4% 4	30.3% 9	13.3% 2	0.6% —	735,972 22	80
Yukon & Northwest Territories	42.3% —	53.8% 2	— 	3.9% —	— —	14,457 2	88 & 73
Totals	3,293,790 128	2,591,614 95	1,037,857 17	940,703 24	30,112 1	7,894,076 265	79

Notes: Rows may not add up to 100 per cent due to rounding.
**Less than 0.1 per cent.

Table B.13: 1965 General Election

Province	Liberal	Progressive Conservative	New Democratic Party	Ralliement des Créditistes	Social Credit	Others	Totals	Turnout (%)
Newfoundland	64.1% 7	32.4% —	1.2% —	— —	1.6% —	0.7% —	147,045 7	66
Nova Scotia	42.0% 2	48.6% 10	9.1% —	— —	— —	0.2% —	417,830 12	82
New Brunswick	47.5% 6	42.5% 4	9.4% —	0.4% —	0.1% —	— —	241,687 10	80
Prince Edward Island	44.1% —	53.9% 4	2.0% —	— —	— —	— —	71,561 4	88
Quebec	45.6% 56	21.2% 8	12.0% —	17.5% 9	— —	3.6% 2	2,037,312 75	71
Ontario	43.6% 51	34.0% 25	21.6% 9	** —	0.3% —	0.3% —	2,743,783 85	77
Manitoba	30.9% 1	40.6% 10	24.0% 3	— —	4.3% —	** —	379,440 14	74
Saskatchewan	24.0% —	48.0% 17	26.0% —	— —	1.9% —	** —	402,325 17	80
Alberta	22.4% —	46.6% 15	8.2% —	— —	22.5% 2	0.2% —	531,427 17	74
British Columbia	30.0% 7	19.1% 3	32.9% 9	— —	17.4% 3	4.6% —	725,984 22	75
Yukon & Northwest Territories	51.9% 1	45.2% 1	2.9% —	— —	— —	— —	14,922 2	86 & 76
Totals	3,099,519 131	2,499,913 97	1,381,658 21	359,438 9	282,454 5	90,334 2	7,713,316 265	75

Notes: Rows may not add up to 100 per cent due to rounding.
**Less than 0.1 per cent.

Table B.14: 1968 General Election

Province	Liberal	Progressive Conservative	New Democratic Party	Ralliement des Créditistes	Others	Totals	Turnout (%)
Newfoundland	42.7% 1	52.7% 6	4.4% —	— —	** —	160,200 7	68
Nova Scotia	38.0% 1	55.2% 10	6.7% —	— —	** —	336,957 11	82
New Brunswick	44.4% 5	49.7% 5	4.9% —	0.7% —	0.3% —	251,979 10	80
Prince Edward Island	45.0% —	51.8% 4	3.2% —	— —	— —	50,766 4	88
Quebec	53.6% 56	21.4% 4	7.5% —	16.4% 14	1.1% —	2,184,292 74	72
Ontario	46.6% 64	32.0% 17	20.6% 6	— —	0.8% 1	2,948,492 88	77
Manitoba	41.5% 5	31.4% 5	25.0% 3	0.2% —	1.9% —	400,393 13	76
Saskatchewan	27.1% 2	37.0% 5	35.7% 6	— —	0.2% —	414,425 13	81
Alberta	35.7% 4	50.4% 15	9.3% —	— —	4.6% —	563,835 19	73
British Columbia	41.8% 16	19.4% —	32.7% 7	— —	6.1% —	798,742 23	76
Yukon & Northwest Territories	57.0% 1	33.4% 1	9.6% —	— —	— —	15,913 2	87 & 69
Totals	3,696,945 155	2,554,880 72	1,378,260 22	361,045 14	134,866 1	8,125,996 264	76

Notes: Rows may not add up to 100 per cent due to rounding.
**Less than 0.1 per cent.

Table B.15: 1972 General Election

Province	Liberal	Progressive Conservative	New Democratic Party	Social Credit	Others	Totals	Turnout (%)
Newfoundland	44.8% 3	49.0% 4	4.7% —	0.1% —	1.3% —	175,046 7	63
Nova Scotia	33.9% 1	53.4% 10	12.3% —	0.3% —	0.1% —	383,087 11	80
New Brunswick	43.0% 5	44.9% 5	5.7% —	5.6% —	0.7% —	292,491 10	77
Prince Edward Island	40.5% 1	51.9% 3	7.6% —	** —	— —	56,653 4	86
Quebec	49.1% 56	17.4% 2	6.4% —	24.3% 15	2.7% 1	2,625,036 74	76
Ontario	38.2% 36	39.1% 40	21.4% 11	0.4% —	0.9% 1	3,578,052 88	79
Manitoba	30.9% 2	41.6% 8	26.3% 3	0.7% —	0.5% —	443,154 13	74
Saskatchewan	25.3% 1	36.9% 7	35.9% 5	1.8% —	0.1% —	432,504 13	79
Alberta	25.0% —	57.6% 19	12.6% —	4.4% —	0.3% —	710,952 19	76
British Columbia	28.9% 4	33.0% 8	35.0% 11	2.6% —	0.3% —	948,289 23	73
Yukon & Northwest Territories	30.4% —	39.0% 1	29.5% 1	— —	1.1% —	22,225 2	79 & 73
Totals	3,718,258 109	3,383,530 107	1,713,528 31	737,972 15	114,201 2	9,667,489 264	77

Notes: Rows may not add up to 100 per cent due to rounding.
**Less than 0.1 per cent.

Table B.16: 1974 General Election

Province	Liberal	Progressive Conservative	New Democratic Party	Social Credit	Others	Totals	Turnout (%)
Newfoundland	46.7% 4	43.6% 3	9.4% —	** —	0.1% —	173,945 7	57
Nova Scotia	40.7% 2	47.5% 8	11.2% 1	0.4% —	0.1% —	386,864 11	74
New Brunswick	46.9% 6	33.0% 3	8.6% —	2.9% —	8.1% 1	287,350 10	71
Prince Edward Island	46.2% 1	49.1% 3	4.6% —	— —	0.1 —	58,253 4	80
Quebec	54.1% 60	21.2% 3	6.6% —	17.1% 11	1.0% —	2,458,675 74	67
Ontario	45.1% 55	35.1% 25	19.1% 8	0.2% —	0.5% —	3,565,537 88	74
Manitoba	27.4% 2	47.7% 9	23.5% 2	1.1% —	0.4% —	446,731 13	70
Saskatchewan	30.7% 3	36.4% 8	31.5% 2	1.1% —	0.2% —	413,934 13	72
Alberta	24.7% —	61.1% 19	9.3% —	3.4% —	1.5% —	682,569 19	67
British Columbia	33.3% 8	41.9% 13	23.0% 2	1.2% —	0.5% —	1,010,881 23	72
Yukon & Northwest Territories	28.0% —	38.7% 1	33.2% 1	— —	— —	21,169 2	67 & 61
Totals	4,102,776 141	3,369,335 95	1,467,748 16	481,231 11	84,818 1	9,505,908 264	71

Notes: Rows may not add up to 100% due to rounding.
**Less than 0.1 per cent.

Table B.17: 1979 General Election

Province	Liberal	Progressive Conservative	New Democratic Party	Social Credit	Others	Totals	Turnout (%)
Newfoundland	40.5% 4	29.7% 2	29.7% 1	— —	— —	201,732 7	60
Nova Scotia	35.5% 2	45.4% 8	18.7% 1	— —	0.4% —	425,609 11	75
New Brunswick	44.6% 6	40.0% 4	15.3% —	— —	** —	337,532 10	74
Prince Edward Island	40.6% —	52.8% 4	6.5% —	— —	** —	64,613 4	81
Quebec	61.6% 67	13.5% 2	5.1% —	16.0% 6	3.7% —	3,204,029 75	76
Ontario	36.4% 32	41.8% 57	21.1% 6	** —	0.6% —	4,142,995 95	78
Manitoba	23.4% 2	43.4% 7	32.7% 5	0.2% —	0.3% —	513,773 14	77
Saskatchewan	21.8% —	41.2% 10	35.8% 4	0.5% —	0.7% —	489,404 14	79
Alberta	22.0% —	65.6% 21	9.9% —	0.9% —	1.5% —	853,177 21	68
British Columbia	23.0% 1	44.4% 19	31.9% 8	0.1% —	0.6% —	1,195,912 28	75
Yukon & Northwest Territories	32.6% —	36.9% 2	29.4% 1	— —	1.0% —	26,926 3	74 & 70
Totals	4,594,319 114	4,111,559 136	2,048,779 26	527,604 6	173,341 0	11,455,702 282	76

Notes: Rows may not add up to 100 per cent due to rounding.
**Less than 0.1 per cent.

Table B.18: 1980 General Elections

Province	Liberal	Progressive Conservative	New Democratic Party	Social Credit	Others	Totals	Turnout (%)
Newfoundland	47.0% 5	35.9% 2	16.7% —	— —	0.4% —	203,045 7	59
Nova Scotia	39.8% 5	38.7% 6	20.8% —	— —	0.6% —	422,242 11	72
New Brunswick	50.1% 7	32.5% 3	16.2% —	— —	1.1% —	335,730 10	71
Prince Edward Island	46.8% 2	46.3% 2	6.5% —	— —	0.3% —	66,205 4	79
Quebec	68.2% 74	12.6% 1	9.1% —	5.9% —	4.2% —	2,957,042 75	68
Ontario	41.9% 52	35.5% 38	21.8% 5	** —	0.7% —	4,000,841 95	72
Manitoba	28.0% 2	37.7% 5	33.5% 7	— —	0.8% —	475,904 14	69
Saskatchewan	24.2% —	38.9% 7	36.3% 7	** —	0.5% —	455,774 14	71
Alberta	22.2% —	64.9% 21	10.3% —	1.0% —	1.6% —	795,445 21	61
British Columbia	22.1% —	41.5% 16	35.3% 12	0.1% —	0.9% —	1,209,812 28	71
Yukon & Northwest Territories	37.2% 2	30.6% 2	31.5% 1	— —	0.6% —	25,874 3	69 & 67
Totals	4,853,914 147	3,552,994 103	2,164,987 32	185,486 —	190,533 —	10,947,914 282	69

Notes: Rows may not add up to 100 per cent due to rounding.
**Less than 0.1 per cent.

Table B.19: 1984 General Election

Province	Liberal	Progressive Conservative	New Democratic Party	Social Credit	Others	Totals	Turnout (%)
Newfoundland	36.4% 3	57.5% 4	5.8% —	— —	0.2% —	241,159 7	65
Nova Scotia	33.6% 2	50.7% 9	15.2% —	— —	0.4% —	460,592 11	75
New Brunswick	31.9% 1	53.6% 9	14.1% —	** —	0.4% —	377,350 10	77
Prince Edward Island	40.9% 1	52.0% 3	6.4% —	— —	0.6% —	73,414 4	85
Quebec	35.4% 17	50.2% 58	8.8% —	0.2% —	5.4% —	3,440,360 75	76
Ontario	29.8% 14	47.6% 67	20.8% 13	** —	1.7 1	4,435,411 95	76
Manitoba	21.8% 1	43.2% 9	27.2% 4	— —	7.7% —	513,834 14	73
Saskatchewan	18.2% —	41.7% 9	38.4% 5	— —	1.7% —	522,800 14	78
Alberta	12.7% —	68.8% 21	14.1% —	0.6% —	3.8% —	1,019,539 21	69
British Columbia	16.4% 1	46.6% 19	35.0% 8	0.2% —	1.6% —	1,433,048 28	78
Yukon & Northwest Territories	24.9% —	47.1% 3	23.7% —	— —	4.2% —	31,214 3	78 & 68
Totals	3,516,486 40	6,278,697 211	2,359,915 30	16,659 —	376,964 1	12,548,721 282	75

Notes: Rows may not add up to 100 per cent due to rounding.
**Less than 0.1 per cent.

Table B.20: 1988 General Election

Province	Liberal	Progressive Conservative	New Democratic Party	Reform	Others	Totals	Turnout (%)
Newfoundland	45.0% 5	42.2% 2	12.4% —	—	0.4% —	256,731 7	67
Nova Scotia	46.5% 6	40.9% 5	11.4% —	—	1.2% —	479,841 11	75
New Brunswick	45.3% 5	40.4% 5	9.3% —	—	4.9% —	383,571 10	76
Prince Edward Island	49.9% 4	41.5% —	7.5% —	—	1.1% —	75,644 4	85
Quebec	30.2% 12	52.7% 63	13.9% —	—	3.1% —	3,501,103 75	75
Ontario	38.9% 43	38.2% 46	20.0% 10	—	2.8% —	4,680,030 99	75
Manitoba	36.5% 5	36.8% 7	21.3% 2	3.3% —	2.0% —	542,941 14	75
Saskatchewan	18.2% —	36.4% 4	44.2% 10	0.7% —	0.5% —	523,753 14	78
Alberta	13.7% —	51.7% 25	17.4% 1	15.3% —	1.8% —	1,164,954 26	75
British Columbia	20.4% 1	35.3% 12	36.9% 19	4.9% —	2.4% —	1,533,026 32	79
Yukon & Northwest Territories	30.0% 2	29.7% —	37.0% 1	—	3.2% —	34,005 3	78 & 71
Totals	4,205,072 83	5,667,563 169	2,685,308 43	275,767 —	341,889 —	13,175,599 295	75

Note: Rows may not add up to 100 per cent due to rounding.

Table B.21: 1993 General Election

Province	Liberal	Progressive Conservative	New Democratic Party	Reform	Bloc Québécois	Others	Totals	Turnout (%)
Newfoundland	67.3% 7	26.7% —	3.5% —	1.0% —	— —	1.5% —	230,590 7	55
Nova Scotia	52.0% 11	23.5% —	6.8% —	13.3% —	— —	4.4% —	453,394 11	64
New Brunswick	56.0% 9	27.9% 1	4.9% —	8.5% —	— —	2.7% —	385,099 10	69
Prince Edward Island	60.1% 4	32.0% —	5.2% —	1.0% —	— —	1.7% —	72,222 4	73
Quebec	33.0% 19	13.6% 1	1.5% —	— —	49.3% 54	2.6% 1	3,744,201 75	77
Ontario	52.9% 98	17.6% —	6.0% —	20.1% 1	— —	3.4% —	4,880,216 99	67
Manitoba	44.9% 12	11.9% —	16.6% 1	22.4% 1	— —	4.2% —	541,056 14	68
Saskatchewan	32.1% 5	11.3% —	26.6% 5	27.2% 4	— —	2.8% —	486,872 14	69
Alberta	25.1% 4	14.6% —	4.0% —	52.3% 22	— —	4.0% —	1,203,829 26	65
British Columbia	28.1% 6	13.5% —	15.5% 2	36.4% 24	— —	6.5% —	1,631,994 32	67
Yukon & Northwest Territories	49.5% 2	16.8% —	21.1 1	10.2% —	— —	2.4% —	38,198 3	70 & 63
Totals	5,647,952 177	2,186,422 2	939,575 9	2,559,245 52	1,846,024 54	488,453 1	13,667,671 295	70‡

Notes: Rows may not add up to 100 per cent due to rounding.
**Less than 0.1 per cent.
‡See note 22 in Appendix A.

Table B.22: 1997 General Election

Province	Liberal	Progressive Conservative	New Democratic Party	Reform	Bloc Québécois	Others	Totals	Turnout (%)
Newfoundland	37.9% 4	36.8% 3	22.0% —	2.5% —	—	0.9% —	220,580 7	55
Nova Scotia	28.4% —	30.8% 5	30.4% 6	9.7% —	—	0.8% —	467,370 11	69
New Brunswick	32.9% 3	35.0% 5	18.4% 2	13.1% —	—	0.6% —	398,715 10	73
Prince Edward Island	44.8% 4	38.3% —	15.1% —	1.5% —	—	0.3% —	70,543 4	73
Quebec	36.7% 26	22.2% 5	2.0% —	0.3% —	37.9% 44	1.2% —	3,659,995 75	73
Ontario	49.5% 101	18.8% 1	10.7% —	19.1% 1	—	1.9% 1	4,633,700 103	66
Manitoba	34.3% 6	17.8% 1	23.2% 4	23.7% 3	—	1.0% —	475,943 14	63
Saskatchewan	24.7% 1	7.8% —	30.9% 5	36.0% 8	—	0.6% —	442,286 14	65
Alberta	24.0% 2	14.4% —	5.7% —	54.6% 24	—	1.0% —	1,056,920 26	59
British Columbia	28.8% 6	6.2% —	18.2% 3	43.1% 25	—	3.7% —	1,522,524 34	66
Yukon & Northwest Territories	34.6% 2	15.6% —	24.1% 1	17.2% —	—	8.5% —	34,388 3	59 & 70
Totals	4,994,377 155	2,446,705 20	1,434,509 21	2,513,070 60	1,385,821 44	211,482 1	12,985,964 301	67

Note: Rows may not add up to 100 per cent due to rounding.

LEADERS OF MAJOR POLITICAL PARTIES

Conservative Party Leaders

John A. Macdonald, 1867–91; PM 1867–73, 1878–91
J.J.C. Abbott, 1891–2; PM 1891–2
John Thompson, 1892–4; PM 1892–4
Mackenzie Bowell, 1894–6; PM 1894–6
Charles Tupper, 1896–1901; PM 1896
Robert Borden, 1901–20; PM 1911–20
Arthur Meighen, 1921–6; PM 1920–1, 1926
Hugh Guthrie, 1926–7
R.B. Bennett, 1927–38; PM 1930–5
R.J. Manion, 1938–40
R.B. Hanson, 1940–1
Arthur Meighen, 1941–2
John Bracken, 1942–8
George Drew, 1948–56
John G. Diefenbaker, 1956–67; PM 1957–63
Robert Stanfield, 1967–76
Joe Clark, 1976–83; PM 1979–80
Brian Mulroney, 1983–93; PM 1984–93
Kim Campbell, June-December 1993; PM 1993
Jean Charest, December 1993–8
Elsie Wayne, April-November 1998
Joe Clark, November 1998–

Liberal Party Leaders

Alexander Mackenzie, 1873–80; PM 1873–8
Edward Blake, 1880–7
Wilfrid Laurier, 1887–1919; PM 1896–1911
William Lyon Mackenzie King, 1919–48; PM 1921–6, 1926–30, 1935–48
Louis St Laurent, 1948–58; PM 1948–57
Lester Bowles Pearson, 1958–68; PM 1963–8
Pierre Elliott Trudeau, 1968–84; PM 1968–79, 1980–4
John Napier Turner, 1984–90; PM 1984
Jean Chrétien, 1990; PM 1993–

CCF Leaders

J.S. Woodsworth, 1932–42
M.J. Coldwell, 1942–60
Hazen Argue, 1960–1

New Democratic Party Leaders

Tommy Douglas, 1961–71
David Lewis, 1971–5
Ed Broadbent, 1975–89
Audrey McLaughlin, 1989–95
Alexa McDonough, 1995–

Bloc Québécois Leaders

Lucien Bouchard, 1991–6
Gilles Duceppe, *chef intérimaire*, 1996
Michel Gauthier, 1996–7
Gilles Duceppe, March 1997–

Reform Party Leaders

Preston Manning, 1987–

INDEX